Dividing United Europe

Pictures of Angela Merkel in a Nazi uniform, the burning of German flags, newspaper articles portraying Southern Europe as work-shy and Northern Europe as tight-fisted: The Eurozone crisis has thrown up old stereotypes; often digging into well-established historical images of 'the other'. The conscious or tacit (ab)use of national prejudices by politicians and parts of the media, and the strong emotional reactions among European citizens have caused a lot of public concern about the likely negative implications of such reawakening of national clichés and the newly hardening boundaries they construct for the process of European integration. It is evident that current and recent crises confront European citizens with profound dilemmas which they seek to make sense of, and in response to which much new political mobilisation takes place. At the same time, some of the interpretative and political reactions thus generated also have the potential to become very destructive processes, putting into question years of integration efforts. This book brings together scholars who examine the nexus between (economic) crisis, national identities and the use of historical images, and prejudices and stereotypes, by focusing particularly on media and political discourses in different European countries. In addition to detailed empirical discussions covering diverse national settings across Europe, the different contributions discuss and offer a variety of conceptual and methodological approaches within the inter-disciplinary study of national identities, prejudice and stereotyping in the context of socio-economic and political crises. This book was originally published as a Special Issue of *National Identities*.

Aline Sierp is Assistant Professor in European Studies at Maastricht University, Netherlands. Before joining Maastricht University, Aline Sierp worked as researcher at the Dachau Concentration Camp Memorial Site. Her research interests cover collective memory, questions of identity and European integration. She is the author of *History, Memory and Trans-European Identity: Unifying Divisions* (Routledge, 2014) and the Founder and Co-President of the Memory Studies Association.

Christian Karner is Associate Professor in Sociology at the University of Nottingham, UK. He has published widely within urban sociology, nationalism, and ethnicity studies. Christian has previously held a Leverhulme Special Research Fellowship, and has been a research associate at the Center for Austrian Studies at the University of Minnesota, USA. His books include *Ethnicity and Everyday Life* (2007), *Negotiating National Identities* (2011), *The Use and Abuse of Memory* (2013), *The Commonalities of Global Crises* (2016), and *National Identity and Europe in Times of Crisis* (2017).

Dividing United Europe

From Crisis to Fragmentation?

Edited by
Aline Sierp and Christian Karner

LONDON AND NEW YORK

First published 2019
by Routledge
2 Park Square, Milton Park, Abingdon, Oxon, OX14 4RN

and by Routledge
52 Vanderbilt Avenue, New York, NY 10017

Routledge is an imprint of the Taylor & Francis Group, an informa business

British Library Cataloguing in Publication Data
A catalogue record for this book is available from the British Library

ISBN13: 978-0-367-00255-8

Typeset in Myriad Pro
by Newgen Publishing UK

Publisher's Note
The publisher accepts responsibility for any inconsistencies that may have arisen
during the conversion of this book from journal articles to book chapters, namely
the possible inclusion of journal terminology.

Disclaimer
Every effort has been made to contact copyright holders for their permission to
reprint material in this book. The publishers would be grateful to hear from any
copyright holder who is not here acknowledged and will undertake to rectify any
errors or omissions in future editions of this book.

MIX
Paper from
responsible sources
FSC™ C013985

Printed in the United Kingdom
by Henry Ling Limited

Contents

Citation information

The following chapters were originally published in the journal *National Identities*, volume 19, issue 1 (January 2017). When citing this material, please use the original page numbering for each article, as follows:

For any permission-related enquiries please visit:
www.tandfonline.com/page/help/permissions

Notes on contributors

Giorgos Bithymitris is currently a Postdoctoral Research Fellow at the Centre for Political Research at Panteion University of Social and Political Sciences, Greece. His current research interests focus on union movement theory, strike events and industrial disputes, organised interests, ideology, and framing processes in the context of crisis. He has published academic articles and book chapters on Greek unionism, public discourse in the context of economic crisis, and employment relations.

Tereza Capelos is a Senior Lecturer in Political Psychology at the University of Birmingham, UK. Her research focuses on the affective, cognitive and motivational determinants of political judgments. She has published articles on the role of emotions and values on political radicalisation and tolerance, the formation and updating of institutional and leaders' political reputations, and the role of trust and confidence on political accountability attributions.

Theofanis Exadaktylos is a Senior Lecturer in European Politics at the University of Surrey, UK. He conducts research on the Europeanisation of foreign policy; politics of austerity in Europe; policy implementation and political trust; the rise of populism; and the emergence of national stereotypes in the media.

Elena Genova is a Teaching Associate in Sociology at the University of Nottingham, UK. She is the co-convenor of the Postgraduate Migration Research Network. Her research interests include highly skilled migration, European citizenship, and identity construction.

Horst-Alfred Heinrich is a Professor of Methods in Empirical Social Research at the University of Passau, Germany. His research areas include national identity, collective memory, and visual analysis.

Christian Karner is Associate Professor in Sociology at the University of Nottingham, UK. He has published widely within urban sociology, nationalism, and ethnicity studies. Christian has previously held a Leverhulme Special Research Fellowship, and has been a research associate at the Center for Austrian Studies at the University of Minnesota, USA. His books include *Ethnicity and Everyday Life* (2007), *Negotiating National Identities* (2011), *The Use and Abuse of Memory* (2013), *The Commonalities of Global Crises* (2016), and *National Identity and Europe in Times of Crisis* (2017).

Zinovia Lialiouti is a Postdoctoral Researcher at Panteion University of Social and Political Sciences, Greece, and at the Centre for Modern Greek History at the Academy of Athens,

Greece. She has published papers on the phenomenon of anti-Americanism, American studies, Cold War culture, the study of political discourse, and Greek political culture.

Asimina Michailidou is a Senior Researcher at the ARENA Centre for European Studies at the University of Oslo, Norway. She is a Political Communications Scholar, whose research focuses on the EU's public communication strategies; online media, mobilisation and crises; online journalism and European elections; and Euroscepticism in the media sphere.

Aline Sierp is Assistant Professor in European Studies at Maastricht University, Netherlands. Before joining Maastricht University, Aline Sierp worked as researcher at the Dachau Concentration Camp Memorial Site. Her research interests cover collective memory, questions of identity and European integration. She is the author of *History, Memory and Trans-European Identity: Unifying Divisions* (Routledge, 2014) and the founder and co-president of the Memory Studies Association.

Bernhard Stahl is a Professor of International Politics at the University of Passau, Germany. His research areas include Comparative European and EU foreign policy, and identity theory.

Matti Van Hecke is a PhD Candidate at University of Antwerp, Belgium. His PhD focuses on explaining success and failure of regional lobbying in the EU. He graduated magna cum laude in a Master of European and Comparative Science and an Advanced Master in International Relations and Diplomacy from the University of Antwerp.

Johanna Tuulia Vuorelma is currently a Postdoctoral Researcher in the Network for European Studies at the University of Helsinki, Finland. Her postdoctoral research is funded by the Finnish Cultural Foundation.

Introduction

National stereotypes in the context of the European crisis

Aline Sierp and Christian Karner

ABSTRACT
In this article we position the contributions to our special issue in relation to existing scholarship on racism and stereotypes. We pay close attention to conceptual strands in the literature that emphasize two cognitive-discursive characteristics of stereotypes: their essentialist reductions and projections and their metonymical qualities. We then extend our conceptual and thematic map further to include recent discussions of the relationships between national and European identifications, particularly in crisis contexts, and the role of memory politics in them. We conclude with a brief mention of the scope and potential dangers of historical analogies in moments of crisis and fragmentation.

Introduction

While readers of *National Identities* need no reminder of the large body of existing, steadily growing and multi-disciplinary scholarship focused on stereotypes, there are two particular conceptual strands that are highly pertinent to the following discussions. As such, brief reminders of those conceptualizations may be useful in framing the ensuing articles.

First, stereotypes have been defined by their *essentialism* – the assumption that there is an 'underlying nature, or category essence … thought to be the causal mechanism that results in those properties that we can see' (Gelman, Coley, & Gottfried, 1994, p. 344). Within such a 'logic', individuals are thus reduced to mere channels or surface manifestations of an assumed core that purportedly defines a collective. Individual variation, agency or negotiations of an ascribed subject position (see Hall, 1996) matter little, or not at all, in such positions, which invariably reify their simple, reductive portrayals of 'culture', 'tradition', 'nation' or 'race'. In the European context, and briefly assuming a history of ideas perspective, the legacy of romanticism (see Gellner, 1998) arguably provides the clearest example of such essentialist thought and its far-reaching political consequences.

This raises the obvious question – to be answered both conceptually and in specific empirical contexts – how and to what extent (or perhaps entirely and inevitably?) such essentialism articulates and overlaps with racism in its different manifestations. As in relation to existing research on stereotypes, constraints of space and our readers' own specialisms make a comprehensive summary of the enormous literature on racism impractical and unnecessary in the present context. Yet, a brief reminder of the complexity of this literature, and of the diversity of theoretical models on offer, is in order.

Essentialism, racism and stereotypes

'Explaining' racisms has turned out to be an enormously difficult matter, pitting competing paradigms in competition and sometimes open confrontation with one another. Racism and xenophobia have thus, for example, been 'located' in the human psyche, as psycho-analytically inflected arguments suggest, with Žižek's (1989) post-Lacanian position perhaps the most influential exemplar. In their potential universalism (i.e. racism's conditions of possibility are here detected in features of the unconscious and its relationship with social forces and are thus present everywhere), such positions are already several steps removed from the arguably most famous and most widely debated contribution to the issue: Adorno, Frenke-Brunswik, Levinson, and Sanford's (1950) outline of a much more particular, distinctly 'authoritarian' personality type, which of course also requires particular biographical and social conditions to manifest. Conversely, and clearly shifting the focus from the psychodynamic to the linguistic and institutional, various forms of discourse analysis (e.g. Reisigl & Wodak, 2001; Wetherell & Potter, 1992) approach racism as a form of social practice that bears the imprint of wider political structures and surfaces in language, from everyday utterances to official documents. Yet other arguments tie ideologies of 'race' and racism yet more squarely to very particular institutional configurations, such as those of capitalist modernity and its deep contradictions (e.g. see Malik, 1996). For our present purposes, it will have to suffice to acknowledge the heuristic value in each of these positions and their potential complementarities as we seek to cast analytical light on particular instances of deeply essentialist thinking, talk and politics.

Cutting across or transcending these explanatory differences, there is of course the more common, 'text-book' definition of racism as entailing the coming together of prejudice and power. Essentialism, then, is an obvious, enormously consequential and near ubiquitous manifestation of prejudice, in its complete interpretative privileging of reified collectives over individuals, contextual variations and complexities. And power, we would like to suggest, must here be understood in dynamic rather than static terms: not as inhering in fully fledged, dominant institutions only, but as defining any distribution of, and struggle over, the allocation of resources (in their widest possible sense) and the ability to make and implement decisions. Weaving these different threads together, and applying them to ongoing European crises, what we are currently witnessing across Europe is arguably more than just the revival of 'old stereotypes': we are in the middle of profound disagreements and struggles over the allocation of resources, decision-making, and the possible, indeed now very probable reconfiguration of a variety of institutional structures. In other words, the crisis has given rise to multiple struggles over power in local, regional, national, transnational and pan-European settings. When such political debates and struggles become inflected by prejudice, as they have done and as testified by the contributions to this special issue, the uncomfortable question arises if what we are faced with may indeed be new forms of racism (or old racisms in new disguise). In general, we are of course all too aware of racism's historical malleability, from the 'scientific' racisms of the nineteenth and early twentieth centuries, to the much-discussed new- or 'cultural' racisms of recent decades, with Islamophobia or arguably also forms of

European Union (EU)-phobia, when directed at fellow European citizens from other member states, their arguably most recent or prominent manifestation. The potential (re)appearance of intra-European racisms therefore remains an undeniable possibility. The extent to which such (re)appearance may already be well under way is one of the larger questions, perhaps the key question, hovering above the analyses developed by our contributors.

The second relevant conceptual strand to be mentioned here is provided by Georg Lakoff's cognitive linguistic work and pertains more immediately to the discursive workings of some stereotypes, essentialisms and racisms. Most helpfully for our purposes, Lakoff speaks of *metonymy* as the process of 'taking a particular member or subcategory as ... [standing] for the whole category for the purposes of making inferences or judgments' (1987a, p. 71). Metonymy, Lakoff elaborates elsewhere (1987b, p. 77), is 'one of the basic characteristic of cognition. It is extremely common for people to take one well-understood or easy-to-perceive aspect of something and use it to stand for the thing as a whole'. A close reading of the articles to follow and of discourses encountered daily in the media, articulated by politicians and on the level of the everyday across Europe reveal a plethora of resentful, national stereotypes, many of which are premised on, and driven by, such metonymies. We see this in frequently recurring claims that a given group of people or a particular incident allegedly 'proves' that purportedly profound differences in 'mentality', 'work ethos', etc. divide Europe. Very similarly, singular examples of misspent public money and much-publicized (and of course profoundly worrying) corruption or tax evasion come to be constructed, in metonymical fashion, as the 'epitome' or 'condensed symbol' of entire national groups and institutions. We need to stress here that northern European, often blatantly self-righteous discourses about inflated Mediterranean public sectors or chronic tax evasion work with metonymy; just as much as does some of the extremely worrying and hugely distasteful rhetoric of anti-German, anti-austerity opposition recorded in Greece and elsewhere, which has not even stopped short of taking images of Hitler and Nazism as postulated metonymies of an assumed 'German-ness' purportedly re-encountered in Merkel's policies. Needless to stress that counter-discourses have a very tough time here: thus far, neither statistical evidence to the contrary nor the more nuanced historical contextualization badly needed in difficult circumstances seem very successful at depriving metonymies of their dangerous and divisive appeal.

What we encounter in many of the discourses examined by our contributors, whether anti-Greek or anti-German or anti-whoever, is a coming together of, and close alliance between, essentialist thinking and metonymical 'reasoning' (the inverted commas are indeed key here). Conceptually, there is further momentum to be derived from the discourse analytical notion of the 'topos' (e.g. Reisigl & Wodak, 2001, pp. 74–75), or the usually circular 'structures of argument' that directly connect pre-existing assumption and premises with the claims and assertions being made. Worryingly, there is usually little or no space for argumentative nuance, evidence, or the weighing up of competing interpretations and positions amidst such topoi. As already mentioned, and by definition, discourse analysis always understands such rhetorical practices and argumentative features in relation to their wider social contexts.

European tensions

National stereotypes, essentialisms, metonymical polemics, new (or actually old) racisms –
it is of course stating the obvious that all of this happens and gets articulated against particular material, institutional and historical backdrops. Our contributors thus rightly stress
that the discourses they examine need to be analysed in the decisive context provided by
the recent, and in many of its manifestations continuing financial and political crises variously affecting different member states of both the Eurozone and the EU more widely.
While the genealogy and context-specific dimensions of the crisis need no summary
here, we would like to draw attention to two competing arguments, which in some of
their articulations pre-dated the crisis and which concern the EU's purported ability – or
inability – to withstand such crises. These competing assessments are indeed currently
being 'tested' by near daily developments. The first of these positions suggested,
already before the beginnings of the crisis in 2008, that European institutions and at
most instrumental and 'embryonic' European identities may not be able to withstand
and survive serious economic difficulties (Guibernau, 2007, pp. 115–116). A similar,
though perhaps slightly more optimistic sentiment defines Toplak and Sumi's (2012,
p. 7) conclusion that a 'reinforcement of a European identity' is an 'impossibility', at
least 'in the current political climate'. Also worth mentioning in this context is recent
work revealing different dimensions of EU-scepticism, which variously relate to anxieties
about the local effects of global market forces, reveal a spectrum of competing (local,
national and European) identifications and forms of memory, and reflect widespread concerns about decision-making on EU-level and the balance of power between the EU and its
constituent member states (Karner, 2013; Sierp, 2016).

Alternatively, by way of a counter-position, it has also been suggested that Europeans'
lifeworlds have begun to display forms of 'banal Europeanism' (Cram, 2009) that may be
'capable of counteracting deeply entrenched nationalisms and the fragmentary forces
generated in difficult times' (Karner, 2011, p. 89). Much of this tension between such contrasting assessments and the uncertainty they reflect was already anticipated much earlier
by Manuel Castells, in his seminal *End of Millennium*:

> Faced with the whirlwind of globalization … European countries came together … to unify
> their currencies, and thus their economies, around the turn of the millennium. However,
> the cultural and political dimensions, essential to … European unification, are still unsettled,
> so that the fate of Europe will ultimately depend … on solving historical puzzles posed by
> … the shift from the nation-state to the network state. (Castells, 2000, p. 3)

Put at its simplest, this is where we are currently at, in terms of the *longue durée* of European history, as reflected in the tensions crystallized by the current crisis and, more particularly, in the national stereotypes and resentments examined by the contributors to
this special issue.

As the EU and her member states try to come to terms with the deep socio-economic
and ideological fractures revealed since 2008, a further crucial dimension is provided by
culturally shared memories or, more accurately, by the availability – or lack of availability
– of particular frames of historical interpretation and hence identity construction, negotiation and reassertion. In other words, the past and how we think about it have tremen-
dous implications for how we cope with current crises and for how we go about
responding to the tension summarized by Castells. Recent work on national and European

memories (e.g. Karner & Mertens, 2013; Pakier & Stråth, 2010; Sierp, 2014; Sierp & Wüsten-berg, 2015) draws attention to the manifold and often contradictory effects and political uses of diverse memories. Such work illuminates the close interplay of past, present and the political blueprints for the future on offer. More immediately, the relevance of the past manifests in the sobering realization that many of the stereotypes discussed in the articles to follow have a much longer history, with current tensions and power struggles merely serving as the catalyst to their rediscovery, resurfacing and re-utilization by politicians, in the media, and by 'ordinary citizens'.

How we cope with crises, then, is likely to be significantly shaped by (sub-)culturally shared frames and categories of interpretation. As such, answers to the question as to which kind of Europe, and what kinds of relationship between its member states, publics deem desirable vary between, and therefore need to be addressed in, particular national contexts. This is, of course, what our contributors do. A crucial part of the context to each of the following discussions thus pertains to the schematic 'ways of seeing' (Brubaker, Loveman, & Stamatov, 2004) that are available and in circulation – with differing degrees of salience – in any given setting. Indeed, illuminating such publicly available, and often profoundly stereotypical frames is also a prerequisite for a meaningful analysis of the rising tide of EU-scepticism and its damaging indifference and opposition to the very idea of European integration. Consequently, memory and awareness of the origins and achievements of the EU are further side-lined, belittled and subverted by political positions that are more or less exclusively focused on national categories and that discursively reduce the EU to a series of negatively connoted phenomena: from the alleged spectre of 'over-regulation', to a purported lack of democratic legitimacy and a range of more specific complaints and anxieties. Some of the stereotypes discussed in what follows are clearly part of this wider anti-European tide.

Conversely, our grasp of these phenomena and their contestation is also likely to benefit from the inverse analytical question: namely, how prominent larger European categories may be in public discourse in any given setting, and how such European-minded (counter)discourses position themselves in relation to the structural status quo and hegemonic austerity discourse in the EU in its current form. Put differently, our contextual understanding arguably also needs to extend to comparatively inclusive discourses, some of which replace national stereotypes with structural and ideological critique that is variously directed at national or indeed European politics and publics. One might further question what the effects of the relative absence of such counter-discourses are: an economic instrumentalism that reduces the EU to the trope of 'the common market'? And might this in turn open the door yet further to negative stereotypes being applied to other European countries and the EU itself? How does all of this intersect with what Gilroy (2004) describes as 'postcolonial melancholia'? While this concept has been applied, for obvious and all too timely reasons, to the British context in particular, it is not difficult to see how other parts of contemporary Europe also struggle with their widely felt decline of former economic might and political influence. The analyses offered by our contributors offer much food for thought on these and related questions that look set to shape the European continent in the years ahead.

Eight contributions have here been carefully selected from a total of over 60 proposals that had reached us after an open call for papers. Earlier versions of all eight articles included in this special issue were presented either at the general conference of the

Council for European Studies (CES) in June 2013 in Amsterdam or at the general conference of the European Consortium for Political Research (ECPR) in September 2013 in Bordeaux. By gathering researchers from universities in the UK, Norway, Portugal, Belgium, Germany and Greece with different disciplinary backgrounds (political science, anthropology, history, media studies and sociology), the aim of the special issue is to examine the nexus between the (economic) crisis and the use of historical images, prejudices and stereotypes from the widest possible angle. In addition to detailed empirical discussions covering diverse national settings across Europe, the different contributions discuss and offer a variety of conceptual and methodological approaches within the inter-disciplinary study of prejudice and stereotyping in the context of socio-economic and political crises.

The contributions

In her article 'A narrative battle: Debating Finland's EU policy during the economic crisis', Johanna Vuorelma examines how metaphors are employed to turn a previously consensus-driven discourse about the EU into a political struggle over dominance between different political forces. According to her analysis of Finnish newspaper articles two different meta-narratives feature in the discussion of Finland's role in the EU: a tragic narrative shaped by a metonymical understanding of the European project and a romantic narrative derived from a synecdochal vision. She argues that the Finnish debate on the Eurozone crisis is essentially about strengthening ontological security, namely Finland's European identity.

Elena Genova's article 'Between a rock and a hard place': Bulgarian highly skilled migrants' experiences of external and internal stereotypes in the context of the European crisis' studies how the anxiety surrounding the negative socio-economic consequences of the European financial crisis has channelled into stigmatizing discourses towards migrants in the UK. It analyses in detail the process of constructing stereotypes in light of their specific spatial and temporal conditions in both home and host societies. Making use of multi-sited ethnographic research, she exposes the progression of double-sided othering and migrants' reactions to this. She contends that Bulgarian highly skilled workers have succeeded in finding a space of their own in between the two simultaneous processes of exclusion in home and host societies.

In their contribution entitled 'A nation under attack: Perceptions of enmity and victimhood in the context of the Greek crisis', Zinovia Lialiouti and Giorgos Bithymitris analyse the ideological function of various interpretative repertoires for the construction, reproduction and contestation of national self-images. Focusing on two seemingly contradictory interpretive repertoires – premised on victimization and self-blaming respectively – they demonstrate how hybrid discursive constructions can coexist. They argue that in the Greek context it is particularly the use of history as an interpretative framework, and more specifically an interpretative scheme of German occupation, that penetrates political discourse and has come to increasingly shape national self-images.

Tereza Capelos and Theofanis Exadaktylos further explore emotions and identity in their article 'Feeling the pulse of the Greek debt crisis: Affect on the web of blame' by focusing on expressive reactions that marked the Greek public agenda during its sovereign debt crisis. Using content analysis and drawing insights from political psychology and political economy, they map the presence of affective expressions in media representations of the debt crisis. Their contribution shows that both citizens and elites engage not only cognitively but also emotionally with the Eurocrisis. They contend that emotional reactions among the public manifest as decreasing levels of trust in the EU and increasingly negative attitudes towards European integration.

This is followed by Asimina Michailidou's investigation of the link between public contestation of the Eurocrisis and the struggle of political elites for public legitimacy in her article '"The Germans are back": Euroscepticism and Anti-Germanism in crisis-stricken Greece'. She traces the surge of Eurosceptic and anti-German sentiments in a country that had been markedly pro-European prior to the outbreak of the crisis in 2009. Adopting a crisis management and communication perspective and using a crisis accountability model of analysis, this article maps how public discourses changed in the context of the EU public legitimation process. Michailidou comes to the conclusion that while anti-German stereotypes are clearly present, the most dominant discourse is one reflecting power struggles taking place on different levels.

Yet another perspective and methodological approach are offered by Horst-Alfred Heinrich and Bernhard Stahl's analysis, entitled 'Pictorial stereotypes and images in the Euro debt crisis', of anti-Greek stereotyping in Germany. By focusing on select images published in German media, they examine both the symbolic register employed by particular stereotypes and their embeddedness in national identity. Basing their conceptual approach on an explorative analysis of cover images from two German weeklies, they show how pictures can contribute to reviving old images of the 'other'.

Matti van Hecke, in his contribution 'Imag(in)ing the Eurocrisis: a comparative analysis of political cartoons', uses a similar approach to examine the articulation of stereotypes and historical images in cartoons. Through a comparative analysis of 400 political cartoons published in twelve different member states, he examines to what extent the political, economic and financial division in Europe runs parallel to a communicational or ideational split. He argues that the causal interpretation and moral evaluation expressed in the different cartoons are constructed along national and cultural lines. While the Euro debt crisis is associated with a crisis of responsibility in Northern Europe, in southern Europe a solidarity crisis frame prevails.

Conclusion

We would like to conclude this introduction by quoting two separate sets of reflections offered by arguably two of the most perceptive literary commentators on Europe's successive tragedies and atrocities in the first half of the twentieth century: Stefan Zweig and Kurt Tucholsky, respectively. Summarizing his memories of the outbreak of the First World War, Zweig recalls with great sadness the sudden destruction of a world of transnational friendships and artistic exchange he had inhabited up until 1914:

> Then, on 28 June 1914, that shot was fired in Sarajevo, and our world of safety and creative rationality, in which we had been brought up and felt at home, began to shatter. (1944/1970, p. 247, *our translation*)

And a quarter of a century later, Zweig reflects on the beginning of the Second World War as follows:

My beating heart felt the last war all over again – in the new one that started today, and whose horror was not yet known to us. And I knew: once again, the past had disappeared, our achievements would yet again be wiped out, Europe, our home, for which we had lived, would be destroyed for a long time to come. (1944/1970, p. 494, *our translation*)

In the intervening years, and writing under one of his journalistic pseudonyms, Kurt Tucholsky had the following to say in 1920:

The thing they call Europe has become a cloth of multi-coloured pieces. Everyone's a stranger as soon as they so much as peak out of their own village. There are more strangers than inhabitants on this blessed continent … After this war … after entire peoples' bloody marches across half of Europe, every town considers its own church tower to be a matter of hellish significance … Everyone thinks their concerns are the most important ones, and nobody's prepared to compromise in any way. Initially we draw a line of demarcation. We separate ourselves from others. We need a boundary … But beneath our stupidity, there is only one earth, and above us just one sky. Borders criss-cross Europe. But no one can keep people apart indefinitely – not those borders, and not the soldiers … (Tucholsky, 1960/2010, p. 110, *our translation*)

Zweig's and Tucholsky's reflections on Europe's history of previous 'disintegrations' are presented here *with a warning, and not (necessarily) as a warning*. We do not here invoke them to suggest that we can or should extrapolate any form of simplistic comparison between then and now. On the contrary, Jan-Werner Müller's warnings (2002) against the use of facile historical analogies, which invariably decontextualize and replace potentially careful analysis with simplistic rhetoric and self-serving politics, need to be taken very seriously and endorsed (also see Karner & Mertens, 2013). And yet, Zweig and Tucholsky nonetheless seem very relevant to the following discussions: not as offering historical analogies or, even more problematically, a template for predicting what may happen next; but as reflections on a previous and different historical context, in which discursive and institutional boundaries hardened quickly, ultimately – in the contexts in question – to disastrous, deadly and genocidal effect.

Disclosure statement

No potential conflict of interest was reported by the authors.

References

Adorno, T., Frenke-Brunswik, E., Levinson, D. J., & Sanford, R. N. (1950). *The authoritarian personality.* New York, NY: Norton.

Brubaker, R., Loveman, M., & Stamatov, P. (2004). Ethnicity as cognition. *Theory and Society, 33*(1), 31–64.

Castells, M. (2000). *End of millennium.* Oxford: Blackwell.

Cram, L. (2009). Banal Europeanism: European Union identity and national identities in synergy. *Nations and Nationalism, 15*(1), 101–108.

Gelman, S. A., Coley, J. D., & Gottfried, G. M. (1994). Essentialist beliefs in children: The acquisition of concepts and theories. In L. A. Hirschfeld & S. A. Gelman (Eds.), *Mapping the mind* (pp. 341–363). Cambridge: Cambridge University Press.

Gellner, E. (1998). *Language and solitude.* Cambridge: Cambridge University Press.

Gilroy, P. (2004). *After empire.* Abingdon: Routledge.

Guibernau, M. (2007). *The identity of nations.* Cambridge: Polity.

Hall, S. (1996). Who needs identity? In S. Hall & P. du Gay (Eds.), *Questions of cultural identity* (pp. 1–17). London: Sage.

Karner, C. (2011). *Negotiating national identities: Between globalization, the past and 'the other'.* Farnham: Ashgate.

Karner, C. (2013). Europe and the nation: Austrian EU-scepticism and its contestation. *Journal of Contemporary European Studies, 21*(2), 252–268.

Karner, C., & Mertens, B. (Eds.). (2013). *The use and abuse of memory: Interpreting World War II in contemporary European politics.* New Brunswick, NJ: Transaction.

Lakoff, G. (1987a). Cognitive models and prototype theory. In U. Neisser (Ed.), *Concepts and conceptual development* (pp. 63–101). Cambridge: Cambridge University Press.

Lakoff, G. (1987b). *Women, fire, and dangerous things.* Chicago, IL: The University of Chicago Press.

Malik, K. (1996). *The meaning of race.* Basingstoke: Macmillan.

Müller, J.-W. (2002). Introduction: The power of memory, the memory of power, and the power over memory. In J.-W. Müller (Ed.), *Memory & power in post-war Europe* (pp. 1–39). Cambridge: Cambridge University Press.

Pakier, M., & Stråth, B. (Eds.). (2010). *A European memory.* New York, NY: Berghahn.

Reisigl, M., & Wodak, R. (2001). *Discourse and discrimination.* London: Routledge.

Sierp, A. (2014). *History, memory and trans-European identity. Unifying divisions.* New York, NY: Routledge.

Sierp, A. (2016). Drawing lessons from the past – mapping change in central and south-eastern Europe. *East European Politics & Societies, 30*(1), 3–9.

Sierp, A., & Wüstenberg, J. (2015). Linking the local and the transnational: Rethinking memory politics in Europe. *Journal of Contemporary European Studies, 23*(3), 321–329.

Toplak, C., & Sumi, I. (2012). Europe(an Union): Imagined community in the making? *Journal of Contemporary European Studies, 20*(1), 7–28.

Tucholsky, K. (1960/2010). *Panter, Tiger & Co.* Reinbek: Rowohlt.

Wetherell, M., & Potter, J. (1992). *Mapping the language of racism.* New York, NY: Harvester Wheatsheaf.

Žižek, S. (1989). *The sublime object of ideology.* London: Verso.

Zweig, S. (1944/1970). *Die welt von gestern.* Frankfurt: Fischer.

1 A narrative battle
Debating Finland's EU policy during the economic crisis

Johanna Tuulia Vuorelma

ABSTRACT

The economic crisis in Europe has resulted in an unprecedented narrative battle in the traditionally consensus-driven Finland. National stereotypes and prejudices have been employed to situate Finland on the shifting political and moral map of Europe with the North–South division taking an important role in the narrative battle. Using a narrative approach to policy debates and following Erik Ringmar's work, this article analyses how Finland's European role has been narratively constructed with romantic, tragic, and satirical interpretations featuring in the debate.

Introduction

This article focuses on the Eurozone crisis debate in Finland as a European narrative battle between tragic, romantic, and satirical visions of the European Union's (EU) future. The Finnish public debate on the financial crisis in Europe, a complex web of government debt crisis, a banking crisis, and a growth and competitiveness crisis that erupted in late 2009 and intensified in 2010, is significant for a number of reasons. The debate should interest us, firstly, because it reflects pan-European concerns and ideas and as such it represents a Europeanised debate on a national level. This means that the debate in Finland is not taking place in isolation from the rest of Europe but instead localises and dramatises European ideas in such a way as to narrate Finland's role and status in the changing Europe. It is about, in Burke's (1969, p. 17) terms, 'localizing or dramatizing the principle of transformation'. It is important to understand how European ideas are narrated on a national level because that knowledge contributes to a more nuanced understanding of the political and identity aspects of the European integration project.

Most importantly, the Finnish case is unique and powerful because it has the potential of undermining the whole European project. Finland has been narrated a European 'model pupil' in strictly abiding by the common rules, seeking cooperation and compromise, and still leading in economic and political performance. In other words, Finland was Europe's chance to show that following the common rules translates to economic and political benefits. The tragic and satirical narratives in the Eurozone crisis debate in Finland challenge the 'model pupil' image and as such questions the desirability and feasibility of the very ideals that the 'European dream' is premised upon.

Finally, in analysing the narrative rupture and its manifestations on a national level, the article extends our understanding of Finland's identity project in the EU and argues that it has concrete policy implications on a European level. What is particularly noteworthy in the narrative battle is the dividing line that runs across North and South instead of the more familiar East–West bifurcation that Finland's policy options have traditionally been framed around. The idea that Europe forms a socially stratified space divided between North and South was part of Max Weber's (2002) classical work *The Protestant Ethic and the Spirit of Capitalism* in the early 1900s, but its impact on Finland's European identity has been marginal compared to the Cold War division between East and West. In fact, Weber left the Lutheran North out of his Protestant ethics, which meant that Finland was not part of Weber's hard-working and rational North that he juxtaposed with economically, politically, and culturally different South. However, in the narrative battle in the early 2010s, Finland was discursively situated firmly at the very core of Weber's North Europe – often as its last defender along with Germany.

The article examines the fierce narrative battle where politicians, journalists, and commentators debate whether to continue cooperating in the EU when its southern member states are struggling financially and big member states are allegedly lacking in moral and political principles. The shift from being a 'model pupil' into a rebel materialised in Finland's controversial and uncompromising demand for an exclusive collateral deal with Greece, finalised in October 2011, before agreeing to join the Eurozone's second financial aid package to Greece. This 'significant stumbling block' (The Telegraph, 6 July 2012) represented an explicit turn in Finland's EU policy and caused great anxiety in many domestic commentators: will Finland now lose its hard-earned status in Europe as a reliable partner?

The article will show how metaphors of war, disease, nature, and capital have been employed, among others, to strengthen the narratives concerning Finland's role and status in Europe. It argues that the stereotypical division between the good Northern Europeans and the bad Southerners has served as a metaphorical tool to reinforce the narratives. The Finnish debate about the Eurozone crisis has demonstrated that policy debates are guided not only by strategic calculations based upon careful analytical deliberations but also by underlying moral and aesthetic preferences concerning Finland's role in Europe.

Domestic policy debates are traditionally treated as ideological exchanges between political parties. Erik Ringmar shows in his article 'Inter-Textual Relations: The Quarrel Over the Iraq War as a Conflict between Narrative Types' (2006) that we should also focus on the linguistic aspect of policy debates and pay attention to their storied form, which leads us to narratives. A narrative approach to policy debates offers a more nuanced interpretation of what exactly is political in the debate because it teases out, as White (1973) has famously argued, the moral and aesthetic preferences that influence the way in which reality is represented. The article is premised on White's (1987, p. 24) notion that any narrative representation of reality contains a 'moralising impulse' and 'a desire to have real events display the coherence, integrity, fullness, and closure of an image of life that is and can only be imaginary'.

The article also relies on Kenneth Burke's understanding of speech acts as persuasive language, especially his *A Rhetorics of Motives* (1969). The Finnish debate on the Eurozone crisis is a particularly good case study of narratives that concern real events but are strongly moral and imaginative as opposed to analytical and neutral. A narrative approach also allows us to study policy debates that do not follow a strict ideological division but run across political parties and ideologies, resulting in, as Erik Ringmar argues, 'unexpected quarrels and strange new alliances' (2006, p. 403).

The data set comprises of around 120 articles that appeared in Finnish newspapers during 2011. The relevant articles – those concerning the Eurozone crisis – were selected from the archives of the Finnish Parliament's internal information service ('eduskunnan sisäinen tietopalvelu'). This service archives all EU related articles that appear in the established newspapers in Finland. In the data set, there are articles from seven different publications, which are listed here in their order of relevance: (1) *Helsingin Sanomat*; (2) *Aamulehti*; (3) *Turun Sanomat*; (4) *Kaleva*; (5) *Nykypäivä*; (6) *Suomenmaa*; and (7) *Vihreä Lanka*. The last three publications are affiliated to political parties.[1] The more sensational but widely circulated *Ilta-Sanomat* and *Iltalehti* are not included in the parliamentary archives. The only criterion for data selection was whether the Eurozone crisis was mentioned in the articles. The data are gathered from and limited to 2011 as the policy debate was particular intense at the time, which allows the articles to talk to one another.

Narratives in politics

The article argues that the Finnish narrative battle is essentially Finland's identity project in the EU, and in order to tease out what this really means, we need to unpack the concept of narrative. The first necessary question is, simply, what *is* a narrative? Sometimes narrative is used interchangeable with 'story', which can eventually mean that it gets 'emptied of all semantic content: if everything is narrative, nothing is' (Rimmon-Kenan, 2006, p. 11; 17; Riessman, 2008, p. 3). Most narrative researchers would agree that for a narrative to exist there must be, first, more than a single metaphor and second, some sort of ordering of those metaphors. We could talk about, for example, contingent sequences. As Erik Ringmar argues: 'To assemble metaphors into sequences and to organise the continuity of life around them is to render an interpretation into *narrative* form, to tell a *story* about the metaphors we have come to embrace' (Ringmar, 2008, p. 72, emphases in original).

Michael Mann formulates this in an even more straightforward way: 'History seems just one damned thing after another. If the damned things are patterned, it is only because real men and women impose patterns' (Mann, 1986, p. 532). Barbara Herrnstein Smith provides an even simpler definition of narrative as 'someone telling someone else that something happened' (Herrnstein Smith, 1981, p. 228). There are also different criteria that can be outlined in the task of defining a narrative (see for example Bruner, 1991; Gergen, 1999; Somers & Gibson, 1994).

Another way to approach narrative is to focus on what it does. There are three overlapping research avenues here: autobiographical, strategic, and ontological narratives. They are not explicitly concerned with what exactly is a narrative but its relation to reality and its function as a tool of representation. They are, unlike purely structural approaches that are concerned with what technically constitutes a narrative, grounded in ethical and aesthetic considerations. This article is particularly concerned with strategic and ontological narratives. To treat narrative as a strategic tool is to focus on how it is being employed by political elites and to examine how narratives are mobilised and framed to discursively create space for new policy options (see for example Barnett, 1999; Nykänen, 2013;

Subotic, 2015). Narrative framing is particularly intense during changes in foreign policy when internal or external conditions are seen to be fluctuating to a different direction. Political, academic, and diplomatic circles are seen as 'narrative entrepreneurs' that attempt to create narratives that are eventually accepted and internalised by the public (Sjursen, 2013).

An ontological approach to narratives concerns the way in which narrative constitutes rather than simply describes or strategically frames reality. Ontological narratives are not always easy to define because they overlap with autobiographical narratives and strategic narratives that also influence how we see the world and develop a sense of the self. However, they are not primarily interested in narrative's ontological function. The ontological approach to narrative, in contrast, is specifically focused on how narrative turns seemingly random and disconnected events into coherent 'facts' about the self and the world. Somers and Gibson (1994, p. 61) define ontological narratives as something that

> are used to define who we are; this in turn is a precondition for knowing what to do. This 'doing' will in turn produce new narratives and hence new actions; the relationship between narrative and ontology is processual and mutually constitutive.

Unlike autobiographical and strategic approaches to narrative, the ontological approach commences the analysis from the notion that reality can only be accessed through narratives. Ringmar (1996), for example, argues that we should no longer make scholarly attempts to tackle the impossible task of finding a way to talk about what something 'really' is and instead talk about what it resembles. This article treats the Finnish narratives of the Eurozone crisis strategic in that they attempt to frame the debate in such a way as to limit the policy options available to Finland. Powerful metaphors that draw from Finnish historical and cultural tropes are important in these narratives. The Eurozone crisis narratives are also ontological in that they construct Finland's European self that is being negotiated in the debate.

The Finnish narrative battle – like all policy debates – is both figurative and performative. As White explains:

> A narrative account is always a figurative account, an allegory. To leave this figurative element out of consideration in the analysis of a narrative is to miss not only its aspect as allegory but also the performance in language by which a chronicle is transformed into a narrative.

This article demonstrates the figurative aspect of the narrative battle by paying attention to different metaphors that are employed in the process. The performative aspect is twofold: policy debates perform not only narrative acts but also policy-making because the two cannot be separated in policy processes. Politicians and influential narrative entrepreneurs take part in narrative battles concerning policies, forming a complex discursive continuum between parliamentary practices and public speech acts.

Ringmar and four narrative types

Following Ringmar, the article distinguishes between different narrative types in examining the Finnish Eurozone crisis debate. In Ringmar's analysis of the Iraq War debate there are four narrative types: romance, tragedy, comedy, and satire. Analysing the decision-makers' arguments, Ringmar argues that

Taking their departure from the same basic facts, the interpretations they reach often vary and the conclusions differ. As a result, stories present different agendas for action and thereby different moral choices. Consequently, it is not surprising that decision-makers who tell different stories end up disagreeing with one another. (Ringmar, 2006, p. 404)

Frye (1957/2000) systematically classified and analysed those four different modes of emplotment in his famous *Anatomy of Criticism: Four Essays*. In this paper, three of them – romance, tragedy, and satire – will be dealt with more closely because of their relevance to the case.

In romance

there are three stages to the quest: first the perilous journey, next the struggle or the conquest, and finally the exaltation of the hero. In all these respects the enemy is the hero's opposite. The enemy represents winter, darkness, confusion, sterility and old age. The remaining characters are either for or against the hero, and obviously there is never any doubt about whose side the audience is on. (Ringmar, 2006, pp. 404–405).

Hayden White further notes that romance 'is a drama of the triumph of good over evil, of virtue over vice, of light over darkness, and of the ultimate transcendence of man over the world in which he was imprisoned by the Fall' (White, 1973, p. 9).

Tragedy, on the other hand, 'provides an entirely different plot structure. Here too there is a hero, but a tragic hero is someone who rebels against the established order and who is destroyed as a result … In the end no one escapes and no one gets away with anything, no matter how good the intentions' (Ringmar, 2006, p. 405). In a tragic narrative, White continues, 'there are no festive occasions, except false or illusory ones; rather, there are intimations of states of division among men more terrible than that which incited the tragic agon at the beginning of the drama' (White, 1973, p. 9).

Finally, as satire assumes

an ironic stance towards the world, it is parasitic on other narrative forms, and since it lampoons the established social order its aims are subversive rather than constructive. The basic strategy is to turn other plot structures inside-out, upside-down, or to deconstruct and reassemble them in unrecognizable patterns. (Ringmar, 2006, p. 406).

White also argues that the 'aim of the Ironic statement is to affirm tacitly the negative of what is on the literal level affirmed positively, or the reverse' (White, 1973, p. 9).

In the Finnish Eurozone crisis debate, tragedians and sometimes satirists highlight the unreachable gap between the selfish elite and the honourable yet downtrodden masses or the hard-working North and wicked South, which will lead to the fall of the naïve hero, either Finland or the EU. For tragedians, the EU in its current structure will inevitably fall because of its elite structure and unfortunate naivety, but what comes after is important. Tragedians advocate a return to a nation-state driven system with national currencies and less if any supranational decision-making mechanisms.

Romantics, on the other hand, foresee a future where the EU manages to solve the current crisis by strengthening and enforcing its structure and values, and emerge as an even more powerful actor in the international system. For romantics, the EU's initial struggle will lead not to its downfall but to a stronger union and deeper integration. But the triumph will not come easily; it requires hard work and painful decisions. Finland is placed at the centre of this battle and represented as a force that can guide Europe out of its nearly impossible impasse.

Finally, satirists turn the whole debate upside down and ironically argue that Finland never was a significant actor in Europe – and never will be. Therefore there is no point in getting nervous about Finland's presumably tarnished reputation in Europe; it simply does not matter. In reverse, we should celebrate Finland's insignificance and laugh out loud to those who actually thought that Finland was 'someone' in the European or global arena. In addition to often being cynical, satire as a narrative type is sentimental, self-conscious, and self-critical.

The Consensus-driven Finland

In order to both situate the narrative battle in the right context and to understand the significance of the alleged shift in Finland's European policy, we need to first shortly discuss Finland's identity project in the EU and what is the role of Europe in the self-identification of those who participate in the narrative battle. Tapio Raunio and Teija Tiilikainen argue that 'Finland has often been characterized as a "model student" of the EU that is always willing to promote common goals and to respect common rules and obligations. Pragmatism and adaptability are the leading qualities of Finnish integration policy' (Raunio & Tiilikainen, 2004 p. 145). The metaphor of model pupil[2] is a popular image of Finland's role in the EU, which is juxtaposed – across the political spectrum and both in romantic and tragic narratives – with the purported Southern troublemakers. Explaining Finland's European policy, Raunio and Tiilikainen continue that the 'Lutheran mentality of the Finns, combined with the small-state identity, clearly reflects itself in Finland's international action' (Raunio & Tiilikainen, 2004 p. 145).

Finland's ideal self-image as a model pupil is connected to the desire to be recognised as a full-fledged member of the international system that, as Christopher Browning argues, stems from the country's challenging geopolitical position as a small state in the European periphery dominated by great power interests (Browning, 2015, pp. 206–207; see also Browning, 2008). Browning also notes that the 'emphasis on problem solving also interestingly resonates with historically ingrained nationalist narratives and stereotypes that depict the Finns as possessing a distinctively practical and pragmatic mindset' (Browning, 2015, p. 209).

In the narrative battle of the Eurozone crisis the narrative of Finland as a practical and consensus driven model pupil is challenged in various ways with different political events being 'woven into the narrative tissue' (Ricoeur, 1981, p. 278) and made to function as part of the counter narrative. The most important event was Finland's aforementioned demand for an exclusive collateral deal with Greece before agreeing to join the Eurozone's second financial aid package to Greece in 2011. The fierce demand collided with the model pupil ideal so radically that it caused a deep sense of ontological insecurity – an insecure sense of the Finnish self in Europe – that is explicit in the narrative battle.

Narrating the Eurozone crisis in Finland

The stereotypical bifurcation between virtuous Northern Europeans and repugnant Southern Europeans has featured prominently and served an important narrative function in the Finnish Eurozone crisis debate. The function has been two-fold depending on the narrator's moral and aesthetic preferences: Either Southerners, especially Greece, have been made the main culprit who must be punished or Northerners, especially Finland, are lifted to a superior role as the only possible saviour. Kenneth Burke's 'scapegoat' well illustrates the metaphorical function of South Europe in the narrative battle:

> as the principle of *any* hierarchy involves the possibility of reversing highest and lowest, so the moralizing of status makes for a revolutionary kind of expression, the scapegoat. The scapegoat is dialectically appealing, since it combines in one figure contrary principles of identification and alienation. (Burke, 1969, p. 140)

From romance to tragedy

The article will first analyse how Finland's role in Europe is represented in romantic narratives and how they interpret Finland's identity project in the EU. Niemeläinen[3] positions Finland at the frontline of Europe as a country that can rescue the continent from economic, political, and moral fall. Europe can only find a way out of its crisis if it increases cooperation between the member states, and Finland, according to Niemeläinen, can take a formative role in the process. Niemeläinen writes in his column 'Leaderless Europe' that it is frightening to follow Europe's destinationless wandering in the midst of the Euro crisis as it weakens the global role of European values – freedom, fratenity and equality – while strengthening the power of nationalist populism, which currently leads Europe (Vihreä Lanka, 30 September 2011). According to Niemeläinen, Europe really has only one choice: harmonising its economic policy, which means 'more Europe'. Finally, Niemeläinen encourages Finland to lead the way, because the lack of will and decision-making will lead Europe to fall apart. The narrative represents the traditional 'model pupil' identity that defined Finland's EU policy in the 1990s and the 2000s. It is therefore unsurprising that Paavo Lipponen, Finland's prime minister from 1995 until 2003, similarly emphasises cooperation and rules as the most important cornerstone of Finland's EU policy.

Lipponen writes in his column in *Turun Sanomat* (7 January 2011):

> It is more beneficial to small states to be part of a strong structure in which clear rules are followed. In a breaking Europe we would end up being managed by some of the big states. A short-sighted nationalist is not a true patriot.

Using size as the determining factor is one of the key components of the 'more Europe' narrative; Finland needs cooperation because small states cannot survive on their own. Also the Finnish MEP Sirpa Pietikäinen (EPP) calls for a more united Europe, arguing that states and economies that withdraw from international cooperation face more economic problems, political aversion, and inefficient global problem solving (Nykypäivä, 23 September 2011). For a small state like Finland, a strong and united EU is the best option. Pietikäinen envisions the current crisis as a disease with a set of different prescriptions offered to the patient: collateral, bankruptcy, or EU bonds. But the patient, according to Pietiläinen, 'cannot be cured by single, targeted medication but holistic treatment including several vaccines and long-term nursing programmes'. In Pietikäinen's narrative, the romantic hero has fallen ill, but will rise again with hard work and dedication.[4] A cooperative and compromising Finland is presented as a state that can positively contribute to curing the EU patient.

It is interesting how the size factor is figuratively turned into a coherent fact about Finland's geopolitical position in Europe, although it is by no means a neutral measure. It prompts many questions: what are we actually measuring and why? If we consider Finland's size by geographical area, it is the fifth biggest member state (out of 28) in the EU. If we consider it by GDP per capita, it was the seventh biggest member state in 2011.[5] In terms of Finland's economic performance, Finland was one of only eight member states in 2011 to have an AAA credit rating.[6] Finally, if we measure Finland's size by population, there are only 10 member states that are smaller. The article argues that it was above all the discrepancy between Finland's economic figures and the narrative of Finland as a small state that needs cooperation that influenced the counter narrative that challenged the 'model pupil' identity.

The opponents, as it will be shown later in the article, relied on the idea of market civilisation where those states that have a competitive economy have the moral right to dictate policies in the EU.[7] The 'small state' narrative was no longer as convincing as before. The government, nevertheless, continued to narrate European policy option through the 'more Europe' trope. Prime Minister Jyrki Katainen argued that 'for the austerity measures represented by Finland and Germany to come true, some sort of common European mechanisms are needed' (Rönkkö, 14 September 2011). In the same article, it was brought up that during their meeting in Berlin, Katainen's tie matched in colour with Merkel's jacket, which fittingly symbolised the united front between the Northerners: Finland and Germany.

Employing metaphors of war, the main editorial in Aamulehti similarly argues that the European spirit, trust, and cooperation must be strengthened in order to win the war against the Eurozone crisis (29 September 2011). There are several war metaphors in the text: fighting on several fronts; building a defence wall; and that tightening fiscal austerity might represent our modern Maginot line if rules are not abided by.[8] The editorial concludes that if common trust is lacking, Europe will not survive its 'baptism of fire'. The war metaphor, as Lakoff and Johnson (1980, p. 4) argue, is often used in everyday language in a variety of forms. They note that 'the things we *do* in arguing are partially structured by the concept of war. Though there is no physical battle, there is a verbal battle, and the structure of an argument – attack, defense, counterattack, etc. – reflects this'. The metaphor of war is a popular linguistic device in Finland where the experiences of the Second World War, in particular, serve as powerful and persuasive narrative resources.

Finally, a main editorial in Aamulehti (11 March 2011) employs particularly dramatic language and uses the Roman Empire as narrative resources, comparing the situation to the murder of Julius Caesar that 'ended the career of the famous war leader and politician'. The editorial continues: 'In the Euro group meetings and the EU summits no life is in danger but the careers of the political leaders and above all the idea of European cooperation.' Mikko Mäenpää, the leader of the largest trade union confederation of salaried employees in Finland (STTK), also makes a passionate call for more European cooperation in his column in Turun Sanomat (17 June 2011): 'Europe must succeed. There are no other options ... The ability to collectively solve problems and sustainably build welfare is the best feature of Europeaness.' This illustrates that, as Burke (1969, p. 17) argues, 'depicting of a thing's *end* may be a dramatic way of identifying its *essence*' (emphases in original). Collective problem solving and cooperative attitude, which have traditionally been at the core of Finland's European identity project – are depicted as the very essence of Europe.

As such, what guides the romantic 'more Europe' narrative is not only the underlying believe in the intrinsic virtue of European values but also the belief that Finland belongs to and deserves to be in the European core – often more so than the less reliable and more disorganised South. But despite Finland's geographical, historical, and cultural ties to Europe together with almost two decades of EU membership, the sense of ontological insecurity as regards Finland's European identity prevails. The insecure sense of the European self-frames the narrative battle and continues to limit narrative imagination and resources both in romantic and tragic narrative types. Instead of focusing on broadening the horizon for different policy options, it easily reduces the debate to the question of whether Finland is or should be European. For example, Esa Stenberg, Professor in Global Finance at the University of Turku, argues that 'we should re-open the debate on whether Finns want to be European or not, and what are the rational and emotional reasons for this' (*Turun Sanomat*, 28 September 2011).

Directing his words towards the populist EU critics, he argues that it is 'cheap' to use the EU as a political weapon when hard work has been put into building a common European identity. Believing in the intrinsic value of the European project – which for him was initially about avoiding new major wars – he writes that it must be remembered that the EU membership benefitted Finland and replaced the earlier ambiguous position between the East and the West. As such, Stenberg contributes to the romantic 'more Europe' vision. Similarly, Juho Rahkonen writes in his *Aamulehti* column that Finnish and European identities are not in conflict with each other – Finland *is* part of Europe. (15 September 2011, emphasis added). But Rahkonen also plays with the East–West bifurcation and asks provocatively 'whether European integration has merely been a failed and impossible experiment that is doomed to fall like the Soviet Union?'

Finally, referring to Finland's Europeaness, *Aamulehti* writes in its main editorial titled 'Finland's place is in Europe' that 'Finland's direction cannot be away from Europe. A well functioning EU benefits small states like Finland' (8 September 2011). However, it also draws a line across the union – which is depicted as running between North and South – when arguing that it is understandable that assisting states that have 'messed up their situations is causing resentment in punctilious states like Finland'. It continues that this causes a sense of unfairness, which can turn to wider distrust towards all cooperation and even democracy. As such, political or economic stability is something that can be established through meticulous behaviour – by being a 'model pupil'.

The next section discusses the tragic counter narrative that challenges Finland's 'model pupil' identity. It will be shown that the Weberian division between North and South is the most important narrative resource in the debate. It is clear that the narratives exemplify Kenneth Burke's thesis concerning identification and division, which suggests that they are not in contrast to one another but part of the same motive. The narratives might call for a more united Europe but offer division as the solution. Burke (1969, p. 22) explains that identification 'is affirmed with earnestness precisely because there is division. Identification is compensatory to division'. In the narrative battle, the dynamics between identification and division are connected to Finland's identity project in the EU with narrative attempts to situate Finland at the core of Europe by juxtaposing it with Southern Europe.

Southern European scapegoats

Olli Nurmi writes that Finland has been a European exception in meticulously abiding by the common rules, and as such, strengthening common European economic policies would suit Finland (Nurmi, 30 September 2011). Nurmi continues that a strong and united economic policy would rightfully weaken the decision-making powers of those states that break the rules, and consequently increase the sense of responsibility in Europe – something that Finland and Northern Europe already represent. As such, Nurmi exploits the 'model pupil' metaphor to simultaneously call for 'more Europe' and 'less Europe'. What Nurmi implies is that we need more North and less South, situating Finland at the forefront of the former.

Ville Vähämäki, a Finns party MP, writes in his column that 'traditionally Finns have lived according to their needs, which is a good advice also to the debt-ridden states' (*Kaleva*, 28 September 2011). The metaphor he employs can be translated as 'you cannot have a mouth bigger than your sack',[9] which implies that the economically fragile states have simply eaten more than they earn, and should cut their cravings. Again, Finland is positioned as the moral vanguard in Europe that can teach the Southern member states how to better manage their political affairs. In its main editorial, *Turun Sanomat* writes that 'Greece must learn if not to love at least to pay taxes' (13 September 2011). Referring to Greece's urgent need to cut spending and increase taxes, Olavi Ala-Nissilä writes that 'long-term benefits surpass short-term suffering' (*Turun Sanomat*, 29 September 2011). There is a religious tone to the narrative, which returns us to Weber dividing Europe into a Protestant North and a Catholic South. Now Finland is firmly positioned as the example to follow if Greece is to avoid a tragic fall. Burke explains in his *The Rhetoric of Religion: Studies in Logology* (1970, p. 218) that 'the terms in which we conceive of redemption can help shape the terms in which we conceive of the guilt that is to be redeemed'. The terms here are narrated through the logic dictated by market civilisation standards, illustrating how the idea of redemption continues in a secular context (see Burke, 1969, p. 31).

The image of Greece as a state that has disregarded the balance between spending and earning is particularly popular in the Finnish debate.[10] The dominant motive is Greece's own action, which is narrated tragically. For example, Markku Kuisma, Professor of Finnish and Nordic history at the University of Helsinki, argues that Greece tried to build a Scandinavian standard of living but with debt money (*Kaleva*, 20 September 2011). Greece and other Southern European states are referred to as 'Southern European madcaps' (Rahkonen, 2011), 'scoundrel states' (Kettunen, 30 August 2011),[11] 'lazy-bone states' (Koistinen & Kähkönen, 15 September 2011), 'baddies' (Rinne, 23 September 2011), 'the weakest links' (Rautio, 9 January 2011),[12] 'prodigal sons' (*Kaleva*, 16 March 2011), 'not as "empty pocket" as the debt crisis make it seem' (*Kaleva*, 28 September 2011), 'living carelessly' (Pekkarinen, 14 September 2011), and 'living as if there's no tomorrow' (Järventie, 8 September 2011). *Aamulehti* also suggests in its main editorial that Greece has not even begun to reorganise its economy by employing a sarcastic Finnish proverb: 'The task is complete, it only needs to be started' (7 September 2011).[13]

All these terms narrate the situation as hopeless and present a stark difference between North and South. The former is elevated to a higher position by presenting the latter as politically, economically, and morally weak. The South's imagined moral failings – laziness, corruption, and inefficiency – are used, at least implicitly, to explain its current political and economic crisis. For example, Paavo Rautio writes in his *Helsingin Sanomat* column that 'the plight of the crisis states is largely self-inflicted' (21 September 2011). Rautio employs a ship metaphor in his column: 'When problems began to emerge, the weak ones started to go under and the strong ones had to come to help – not out of sympathy but because the Euro-zone was sinking and the whole monetary union was about to take in water'.[14]

Helsingin Sanomat writes in its main editorial in January 2011 that Finland is in 'the core of the European core' – 'the AAA club' – that is inevitably breaking away from the rest of the union and acts as a 'beacon' to member states that are struggling in the 'storm'. It further argues that 'those states and regions that had the potential to make it now rise like a cork in the water (24 January 2011). Those state that already had troubles to survive are sinking'. Sports metaphors support the idea of market civilisation with physical attributes being intertwined with economic performance and durability. As Pekka Kymä-läinen writes in his column in *Aamulehti* (6 January 2011):

> Luckily (Finland's then European Commissioner for Economic and Monetary Affairs and the Euro Olli) Rehn is a footballer and sustained a good condition because now it is needed. The cold economic figures from the last days of the previous year are a burden to Rehn and his team, and there are no substitute players.

Finally, the ontological insecurity concerns regarding Finland's European identity are invoked in a *Helsingin Sanomat* article in which the then Viviane Reding, European Com-missioner of Justice, is quoted as saying that 'the Finns are true Europeans' (Kähkönen, 8 September 2011). In the article, she affirms that 'the Finns have always been firm and loyal Europeans', but subsequently notes that she hopes that they 'will remain that way'. The fear of losing the status as true Europeans takes hold when established predictions fail to materialise (Roe, 2008, pp. 778; 782). The prediction of Finland being a consensus-driven and compromising model pupil did not materialise when the controversial demand of the Greek collateral was brought to the table. Finland was seen to turn from a model pupil to a rebel, which was a position more commonly or stereotypically associ-ated with Southern Europe. In other words, the ontologically important narrative line between the exemplary North and troublesome South was challenged.

Narrating 'political capital'

In the debate about Finland losing its model pupil status in the EU, the term 'political capital' comes up regularly. It was argued that Finland worked hard to build up its political capital – as reflected in the image as a model pupil that can be trusted – and now all that was wasted for an unreasonable demand. For example, *Helsingin Sanomat* writes in its main editorial that small states like Finland need to acquire political capital in order to be heard in the EU (3 September 2011). Until recently, Finland had stayed true to that with its constructive and compromise-driven EU policy and by positioning itself in the decision-making core. The editorial continues that Finland's uncompromising demand for the Greek collateral is a stark exception to the familiar way of thinking. It concludes with a warning that

> This way of acting will be remembered. It might not be worthwhile to talk about revenge but in the EU it takes a long time to acquire political capital and a short time to spend it. It is not

only about tarnishing the reputation or an ambiguous loss of image. Finland's negotiation position might weaken in actual issue areas.

The idea of transformation is dramatised and localised to Finland with dire consequences if the 'model pupil' behaviour is not followed. Such dramatic and persuasive language clearly resonates in Finland where a poll showed that over half of the population expressed concern that Finland 'will be side-tracked and end up in a deadlock in the EU' as a result of the collateral demand (Pokkinen & Palovaara, 7 September 2011). Olli Kivinen, a political columnist, similarly defends the 'model pupil' metaphor and argued that 'Finland should be a reasonable builder, not a troublemaker that rocks the boat' (*Helsingin Sanomat*, 13 September 2011). For Katarina Baer, 'Finland is drifting further away from Europe' (*Helsingin Sanomat*, 30 September 2011). Jaakonsaari (Simola, 6 May 2011) notes that Finland's nation branding committee headed by the then foreign minister Alexander Stubb concluded that Finland can solve all the problems but now worryingly 'Finland is the problem'.

Even the then Prime Minister Jyrki Katainen admitted that the demand for the Greek collateral 'will leave a mark' (*Helsingin Sanomat*, 4 September 2011). In this narrative, the tragic hero, Finland, committed a crucial mistake – it punched above its weight – that will cost its hard-earned status as a core state in the EU. The then Foreign Minister Erkki Tuomioja, on the other hand, emphasised that there has been no negative signs resulting from Finland's uncompromising attitude (Huhta, 4 September 2011).[15] According to Tuomioja, Finland is actually 'doing a favour to the whole Europe' as the Greek collateral would pave the way towards more economic strength. According to this narrative, the hero, Finland, is sacrificing its hard-earned position for the sake of the whole Europe.

Satirists in the narrative battle

A satirical response to the debate highlights Finland's naïve and essentially insignificant role in the EU where small states are subservient to the big member states. As such, the elite-masses bifurcation exists also among member states where the big ones allegedly represent the powerful elite. The satirical narrative turns the desirability of the 'model pupil' metaphor around in an ironic and even resentful way. Rorty (1989, p. 88) notes that irony is 'if not intrinsically resentful, at least reactive Ironists have to have something to have doubts about, something from which to be alienated'. This means that being a model pupil in the EU only benefits the powerful elite, not the peripheral pupil – not at least the majority population in the country.

Helsingin Sanomat employs a vehicle metaphor when noting that it is not the then President of the European Commission José Manuel Barroso who is 'on the driving seat' when the EU is trying to 'navigate its way off the debt road' but the big member states: Germany's Merkel and France's Sarkozy (Kähkönen, 29 September 2011). A few months earlier its main editorial (8 February 2011) speculated:

> A question arises as to how much the list (of economic and fiscal reforms delivered to the European Council by Germany's Angela Merkel and France's Nicolas Sarkozy) reflects the desire of Germany and France to strengthen their own competitiveness vis-à-vis the other EU states rather than a genuine attempt to strengthen Europe's banking sector or the economy of the struggling Euro countries.

Similarly, *Aamulehti* writes in its main editorial that 'all roads lead to Berlin' (14 September 2011) whilst Mitro Repo, then a Finnish MEP in the Group of the Progressive Alliance of Socialists and Democrats, notes: 'Who decides? Germany, Germany, Germany' (13 September 2011). In February 2011 *Aamulehti* ironically writes: 'Next will be the harmonisation of dress code (*Aamulehti*, 8 February 2011). This means a compulsory outfit of leather trousers and a beret to everyone in the European Union' with the first, of course, referring to Germany and the latter to France.[16]

Vesa Kanniainen, Professor of Economics at the University of Helsinki, writes in *Helsingin Sanomat* (10 May 2011) that Finnish decision-makers have been threatened that Finland's role might weaken in the EU if the financial aid package to Portugal fails. Kanniainen continues sarcastically that 'it is possible that the only thing that weakens is the status of those politicians and civil servants that have built their careers in the EU'. The EU is represented as an elite-driven project that supposedly benefits all members but in reality only produces a new political and economic EU elite. Mauri Pekkarinen, a veteran Centre Party politician, writes that the government's demand for the Greek collateral has merely served as 'emperor's new clothes', hiding the real attempt to increase Finland's economic liabilities towards other EU member states (*Aamulehti*, 14 September 2011). Greece, he argues, should be allowed to declare 'bankruptcy' and Finland should refrain from giving out more financial aid to other Eurozone states.

Also the importance of building 'political capital' in the EU, which formed the cornerstone of Finland's EU policy since the 1990s, is challenged with satirical narrative strategies. Pekka Pihlanto, Emeritus Professor at the Turku School of Economics, ironically asks that when it comes to Finland's supposed loss of trust in the EU, what have we actually achieved with our political capital so far? (Pihlanto, 7 September 2011). Furthermore, although the Greek collateral demand is justified, we would probably only achieve a superficial solution that our politicians were forced to accept. Finally, he probes why Finland needs to get into more debt just to rescue French and German banks.

In the satirical narratives, the idea that Finland is at the core of Europe is presented in a carnivalesque manner.[17] The 'model pupil' metaphor attains a negative connotation and is presented as the dominant motive for Finland's allegedly subservient position in the EU. For example, Arvi Marjamäki, a Finns party[18] supporter, employs a Soviet reference and calls for Finland to abandon the Euro 'kolkhoz' and its socialist policies, where a 'central committee' is giving out crumbs to the masses while the elite and 'duuma' continue to party with no regard for the well-being of the taxpayers (*Aamulehti*, 30 September 2011).

Veikko Vuorikoski employs the beacon metaphor when he, in an ironic manner, asks in his column in *Aamulehti* (21 January 2011): 'What has made (the British Prime Minister David) Cameron interested in the cold North? Is there a new light shining from the north that is brighter than the previous guiding stars?' Vuorikoski refers to Cameron inviting all Nordic and Baltic leaders to an unofficial meeting in London on 20 January 2011. Vuorikoski continues that according to the then Foreign Minister Alexander Stubb, small states are always flattered when big member states approach them and that it is important to have big friends because 'we benefit from it'. Vuorikoski concludes: 'Surely so, but one needs to choose also big friends carefully. There might be secret motives behind those smiles.'

Also employing an ironic narrative, Paavo Lintula writes in his commentary that Finland's alleged tarnished reputation is merely political elite's babbling (*Aamulehti*, 9

September 2011). He continues that if the reputation is about being submissive and obe-dient, it deserves to be lost. He writes that France and Germany have humiliated Finland and other small member states by negotiating all the deals beforehand and only informing the rest what the EU has decided. The only role for the rest of the member state leaders has been to pretend a unified front by looking important in the official portraits. Finally, he refers to the Second World War and notes that history is quickly forgotten: Finland was left alone to fight against the Soviet Union; why would you trust the European powers this time around? Hannu Kahra, Professor in Finance at the University of Oulu, notes that the Euro system reminds the Soviet Union in that crucial decision cannot be made and rules are not followed' (Sajari, 28 September 2011).

When the Greek collateral deal was finally completed and after immense political pressure to make the initially confidential documents public, the Finns Party chairman Timo Soini published a rare full-page notification on the front page of the Sunday edition of *Helsingin Sanomat*, arguing that Finland's deal – which according to him was not really a traditional collateral deal at all – was so expensive that no other member state even wanted it. Finland was, once again, foolish and naïve.[19] In the narrative of Unto Valpas (2011), a Left Alliance MP, Finland's foolishness can be traced back to the elite-driven decision to adopt Euro in 2002 when 'in a Euro ecstasy people were led to believe that the common currency will become a supreme method of payment and its critics were considered mainly fools.' As a result Finland is now 'tethered' to 'rescuing the muddy economies' of member state after member state.

It was initially the Finns party that made the more conflict-focused tragic and satirical narratives a popular discursive frame in the Finnish Eurozone crisis debate. Finland's tragic fault is here attributed to either its naïve nature or a morally corrupted elite that keeps Finland in the EU where the elites and Southern European states are taking advantage of it. *Kaleva* suggests in its main editorial that Greece is actually not as poor as we think, and that the bailout 'tap' should be turned off (28 September 2011). Employing metaphors of marshlands, which have strong cultural resonance in Finland, it notes that 'we are in a deep swamp up to our necks, and will not stay dry. Now we can only guess how badly we will get wet'.[20] The editorial concludes that the solution is for Greece to continue with its economic modernising including cuts and tax increases as well as selling its national property. No more financial aid should be expected from the other Euro countries.

In his commentary in *Aamulehti*, Reijo Kauppila similarly argues that Greece is actually richer than Finland, but is not willing to pay back the loans (30 September 2011). Still the 'blue-eyed' (metaphor for naïve) and 'foolish' Europeans are planning to lend more money to Greece. These loans, he continues, will turn into gifts. Kauppila concludes that 'the Greeks are tricking European states as much as they can. This is the Greek economic policy'. Also Kauppila employs the popular tap metaphor to describe the financial aid packages: Greece only needs to turn the tap on to receive more money. For Leena Tikka, writing in her commentary in *Turun Sanomat*, Finnish taxpayers have been 'misled' to pay for Greece's 'prodigal way of living' (29 September 2011).

Ringmar (2006, p. 415) argues that as tragedies and satires are 'the obvious fall-back options', stories in international relations tend to 'turn both darker and ironic'. This is true also in the Finnish case. Ringmar continues that tragedies and satires are not necessarily more accurate descriptions of world politics but they are less likely to suffer reversals and are for that reason alone more attractive. In this sense it is easy to understand why the most persuasive stories of international relations have often been told in these two modes.

It was particularly the Finns party that recognised the attractiveness of telling dark and ironic stories of European integration and ideals, introducing the narrative types to the Eurozone crisis debate. Their countering effect was successful that they soon represented hegemonic interpretations of the crisis, shared across different political parties.

Hayden White argues that narratives have ideological implications with the term 'ideology' being employed to refer to 'a set of prescriptions for taking a position in the present world of social praxis and acting upon it' (White, 1973, p. 22). In the Eurozone crisis debate in Finland, the 'more Europe' narrative represents a conservative mode of ideological implication in that it aims to maintain the current state of affairs and it is not restricted to particular parties. The tragic narrative, on the other hand, represents a radical mode of ideological implications as it aims to completely reverse Finland's EU policy. The Finns party most prominently but not exclusively embodies the radical mode of implication with its uncompromisingly critical approach towards the EU. It frequently uses a slogan 'Where the EU, there the problem'.[21] Employing a biblical metaphor, the party chair Timo Soini has demanded the prime minister to tell Angela Merkel 'to let my people go!' – a reference to Moses meeting Pharaoh as written in the Old Testament of the Bible (Pokkinen, 13 September 2011).[22]

Markets as the scapegoat

Finally, there are narratives in the Finnish debate that shift the responsibility from agencies to structure – the markets. These narratives pay less attention to the character or conduct of single agencies and emphasise the role of the uncontrollable, faceless, and unethical market forces. They demand more political leadership and decision-making either on a national or supranational level. As such, they can have either conservative ('more Europe') or radical ('let our people go!') implications. Belonging to the first camp, Raimo Väyrynen argues that strengthening economic coordination in the EU is essential for saving the Eurozone and calming down market forces that in crisis situations are only concerned with their own benefits. According to Väyrynen, the main problem has been weak and opportunistic political leadership both nationally and across the Eurozone. He also notes that market forces limit political communication, which widens the gap between the elite and the masses and threatens democracy (Väyrynen, 3 September 2011).

Liisa Jaakonsaari, a Finnish MEP, notes that irresponsible banks are widely held as the 'chief war culprits' and calls for more political intervention (Jaakonsaari, 20 September 2011). Metaphorically comparing the economic crisis to a fire that threatens the Eurozone, *Turun Sanomat* writes in its main editorial that 'weak state power has allowed the market forces to assume more power and hold political decision-makers to ransom. Unfortunately the market forces have in the process gained support from nationalist politicians' (29 September 2011). Matti Mörttinen writes that 'the market forces demanded a victim, and political decision-makers were ready to sacrifice Greece' (Aamulehti, 11 September 2011). He continues that the market forces did not like the Euro currency in the first place as it reduced currency trading: more currencies, more trading. As such, a return to national currencies would mean more trading opportunities for bankers.

In these narratives, the underlying moral vision depicts market forces as intrinsically unethical, greedy, and wicked. Burke's (1969, p. 5) 'all-pervasive generating principle' is the markets that are an uncontrollable force. The narratives use 'personification' as their narrative strategy, which allows them to 'comprehend a wide variety of experiences with nonhuman entities in terms of human motivations, characteristics, and activities' (Lakoff & Johnson, 1980, p. 33). Treating the markets as a person is a more accessible explanation that can be presented in narrative terms. As Lakoff & Johnson (1980, p. 34) continue:

> Viewing something as abstract as inflation in human terms has an explanatory power of the only sort that makes sense to most people. When we are suffering substantial economic losses due to complex economic and political factors that no one really understands, the INFLATION IS AN ADVERSARY metaphor at least gives us a coherent account of why we're suffering these losses.

What is interesting about the narratives that treat the markets as the adversary is that they have the most potential for unifying North and South Europe as well as to opening new narrative horizons for a debate about Finland's EU policies. They are less concerned with Finland's identity project in the EU and render the 'model pupil' metaphor less meaningful. At the same time, they contain the risk of reducing the complexity of economic and political processes into a coherent yet far too simplified narrative of 'what it all boils down to' (Burke, 1969, p. 15).

Conclusion

To tease out the narrative structure of policy debates is important because stories are a particularly powerful tool in constructing reality. When a policy option is woven into a narrative that employs cultural metaphors and national stereotypes it acquires political potency that is often lacking in purely analytical statements that rely on statistics and facts. The eruption of European financial crisis has seen a rise in narratives that exploit the North–South division in such a way as to elevate Finland and other Northern European states to a higher political, moral, and economic status vis-à-vis Greece and other Southern European states. The narratives rely on a market civilization logic of economic performance rather than immaterial values determining who has the right to dictate policies in Europe.

Both tragic and romantic narratives of Finland's role and status in Europe follow a market civilization thinking with their emphasis on Finland's highest possible credit rating, which is indicated with three As, but their emplotment is different. Tragedians focus on Finland's naïve faith in European ideals that are being challenged by the greedy and untrustworthy Southerners. Romantics, on the other hand, situate Finland at the very core of Europe where it can rescue the whole union with its vision and determination. Satirists reverse the whole plot and represent Finland's European self in a carnivalesque fashion: Finland has no role to play in the faith of Europe and should stop pretending otherwise. What is in common with all the three narratives is that the actual moral focus is less on the Eurozone crisis and more on the nature and future of Finland. In other words, in narrating the Eurozone crisis, they are narrating themselves.

It is paradoxical that ontological concerns regarding Finland's European identity are narrated through European metaphors and ideas ranging from the fate of Julius Caesar to the Maginot Line and the works of Max Weber. The article therefore calls the Finnish narrative battle an Europeanised debate on a national level. The article further suggests the narrative battle has important policy implications not only on a national but on the European level because Finland's desire – or the lack of it – to act as a European 'model pupil' provides powerful narrative resources to EU critics across Europe. Like Julius Caesar or the Maginot Line, different interpretations of Finland's model pupil-ness can eventually become European narrative resources that are used to localise or dramatise the principle of transformation anywhere in Europe.

Notes

1. *Nykypäivä* is affiliated to the National Coalition Party, a centre-right party belonging to the European People's Party in the European Parliament. *Suomenmaa* is affiliated to the Centre Party, an agrarian party belonging to the Alliance of Liberals and Democrats for Europe in the European Parliament. *Vihreä Lanka* is affiliated to the Green Party.
2. For example, *Aamulehti* writes that 'Finland is one of the stars in the Commission report', 13 September 2011; Allan Rosas (Turun Sanomat, 19 September 2011) notes that Finland is among the model pupils in the EU with 'Greece famously being the most sinful' ('suurin syntipukki'); and Esa Stenberg (*Turun Sanomat*, 28 September 2011) writes that Finland received positive fame for fulfilling the EMU criteria among the best.
3. 'Niemeläinen' was Pekka Sauri's, a Green League politician, pseudonym in Vihreä Lanka between 2000 and 2012.
4. The disease metaphor is ubiquitous in the policy debate. For example, Riikka Manner (2011), a Finnish MEP, writes that 'Barroso was expected to present miraculous medicine to cure Europe's acute state'. *Suomenmaa*, 30 September 2011. Also Timo Kalli, a Centre Party MP, uses the disease metaphor to argue that the current medicine taken for the EU's debt crisis, financial aid, should be abandoned and notes that 'a competent and good doctor can rewrite the prescription if the patient is not cured with the existing medicine. (Kontio, 28 September 2011)
5. See Eurostat http://ec.europa.eu/eurostat/tgm/table.do?tab=table&init=1&language=en&pcode=tec00001&plugin=1 (5 January 2016).
6. See http://www.treasuryfinland.fi/en-US/News_and_publications/News_archive/Fitch_Ratings_affirms_AAA_rating_for_Fin(48130) (5 January 2016).
7. More on the idea of market civilisation, see Bowden and Seabrooke (2006), Gill (1995), and Kangas (2013).
8. Other examples of the war metaphors are Veikko Räntilä writing in *Aamulehti* that in South-Europe there is a 'wide minefield', 24 September 2011, and Toni Viljanmaa writing in *Aamulehti* (5 May 2011) that Jyrki Katainen, the then prime minister, being 'ambushed'.
9. 'Suu säkkiä myöten'.
10. This image is a useful political tool in Finland where, according to Juho Saari, Professor in Sociology at the University of Eastern Finland, the least empathy on a societal level is felt towards the debt burdened because they are seen as having brought their misery upon themselves. As such, only a minimum amount of public money should be spent to assist them. Nykänen (2013).
11. Also Anneli Jäätteenmäki, an Alde MEP, employed the term when arguing that

    it is not the responsibility of the states that have managed their economies well to pay the bills and debts of the scoundrel states. It is time to admit that Greece cannot pay all its bills and letting it declare bankruptcy is for the benefit of Greece and the whole of Europe. (Suomenmaa, 16 September 2011)

12. More specifically, it is Greece and Ireland that are the 'weakest links'.

13. 'Talouden saneeraus on Kreikassa savolaisittain aloittamista vaille valmis.'
14. Others employing the ship metaphor include Juho Rahkonen who asks whether Greek economy will sink to the bottom of the Aegean Sea, *Aamulehti*, 15 September 2011; and the main editorial in *Helsingin Sanomat*: 'While watching horrifyingly Greece to sink, we have forgotten to follow the economic development in Ireland', 9 September 2011.
15. Also Sirpa Pietikäinen argues that Finland's EU position has not suffered because of the Greek collateral demand. For her, Finland does not have enough power to bring down the whole Eurozone, as many critics have warned. The whole debate, according to her, has reflected Finland's prevailing 'what do they think about us' syndrome (Niemitalo, 3 September 2011).
16. Sami Metelinen argues in his counter narrative in *Nykypäivä* (17 June 2011) that it is politically and morally right for Germany to lead the way in Europe: 'Why economically the most successful state would not take the leading responsibility for Europe's future?'
17. More on the theory of carnivalesque, see Mikhail Bakhtin, *Rabelais and his world*, transl. Helene Iswolsky (Bloomington: Indiana University Press, 2008).
18. A newcomer in Finland's mainstream politics, the Finns party is a nationalist, EU critical party that belongs to the Europe of Freedom & Democracy (EFP) group in the European Parliament.
19. Also the media has criticised the governmental EU policy. Referring to the demand for the Greek collateral as the then Finance Minister 'Urpilainen's fruitless crusade', *Aamulehti* writes in its main editorial that the governmental approach to the crisis has been too narrow and without any vision (7 September 2011). It has obsessively pushed through with the demand as if nothing else matters for Finland. In another editorial it notes that the government is now imprisoned by the collateral demand because 'the Coalition Party needs to maintain the collateral façade set up by Urpilainen (SDP) as giving up on the demand could mean a death sentence to Katainen's (KOK) coalition government that was half forcibly formed (*Aamulehti*, 3 September 2011). Also Riitta Järventie writes that 'amid the collateral battle the government has managed Finland's own economic matters with a left hand (a metaphor for being careless)' (*Aamulehti*, 8 September 2011).
20. Also *Helsingin Sanomat* (13 March 2011) writes in its main editorial that as a result of the financial aid to Greece 'the forest fire was avoided but the marshland fire does not get extinguished'.
21. See for example Vähämäki (2011).
22. The are several biblical metaphors in the narrative battle. For example, *Turun Sanomat* (25 February 2011) writes in its main editorial that 'in the Brussels meeting the EU leaders need the wisdom of Solomon'. Or as Anni Lassila (2011) writes in her *Helsingin Sanomat* column in reference to Greece's debts, Erkki Liikanen, head of the Finnish Central Bank, 'denied three times', a biblical reference to the denial of Peter.

Disclosure statement

No potential conflict of interest was reported by the author.

References

Ala-Nissilä, O. (2011, September 29). Valtioiden velkapommit purettava hallitusti. *Turun Sanomat*.
Baer, K. (2011, September 30). Saksa hyväksyi EU:n laajennetun tukivälineen velkamaille. *Helsingin Sanomat*.
Barnett, M. (1999). Culture, strategy and foreign policy change: Israel's road to Oslo. *European Journal of International Relations, 5*(1), 5–36.

Bowden, B., & Seabrooke, L. (Eds.). (2006). *Global standards of market civilization*. Oxon: Routledge.

Browning, C. (2008). *Constructivism, narrative and foreign policy analysis. A case study of Finland*. Bern: Peter Lang.

Browning, C. (2015). Nation branding, national self-esteem, and the constitution of subjectivity in late modernity. *Foreign Policy Analysis, 11*(2), 195–214.

Bruner, J. (1991). The narrative construction of reality. *Critical Inquiry, 18*(1), 1–21.

Burke, K. (1969). *A rhetoric of motives*. Berkeley: University of California Press.

Burke, K. (1970). *The rhetoric of religion: studies in logology*. Berkeley: University of California Press.

Euroalue natisee liitoksissaan. (2011, September 13). *Turun Sanomat*.

Finland could leave the eurozone rather than pay other nations' debts, says Jutta Urpilainen. (2012, July 6). *The Telegraph*. Retrieved from http://www.telegraph.co.uk/finance/financialcrisis/9380851/Finland-could-leave-the-eurozone-rather-than-pay-other-nations-debts-says-Jutta-Urpilainen.html

Frye, N. (1957/2000). *Anatomy of criticism: Four essays*. Princeton: Princeton University Press.

Gergen, K. (1999). *An invitation to social construction*. London: Sage.

Gill, S. (1995). Globalisation, market civilisation, and disciplinary neoliberalism. *Millennium – Journal of International Studies, 24*, 399–423.

Hallitus on vakuusvaateiden vanki. (2011, September 3). *Aamulehti*.

Hätärahalla on rajansa. (2011, September 28). *Kaleva*.

Hermot pinnalla Euroopassa. (2011, March 11). *Aamulehti*.

Herrnstein Smith, B. (1981). Narrative versions, narrative theories. In W. J. T. Mitchell (Ed.), *On narrative* (pp. 213–236). Chicago: University of Chicago Press.

Huhta, K. (2011, September 4). Tuomioja odottaa kiitosta Suomen linjalle eurokriisissä. *Helsingin Sanomat*.

Irlanti nieli talouslääkkeensä. (2011, September 9). *Helsingin Sanomat*.

Isotalus, P. (2011, September 13). Euromaiden velkavuori kasvaa ensi vuonnakin. *Aamulehti*.

Jaakonsaari, L. (2011, September 20). *Kaleva*.

Jäätteenmäki, A. (2011, September 16). Kuka johtaa Suomen EU-politiikkaa? *Suomenmaa*.

Järventie, R. (2011, September 8). Kansa tietää, vai tietääkö? *Aamulehti*.

Kähkönen, V. (2011, September 8). Komissaari Reding: Suomalaiset ovat aitoja eurooppalaisia. *Helsingin Sanomat*.

Kähkönen, V. (2011, September 29). Euroopalta puuttuu selkeä johtaja. *Helsingin Sanomat*.

Kangas, A. (2013). Market civilisation meets economic nationalism: The discourse of nation in Russia's modernisation. *Nations and Nationalism, 19*(3), 572–591.

Kanniainen, V. (2011, May 10). EU:n pelottelu on epäuskottavaa. *Helsingin Sanomat*.

Katainen: Vakuusjupakka jättää pienen jäljen. (2011, September 4). *Helsingin Sanomat*.

Kauppila, R. (2011, September 30). Lainat Kreikalle muuttuvat lahjaksi. *Aamulehti*.

Kettunen, O. (2011, August 30). Eurobondit – askel liittovaltioon. *Kaleva*.

Kivinen, O. (2011, September 13). Mustaa Pekkaa metsästämässä. *Helsingin Sanomat*.

Kohti hallittua velkajärjestelyä. (2011, September 14). *Aamulehti*.

Koistinen, O., & Kähkönen, V. (2011, September 15). Eurobondeista Suomelle lisäkulu. *Helsingin Sanomat*.

Kontio, P. (2011, September 28). Keskustalta vihreää valoa Kreikan velkajärjestelylle. *Suomenmaa*.

Kymäläinen, P. (2011, January 6). Miten kauan Euro-Olli jaksaa? *Aamulehti*.

Lakoff, G., & Johnson, M. (1980). *Metaphors we live by*. Chicago: University of Chicago Press.

Lassila, A. (2011, June 16). Liikanen kielsi kolmesti. *Helsingin Sanomat*.

Lintula, P. (2011, September 9). Suomen maine joutaakin mennä. *Aamulehti*.

Lipponen, P. (2011, January 7). Kriisistä tietoisuuteen. *Turun Sanomat*.

Mäenpää, M. (2011, June 17). 'Euroopan pitää onnistua'. *Turun Sanomat*.

Mann, M. (1986). *The sources of social power: A history of power from the beginning to AD 1760*. Cambridge: Cambridge University Press.

Manner, R. (2011, September 30). Federalismi ei ole oikea tie. *Suomenmaa*.

Marjamäki, A. (2011, September 30). Hallitus on vajonnut euron syövereihin. *Aamulehti*.

Metelinen, S. (2011, June 17). Saksalle Euroopan johtovastuu. *Nykypäivä*.

Mörttinen, M. (2011, September 11). Uutta 'uhrimieltä' euroalueella. *Aamulehti*.

Näennäinen ristiriita. (2011, March 13). *Helsingin Sanomat*.

Nahkahousut ja baskeri. (2011, February 8). *Aamulehti*.

Niemeläinen. (2011, September 30). Johtajaton Eurooppa. *Vihreä Lanka*.

Niemitalo, M. (2011, September 3). Suomi tuskin kaataa euroa. *Kaleva*.

Nurmi, O. (2011, September 30). Kriisit keskittävät valtaa. *Nykypäivä*.

Nykänen (Vuorelma), J. (2013). Identity, narrative and frames: Renegotiating "firmness" in Turkey's Kurdish initiatives. *Insight Turkey, 15*(2), 85–102.

On tullut maksun aika. (2011, February 8). *Helsingin Sanomat*.

Outo viesti takausvastuista. (2011, March 16). *Kaleva*.

Papandreu vakuutteluvisiitillä. (2011, February 25). *Turun Sanomat*.

Pekkarinen, M. (2011, September 14). Avustusunionilla ei ole tulevaisuutta. *Aamulehti*.

Pietikäinen, S. (2011, September 23). Eurooppa tienhaarassa. *Nykypäivä*.

Pihlanto, P. (2011, September 7). Vakuusvaatimus on oikeutettu. *Turun Sanomat*.

Pokkinen, P. (2011, September 13). Ei arvuuttelua velkajärjestelyllä. *Helsingin Sanomat*.

Pokkinen, P., & Palovaara, J. (2011, September 7). Kansaa huolettaa, että Suomi ajautuu EU:ssa sivuraiteelle: euron vastustus lisääntyy. *Helsingin Sanomat*.

Rahkonen, J. (2011, September 15). Kansanäänestys menisi tiukaksi. *Aamulehti*.

Räntilä, V. (2011, September 24). Velkakriisi rahoitusalan luoma miinäkenttä. *Aamulehti*.

Raunio, T., & Tiilikainen, T. (2004). *Finland in the European Union*. London: Routledge.

Rautio, P. (2011, January 9). Eurobondit palaavat esityslistalle. *Helsingin Sanomat*.

Rautio, P. (2011, September 21). Euron tuho repisi koko unionia. *Helsingin Sanomat*.

Repo, M. (2011, September 13). Kuka päättää? Saksa, Saksa, Saksa. *Aamulehti*.

Ricoeur, P. (1981). *Hermeneutics & the human sciences: Essays on language, action & interpretation*. Cambridge: Cambridge University Press.

Riessman, C. (2008). *Narrative methods for the human sciences*. Thousand Oaks: Sage Publications.

Rimmon-Kenan, S. (2006). Concepts of narrative. In Matti Hyvärinen, Anu Korhonen, & Juri Mykkänen (Eds.), *The travelling concept of narrative* (pp. 10–19). Helsinki: Helsinki Collegium of Advanced Studies.

Ringmar, E. (1996). On the ontological status of the state. *European Journal of International Relations, 2*(4), 439–466.

Ringmar, E. (2006). Inter-textual relations: The quarrel over the Iraq War as a conflict between narrative types. *Cooperation and Conflict, 41*(4), 403–421.

Ringmar, E. (2008). *Identity, interest & action: A cultural explanation of Sweden's intervention in the thirty years War*. Cambridge: Cambridge University Press.

Rinne, J. (2011, September 23). Halla-Ahon kirjoitus auttoi koko Eurooppaa. *Aamulehti*.

Roe, P. (2008). The 'value' of positive security. *Review of International Studies, 34*, 777–794.

Rönkkö, P. (2011). Suomelle ei tippunut ikiomia Kreikka-takuita. *Aamulehti*.

Rorty, R. (1989). *Contingency, irony, and solidarity*. Cambridge: Cambridge University Press.

Rosas, A. (2011, September 19). Johtuuko velkakriisi yhdestä virkkeestä?. *Turun Sanomat*.

Sajari, P. (2011, September 28). Kreikka-tuki on suotuisa pankeille. *Helsingin Sanomat*.

Simola, A. (2011, May 6). Maineessa ei vielä lommoa, mutta neuvotteluasema voi heiketä. *Aamulehti*.

Sjursen, H. (Ed.). (2013). *The EU's common foreign and security policy: The quest for democracy*. London: Routledge.

Somers, M., & Gibson, G. (1994). Reclaiming the Epistemological "Other": Narrative and the social construction of identity. In Craig Calhoun (Ed.), *Social theory and the politics of identity* (pp. 37–99). Oxford: Blackwell.

Stenberg, E. (2011, September 28). Suomen EU-keskustelu muuttunut jäsenyyden alkuajoista. *Turun Sanomat*.

Subotic, J. (2015). Narrative, ontological security, and foreign policy change. *Foreign Policy Analysis*. doi:10.1111/fpa.12089.

Suomen paikka on Euroopassa. (2011, September 8). *Aamulehti*.

Suomi haaskaa vuosia kerättyä pääomaansa. (2011, September 3). *Helsingin Sanomat*.

Suomi on EU:n ytimen ytimessä. (2011, January 24). *Helsingin Sanomat*.

Tikka, L. (2011, September 29). Meistäkö maksumiehiä. *Turun Sanomat.*
Tukipäätösten toimeenpano ontuu. (2011, September 29). *Turun Sanomat.*
Urpilaisen hedelmätön ristiretki. (2011, September 7). *Aamulehti.*
Vähämäki, V. (2011, September 28). Velkakriisi. *Kaleva.*
Valpas, U. (2011, January 19). Horjuva euro. *Kaleva.*
Väyrynen, R. (2011, September 3). Eurokriisi ja demokratia. *Kaleva.*
Viljanmaa, T. (2011, May 5). Katainen jäi väijytykseen. *Aamulehti.*
Vuorikoski, V. (2011, January 21). Kylmän Euroopan kriittinen kerho. *Aamulehti.*
Weber, M. (2002). *The protestant ethic and the spirit of capitalism: And other writings.* New York: Penguin Books.
White, H. (1973). *Metahistory: The historical imagination in the nineteenth-century Europe.* Baltimore, MD: The Johns Hopkins University Press.
White, H. (1987). *The content of the form: Narrative discourse and historical representation.* Baltimore: Johns Hopkins University Press.
Yhtenäisen Euroopan tulikaste. (2011, September 29). *Aamulehti.*

2 'Between a rock and a hard place'

Bulgarian highly skilled migrants' experiences of external and internal stereotypes in the context of the European crisis

Elena Genova

ABSTRACT

The intensification of intra-European migration has more recently coincided with the negative socio-economic consequences of the European economic crisis. The latter has revitalised dormant national stereotypes, employed into the scapegoating of migrants across Europe. Drawing on multi-sited ethnographic research, this article focuses on young, highly skilled Bulgarian migrants in the UK. Their experiences of internal and external national stereotypes are examined in detail. This article argues that this results in a process of double-sided othering, which has implications upon the identities of young skilled Bulgarians as they employ various strategies to make sense of their migratory choices.

The intensification of European integration and the end of the Cold War, have enabled Europeans to study, work and live in other member states, transforming the EU into the epitome of the 'network state' (Castells, 2004). While visa restrictions among the 28 EU member states are now a relic from the (not so distant) past, their non-existence can hardly be proclaimed in a Fukuyamian (1992) manner as the end to intra-European cleavages. Instead, Balibar (2010) argues that borders are more prominent than ever – a claim that becomes more evident in light of the implications of the ongoing European economic crisis. The latter coincided with high levels of migration both within and outside the EU, thus producing an array of emotional responses with markedly negative connotations both on governmental and local level in many countries (Datta, 2011). Therefore, the economic crisis has tested the core principles of the EU as across its member-states nationalism (s) have gathered more momentum. This has in turn prompted the rebirth of (old) national stereotypes, covered with a thin veneer of Eurosceptic rhetoric.

Correspondingly, Bulgarian migration to the UK is an interesting case. Although not a new phenomenon as Maeva (2010) notes, Bulgarian migratory flows to Britain have significantly intensified since the country, together with Romania, joined the EU in 2007. Notably, the latest data from the Bulgarian National Statistical Institute shows a clear shift in the direction of migratory flows away from 'traditional' destinations such as Spain, Italy and Greece (Club, 2015). In 2015, Germany and the UK emerge as top receiving countries for young and highly skilled migrants (Club, 2015). This change in the pattern of the newest Bulgarian migratory flows is credited not only to Bulgaria's membership in the EU but also to the impact of the European economic crisis on countries in Southern Europe.

While the literature on the topic is growing (see Genova, 2015; Chongarova, 2010; Ivancheva, 2007; Maeva, 2010; Markova, 2010), Bulgarian migration to the UK is still less researched in comparison to migratory flows from other Central and Eastern European (hereafter CEE) countries such as Poland, Hungary and Romania (among many, see Csedő, 2008; Fox, Moroşanu, & Szilassy, 2012; McGhee, Heath, & Trevena, 2012; Moroşanu, 2013a, 2013b; Moroşanu & Fox, 2013; Ryan, 2010). Additionally, there are two further problems associated with the knowledge of Bulgarian migration: both public and academic discourses tend to mention Bulgarian migrants briefly either in conjunction with Romanians or under the much broader term 'Eastern European'. While this is largely a reflection of the processes of Eastern enlargement of the EU, such assumptions should nonetheless be treated cautiously for a number of reasons. Firstly, the umbrella term 'Eastern European' is often used as a catch-all phrase to denote all migrant groups originating east of Germany and Austria. Undoubtedly, many of the countries in that region share a lot of socio-political and economic similarities, however, the essentialist nature of the term disregards any differences that are often key elements in migrant experiences. Secondly, the term 'Eastern European' has arguably developed negative connotations in the British context in light of strong anti-EU sentiments, as tensions emerge between the freedom of movement and claims for social rights (BBC, 2014a, 2014b). Thus, the homogenising effect of umbrella terms such as 'Eastern European' in relation to migrants not only emerges as highly contested but it also highlights potential pitfalls in treating different ethnic groups in an essentialist manner.

Therefore, this paper aims to contribute to the literature on newer European migratory flows by focusing on a migrant group that receives comparatively less attention – young, highly skilled Bulgarians in Britain. Based on empirical data gathered through a multi-sited ethnography with Bulgarian university students and young professionals, this paper has three main goals. Firstly, it will explore the external and internal, socially constructed perceptions that young Bulgarians are subjected to both in their host and home societies in the context of the European economic crisis. It will be argued that the participants in the study experience double-sided othering, whereby simultaneous processes of external and internal stereotyping delineate the contours of a temporally- and spatially-bound discursive realm based on constant power renegotiations, which thus impact upon their sense of identity. Secondly, I will analyse the techniques and strategies that the respondents utilise to respond to the dominant stereotypical discourses. While similarities with other CEE migrants will be noted, particular attention will be paid to the differences which outline the problematic nature of the term 'Eastern European'. Ultimately, I will argue that while young Bulgarians in the UK experience double-sided othering, they employ a range of techniques which allow them not only to negotiate their identities in that context but also to make sense of their complex realities.

The article begins by theoretically and contextually exploring the nature and characteristics of stereotypes as well as conceptualising the notion of double-sided othering. A brief summary of the research is provided, followed by two empirical sections: the first one will analyse the reactions to and experiences of both external and internal stereotypes, and the second one will focus on counterbalancing strategies and implications for identity. The conclusion summarises the findings and outlines some areas that require further research.

From stereotypes to double-sided othering: theoretical and contextual framework

The heightened levels of migration within and outside the EU, combined with the effects of the ongoing economic crisis, have not only made the presence of the Other(s) more visible and threatening in host societies but also their absence from the home society – more painful. Thus, arguably, the European economic crisis has become a catalyst for anxiety channelled into various stereotypes towards migrants, which have subjected them to processes of othering in both societies. Othering and stereotypes are not only intrinsically interrelated but their nature and characteristics also impact upon identity formation. Moreover, stereotypes are arguably an integral part of othering and as such – a key element that serves to provide differentiation. Therefore, I will first explore the notion of stereotypes as a way of understanding the basis upon which othering operates. Drawing largely on Jensen (2011), I will trace the relationship between othering, identity and power. Next, the notion of double-sided othering will be conceptualised, arguing that it provides a useful analytical framework for the understanding of migratory experiences. The concept will then be contextualised to provide a better understanding of Bulgarian highly skilled migrants' experiences, highlighting the importance of the spatial and temporal conditions within which othering occurs. Finally, some considerations will be mentioned in relation to the problematic nature of the concept of highly skilled migration.

Stereotypes and (double-sided) othering: theoretical postulations

The ontological foundations of stereotypes can be traced to the 1920s when Walter Lippmann defined the concept as 'pictures in our heads' (Seiter, 1986, p. 16), thus highlighting the inflexibility of stereotypical perceptions, usually related to images and ideas that are incorrect and rather simplistic. Consequently, stereotypes not only '[...] erase a person's individuality', but they also '[...] control and constrain people' (Anderson, 2010, p. 19). Evidently, the concept involves the establishment of a power relationship, which implicates upon one's identity. Three further key points emerge when scrutinising the concept of the stereotype. Firstly, ' ... social stereotypes exaggerate and homogenise traits held to be characteristic of particular categories and serve as blanket generalisations for all individuals assigned to such categories' (Pickering, 2001, p. 10). This observation underlines two of the most prominent characteristics of stereotypes – their metonymic and essentialist properties. Thus, national stereotypes not only 'label' groups of people by ascribing characteristics, but they also claim uniformity of 'packaging'. Secondly, again claimed by Pickering (2001), stereotypes dwell in the realm of the politics of representation and as such, they are sensitive to socio-temporal conditions (p. xiv). While the first argument highlights the intricate relationship between stereotypes and identity, the second one points to the need to contextualise the emergence of such perceptions. The terms stereotypes and the Other will be used interchangeably throughout the paper as Pickering (2001) rightfully observes that both concepts entail the same processes of categorisation and differentiation (2001, p. xiv). These processes of othering, however, require further clarification.

In that sense, Jensen's (2011) study of ethnic minority men in Denmark is particularly instrumental as it focuses on the potential of othering to describe identity formation, simultaneously highlighting ideas of agency and power. Providing a thorough ontological and epistemological overview of the notion of othering, Jensen (2011) affirms its postcolonial roots, noting that Spivak was the first scholar to use it in a systematic way in 1985 to denote a multidimensional process, involving various forms of social differentiation (pp. 64–65). This observation revolves around the idea of inferiority and subordination which emerge as the aimed result of such processes of categorisation. More modern conceptions of the idea continue this line of thought and describe othering as a 'process of differentiation and demarcation, by which the line is drawn between "us" and "them" – between the more and the less powerful – and through which social distance is established and maintained' (Lister cited in Jensen, 2011, p. 65). The value of this definition lies in the fact that it highlights the mechanics of identity formation which operate within the process of othering. In that sense, the establishment of an *us* and *them* rhetoric strongly relies on employing a reductionist approach. The latter is achieved through the use of stereotypes, whose homogenising properties play a crucial role in establishing relations of superiority and subordination. Jensen's (2011) own definition aims to highlight both the power dynamics and the embeddedness of identity in the process of othering, which entails:

> […] *discursive processes by which powerful groups, who may or may not make up a numerical majority, define subordinate groups into existence in a reductionist way which ascribe problematic and/or inferior characteristics to these subordinate groups. Such discursive processes affirm the legitimacy and superiority of the powerful and condition identity formation among the subordinate.* (italics in original, p. 65)

Consequently, the conditionality of identity is located in the power dynamics of the discursive realm of social differentiation. Jensen recognises the need to move away from dichotomous understandings of both othering and identity, which rely solely on binary oppositions (p. 66). Thus, a critical engagement with the process of othering allows the recognition of agency. The latter not only questions the ability of othering to draw the boundaries between superiority and subordination, but it also blurs them by enabling resistance.

Indeed, Jensen's (2011) work raises some valid points with regards to the process of othering such as its nexus with the notions of power and identity. Yet, his analysis remains rather limited due to its narrow contextualisation. In the age of reinvention (Elliott, 2013), characterised by the incessant need to re-formulate and update, the focus is very much on constant change and multiplicity – multiple identities, citizenships, movements, transactions and locations. The latter in particular points to the need of a broader conceptualisation of the processes of othering, one that takes into account various contexts. Consequently, in the case of migration, Triandafyllidou (2006) has rightfully argued that: 'In a world organized into nations and national states, th[e] absence from the country of origin and presence in a foreign one lead to the exclusion of the immigrant from either society' (p. 287). Evidently, to understand migrant experiences, it is important to consider the context and implications of both dominant external stereotyping discourses (those produced by the host society) and the internal ones (those produced by the home society). Therefore, it is necessary to stretch the concept of othering to allow a wider contextualisation. I argue that a particularly useful critical lens is provided by the concept of double-sided othering, which I define in the following way: the simultaneous processes of external and internal stereotyping, which delineate the contours of a temporally- and spatially-bound discursive realm, based on constant power renegotiations, which imminently impact upon migrants' identities. Besides the centrality of stereotypes, this definition highlights the dynamic nature of double-sided othering. More importantly, it captures the fluid essence of the power relationships between the Othering and the Othered, which emerge as a result from double-sided othering. Finally, it highlights the importance of contextualising the occurrence of double-sided othering to fully understand migrants' experiences. Thus, the next section will provide an overview of the spatial and temporal conditions that shape the othering that is experienced by young, highly skilled Bulgarian migrants in Britain.

Contextualising double-sided othering

A closer look at Bulgaria's and Britain's socio- political and economic reality reveals that both countries are entrenched in the legacy of their past, which coupled with the after-effects of the ongoing European crisis, has established migration as a controversial issue.

An analysis of the Bulgarian context reveals complex and rather contradictory perceptions about migration. On the one hand, Bulgarian governments have consistently focused on encouraging migrants' return, thus recognising their importance. Such initiatives include the establishment of the State Agency for Bulgarians Abroad and the adoption of a number of national strategies, the latest of which – the National Migration, Asylum and Integration Strategy (2011–2020) – features the return of highly skilled migrants as a key priority (OECD, 2012). Yet, on the other hand, there are negative connotations in relation to outward migration which have resurfaced in the Bulgarian public space, prompted by the after-effects of the European economic crisis. At the beginning of 2013, a series of austerity measures and high electricity prices triggered unrest in the country, culminating in the resignation of the centre-right Borisov government (BBC, 2013). The nationwide protests gained new momentum in 2013 under the motto #DANS-withme.[1] Amidst these turbulent events, another, less favourable image of the migrant came to the fore (Nikolov, 2013). The re- awakened old national stereotypes of emigrating co-nationals, typical of pre-1989 socialist era, which came in the form of a popular anecdote: 'Question: What are the two exits of the crisis in Bulgaria? Answer: Terminal 1 and Terminal 2 of Sofia Airport' (Bozhidarov, 2012). This anecdote has provided the basis of a stereotype of migration as a form of escapism, often interpreted more negatively as national betrayal. Moreover, this discourse has created a rupture between those who stay and those who leave by questioning the identity and belonging of the latter group.

Similarly, Britain is also facing the consequences of its past, which albeit different, reveal several worrying trends. Arguably in a state of 'postcolonial melancholia' (Gilroy, 2006), the British discourse is saturated with anxieties about the inability to cope with larger, globalisation processes that imminently erode the power structures of the nation-state. British public discourse has focused on objectifying its anxieties and transforming them into concrete fears, resulting in a resurgence of a defensive national identity. Three specific trends not only illustrate this nationalist turn but have also more recently contributed to the othering of European migrants, and Bulgarians in particular. Firstly, stricter border control and immigration policy have been central to the Coalition government's approach and continue to feature in the current Conservative majority cabinet. Secondly, a shift away from multiculturalism can be observed, which has arguably led to a neo-assimilationist turn in the UK's immigration policy. Such a re- orientation has been defined by ' ... populist scapegoating of minorities and migrants for the shortcomings of complex social transformations and its nostalgic sense of "loss" for a mythical cohesive past ... ' (Però, 2008, p. 76). Finally, anxieties about social welfare, crime and migration have generated scepticism, camouflaged as anti-EU rhetoric, and forging a vision of the pillars of the nation-state being corroded and hence in need of patriotic protection.

More recently, the removal of labour restrictions for Bulgarian and Romanian nationals in 2014, which coincided with the ongoing economic crisis, strengthened even further anti-EU sentiments. Furthermore, it triggered a negative discourse, reliant on stereotypical representations of Bulgarian migrants. It should be noted, however, that Bulgarians are not the only migrant group in the UK that experiences such stereotypes. In fact, a brief glance at the literature (Csedő, 2008; Fox et al., 2012; Moroşanu, 2013a, 2013b; Moroşanu & Fox, 2013; Ryan, 2010) reveals that other CEE migrants are subjected to the same stereotypes, establishing the symbolic boundaries of the Eastern European in Britain as the Other. This image is rigidly framed and cumulatively constructs a poor, badly educated, benefits-driven, potentially dangerous, unskilled migrant. Significantly, this stereotype not only disregards the myriad of migratory paths that people take but it also establishes 'Eastern European' as an umbrella term with markedly negative connotations.

Thus, the analysis of the dominant discourses in both the host and home societies, reveals that two processes of othering are occurring simultaneously, subjecting migrants to both internal and external stereotypes.

Defining highly skilled

Despite the proliferation of typologies, it has become increasingly difficult to pin down who can be categorised as a highly skilled migrant (Csedő, 2008). Given the focus of this study, it is necessary to clarify the use of this term.

The British government has adopted a comprehensive list of criteria within its Points-Based Immigration System where factors such as age, education, work experience and earnings tilt the scales either way (UKBA, 2011, p. 2). Within academia, however, a greater diversity can be observed which contributes to the general confusion regarding the term. While Salt (1992) is primarily concerned with people within certain occupations (professional, managerial and technical migrants) who accept job positions adequately matching their skills, Iredale (2001) strives to escape this narrow approach by developing a rather comprehensive typology to accommodate various migratory patterns. Ultimately, she also fails to recognise that being a highly skilled migrant does not represent a given status but rather an outcome of a dynamic relationship between the employer and the employee in migratory contexts. In that sense, Csedő's (2008) study adequately differentiates between highly skilled and highly qualified migrants, where the first group possesses not only general (level of education) and specific (work experience) skills but are also able to successfully negotiate their credentials in migratory contexts. Additionally,

Wolfeil (2009), Chongarova (2010) and Iredale (2001) highlight that students are a subset group of privileged migrants. Drawing on Csedő (2008), I adopt a broad definition, whereby both university students and professionals are considered as highly skilled migrants due to the fact that in both cases they have successfully managed to negotiate their skills in the migratory context. With that in mind, the next section discusses the 'mechanics' underpinning this research.

The study

The study is a multi-sited ethnography (Marcus, 1995) that incorporates offline and online participant observation as well as semi-structured interviews. Such a research design not only enables the researcher to 'follow' their participants and to get an in-depth knowledge of their experiences, but it also takes into account the specificities of different locations (Elwood & Martin, 2000). The latter is crucial, given the strong regional differences in Britain.

Researching highly skilled Bulgarian migrants in the UK represents a rather challenging task. Like their French counterparts (Ryan & Mulholland, 2014, p. 588), the lack of a single systematic mechanism accounting for their number in Britain renders them invisible. While the Office for National Statistics claims that in July 2012 there were 47,000 Bulgarian-born people in the UK (BBC, 2014a), the National Institute for Economic and Social Research asserts that their number was 26,000 in 2013 (Rolfe et al., 2013, p. 21). The demonstrated discrepancy in data not only reflects the unreliability of statistics but it also highlights further problems associated with the lack of information regarding Bulgarian migrants' geographical location and their status in relation to skills. As it will be demonstrated below, this required the use of a range of sampling techniques.

The sample(s) of the study consist(s) of both students and young professionals in order to capture the wide spectrum of young Bulgarian skilled migration. Drawing on Csedő (2008), Chongarova (2010) and Rolfe et al. (2013), the sample criteria focused on Bulgarian nationals, aged between 18 and 35 who were either in the process of obtaining a higher education degree or had already received one, and were living in the UK at the time of the study. In accordance with Csedő (2008), the participants who were students and had a low skilled part-time job to support their studies were still considered as 'highly skilled' because their primary goal for migrating to Britain was not to join the low skilled labour force but to receive education, and that is a position which requires one's negotiation of skills in the host society context.

I utilised purposive sampling to ensure a sufficient range of informants from key demographic characteristics: age, gender, occupation, UK location and length of stay. As can be seen in the Appendix, I have interviewed 37 participants, aged between 19 and 32 years old: 18 male and 19 female, of which 16 were young professionals and 21 students, based in 6 regions in the UK.

In addition to interviewing participants, I have spent extended periods of time with them, occasionally attending social events and celebrations with them. Moreover, the majority of them have either befriended me on Facebook and/or added me to student and young professionals' groups they belong to. This imminently raises ethical implications, which I addressed by adopting a reflexive approach (Aull Davies, 2002) and treating consent as a constantly negotiated relationship rather than a one-off given permission.

Thus, both online and offline participant observation has allowed me to get more in-depth knowledge about respondents' everyday lives, where social media serves as a key factor for communication in both home and host societies, adjustment to life in the UK and maintaining social networks. I was particularly interested in exploring how participants respond to dominant stereotypical discourses in both the host and home society, and what the implications are of this process of double-sided othering.

A thematic analysis was carried out whereby codes were firstly generated inductively, followed by a ' … deductive re-examination of the data, to produce rigorous and analytically informed findings' (Ryan & Mulholland, 2014, p. 589). This has produced rich data whereby various techniques to manage national stereotypes as well as their implications for participants' identities have emerged as prominent themes. The latter is considered in detail in the next section.

Reactions to and experiences of double-sided othering

This section explores whether and how double-sided othering affects the experiences of young skilled Bulgarian migrants in the UK. Both external and internal stereotypes are considered. More specifically, the data will highlight the problematic nature of the term 'Eastern European' and the importance of location in the case of external stereotypes as well as the deepening rift between stayers and leavers in the case of internal categorisations.

External stereotypes

Unsurprisingly, initially many of my participants respond that despite being aware of external stereotypes, they have not been affected by them. This could be explained by the fact that unlike Datta's (2011) 'last hired and first fired' respondents, young skilled Bulgarians tend to find themselves in less precarious positions both while at university and at the workplace. In fact, 20-year-old student Maria[2] shares that she has experienced a lot of positive attitude precisely because she is Bulgarian. Others, such as young professional Vasil demonstrate a very understanding attitude toward external othering: 'I have not been affected directly. […], I do think however that this [othering] is because their country, Britain, has had a lot of negative experience with immigration'. While such a rational reaction is demonstrated by the majority of respondents, their reasoning varies. While Maria cites the power of the media to frame discourses, marketing specialist Kalina sarcastically remarks: 'They envy us! Because we are so pretty and smart, they envy us for being so poor!' However, the data highlights that while reactions tend to be more rational, actual daily experiences point to either subtle (*perception of* discrimination/condescending attitude) or direct effects (*experiences of* discrimination). In fact, a prevalence of the first over the second can be noticed.

For example, 23-year-old professional Dessie shares that external stereotypes about foreigners, and Bulgarians in particular, had initially established an *expectation* of discrimination, which resulted in low self-esteem. This feeling was additionally strengthened by one of her friends who kept joking about her accent. Interestingly, when Dessie confronted her friend, he justified his actions as a way for him to manage his own self-esteem as he felt intimidated by her achievements. Evidently, discourses of othering, whether or not they result in different treatment, produce a range of sensitive reactions, often compromising the emotional well-being of those subjected to them.

Bilyana's story further illustrates that point. She came to the UK as an undergraduate student through the Seasonal Agricultural Worker's Scheme to work on a broccoli farm in Scotland, and save money to obtain a British master's degree. It took her a few years to achieve this, during which she worked on a mushroom farm in Southern England, bartended in a working men's club in London and had other low skilled positions until she completed her degree and secured a graduate scheme position. With the increasingly negative portrayal of Bulgarians in the media, she found herself in situations where attitudes toward her changed as soon as she mentioned her nationality. This has strengthened her own perception of experiencing condescending attitude:

> Bilyana and I decided to conduct the interview in a newly opened café. Immersed in our conversation, we did not notice that they had a poetry reading event that day, so it was not until it had already begun that we realised what was going on. We lowered our voices and I quickly asked my final questions. Upon exiting the café, we had the following conversation:

Bilyana: 'You probably didn't notice but the lady sat behind you was giving us nasty looks'.
Researcher: 'Really?'
Bilyana: 'Yes! It was because we were speaking in Bulgarian. Such a good example of condescending attitude!'
Researcher: 'Did you not think that was because we were disrupting their event and not because we were speaking a foreign language?'
Bilyana: 'Maybe, but it felt like it was because we were speaking a different language'. (Memo, March 21, 2014)

Given the context of this everyday situation, it is very likely that the annoyance of the lady in the café was provoked by our lack of consideration for the ongoing poetry event. Nonetheless, Bilyana interpreted it as an act of condescending attitude rather than a reaction provoked by our socially inadequate behaviour. This episode clearly demonstrates how the negative macro context that participants live in has increased their sensitivity to othering. The realm of the everyday thus transforms into an arena where social interactions in a public space blur the line between perceptions of othering and actual discrimination.

Although less, my participants reported a few experiences of actual discriminatory attitude. Interestingly, they do not interpret it as resulting from being members of a specific national group. Rather, they view it as stigmatisation associated with the socially constructed image of the migrant as a foreigner. While Bulgarians remain relatively 'invisible' in terms of phenotypic markers, the most obvious difference that becomes a tool for othering is their accent. Emanuela, reflecting upon the process of looking for a job, mentions that a few potential employers terminated scheduled phone interviews as soon as they heard her accent. Once she was told by a prospective employer that 'there is no point in continuing this interview. The experience that you have is great but my clients are not gonna be impressed by the fact that you're Eastern European'. This clearly highlights how in social contexts 'Eastern European' is used as a catch-all phrase. Furthermore, young professional Ivan adds: 'Actually, I think that Eastern European is used as a term with a derogatory meaning, which is not right'. Therefore, many of my respondents claim that the term is a metonymical referral with negative overtones to a very large group of people with different cultural, social and national backgrounds.

Furthermore, the data accentuates the importance of the spatial dimensions of external stereotypes. For example, while working at large company in the Midlands, Emanuela recalls a particularly distressing case when one of her work colleagues repeatedly asked her to pronounce words containing the letter 'r'. Imitating her accent, he commented: 'You [migrants] all need to learn how to speak with a **normal** accent 'cos **you** have chosen to come here [...]' (participant's emphasis). Emanuela recollects that her manager excused her colleague's behaviour with the fact that as a Northerner he has had limited communication with foreigners. In this particular instance, regional differences in levels of diversity appear as factors influencing the attitude towards foreigners, even if the latter are highly skilled. Bilyana makes a similar point reminiscing about living and working in Southern England. In contrast, London is described by 23-year-old Boris as a 'transmission centre' and a 'hub', where people not only 'come for a while and leave' but also where one experiences a lot of diversity, which results in less visibility and exposure to stereotypes. In line with Barker (2015), the Scottish context appears as more migrant-friendly as my participants describe the locals as more 'warm-hearted than the English'. Final year student Marko explains that 'Bulgarian students in Scotland as European citizens are treated equally to Scottish students and are not required to pay tuition fees.'[3] This not only makes them feel welcome but it also diminishes the symbolic boundaries between them and locals.

Evidently, the socio-political regional differences, combined with ascribed personality traits of the locals, emerge as key factors in positive attitudes towards migrants in Scotland. Regardless, students who both study and work part-time appear more likely to experience condescending attitudes. An example is provided by Delyan, an undergraduate student who works part-time at Subway, where on a number of occasions customers have made derogatory comments upon hearing his accent. Thus, migrants' skills and status are automatically judged on the basis of a setting, where people can expect to find low skilled labour.

Consequently, the data reveals that external stereotypes have increased the respondents' sensitivity toward differential treatment. While the cases of perceived outweigh those of actual discrimination, the findings point out that location in the form of specific contexts plays a key role in determining the Other.

Internal stereotypes

Interestingly, while external stereotypes generate more emotional reactions, the internal ones were categorically dismissed on the basis of narrow-minded thinking and lack of understanding of the difficulties that one encounters in migration. With regards to the latter, Ivan contends:

> Firstly, I can bet anyone who lives in Bulgaria that they couldn't do what many here have experienced, and secondly, it's not as easy as they think. I mean, most of my good friends here have not only studied hard but they have also had two jobs while doing so to support themselves.

This demonstrates that negative internal stereotypes are not only dismissed on the basis of lack of knowledge but also that the experience of migration is seen as a rite of passage. To leave Bulgaria, for many of my respondents such as Kalina and Ivan, requires courage, determination and strong will. Furthermore, as Ivan's remark suggests, while migrants are being othered, they themselves rely on sweeping generalisations to respond to dominant discourses. Investment banker Paula goes even further when she contends: 'There are a few *quality* people of those who have decided to stay in Bulgaria, I think. Those who have stayed are those who for some reason could not leave' (my emphasis). Evidently, internal stereotypes reveal that othering is two-sided, simultaneously highlighting the presence of a strong cleavage between stayers and leavers.

Moreover, similar to Moroşanu's (2013a, 2013b) account of the experiences of Romanians, internal stereotypes lead to feelings of estrangement upon return to the home country. Such is the case with Svetla when she goes back to Bulgaria. Svetla is a PhD student who is divorced and has a 6-year-old daughter. She recalls a situation when after spending only a year in England, upon going back to her hometown a friend told her that she spoke like an 'English girl' and with an accent. Such comments question the respondents' national identity and belonging, subjecting them to processes of othering. On another occasion, 32-year-old young professional Teodora recollects her frustration at the impossibility of buying a return ticket for the metro, which is a standard practice in London and anywhere else. The cashier's response of – 'You can do that when you go back in London. Now you are in Bulgaria' – not only made Teodora feel judged but also out of place. Furthermore, this story reveals that everyday situations upon return often provide contexts which exacerbate the division between migrants and non-migrants, often generating stereotypes on both sides.

Comparatively, the participants' reactions to and experiences of othering produced by the home society are less varied than attitudes towards similar processes in the host society. Those two simultaneously processes nonetheless affect young Bulgarian's experiences of migration. Moreover, the process of double-sided othering leads to a number of reactive, counterbalancing strategies which allow the Othered to renegotiate and reverse the power dynamics of 'us' and 'them'. As the section below will demonstrate, this ultimately affects identity formation.

Double-sided othering: counterbalancing strategies and implications for identity

The analysis of the effects that double-sided othering has on young Bulgarian highly skilled migrants Britain, reveals four key strategies that they employ to respond to stereotypes: assimilationist, segregationist, integrationist and proactive approaches. Consequently, while the first part of this section will consider each of the strategies in turn, the second one will focus upon the implications they have had upon young Bulgarian migrants' identities, arguing for a tendency toward particularism and situationalism.

Strategies

Those of the respondents who utilise an assimilationist strategy to counterbalance double-sided othering focus their efforts on adopting elements of the host society culture. This often entails an attempt to diminish obvious markers such as accent, cultural practices or name, which increase visibility and thus could potentially serve as the basis of othering. Svetla relies on such an assimilationist strategy, trying to avoid potentially being othered on the basis of being a foreigner. Thus, she considers her marriage to Rob as a turning point:

> The biggest difference I saw was when my [last] name changed from Petrova to Jones. People think you are from here [...] You are not so much a foreigner [...] As far as jobs are concerned, the name makes a big difference.

Consequently, for Svetla the change of a family name has meant mostly an opportunity to be treated equally. Moreover, it has helped her to camouflage her background, thus protecting her from being exposed to various processes of othering. This is also the reason why even after getting divorced, she has decided to retain her ex-husband's family name. This assimilationist strategy allows her to blend in without being judged on the basis of her nationality.

Another technique for counterbalancing double-sided othering that emerges from my data is segregation. It entails a practice whereby some of the respondents try to actively disengage from compatriots in order to avoid stereotypes attached to this migrant group in Britain. A similar practice is observed by Ryan (2010) in the case of Polish migrants in London. Young highly skilled Bulgarians, however, drawing on their professional background, predominantly disassociate their migration experiences on the basis of class. This leads marketing specialist Kalina to remark that she does not feel as a migrant as this is: '[...] someone who has come here in order to stay here [...] to have a better life [...] but a bit lower class in general. Someone who works at Tescos'. Her disengagement with compatriots employed in the service sector is evident in the following episode:

> I was visiting Kalina and she suggested that we grab lunch from the local Turkish takeaway in [borough in London]. We were speaking in Bulgarian while deciding what to order and then the girl at the till, also Bulgarian, introduced herself. While were waiting for our order, the girl came over to ask us whether we knew any other Bulgarians who were looking for a job. Kalina quickly replied: 'I already have a job and I don't know any other Bulgarians'. Interestingly, her body language also changed, signifying annoyance with the girl's presence. When we left I asked Kalina why she was so reserved towards the girl, which she explained in the following way: 'I just don't like it when people just come over like that and act as if they know you just because you are both Bulgarian. I don't want anything to do with those people'. (Memo, August, 2014)

The fact that Kalina felt very uncomfortable in this situation, combined with the effort of establishing a boundary, signifies that membership in the same ethnic group does not presuppose similarities (Moroşanu, 2013a). Right on the contrary, this segregationist strategy in relation to co-nationals suggests that the processes of othering affect negatively interethnic cohesion, accentuating class divisions.

Furthermore, such a segregationist approach can be also observed in relation to other CEE migrants, tarred by the same stereotypical social constructions. In an attempt to disassociate themselves, many of the respondents draw on cultural markers and everyday practices to emphasise differences. Ivan, for example, remarks:

> We have more in common with Greeks and Turks than with Poles and Lithuanians ... despite language [similarities]. On the whole, there is a huge difference. [...]. I usually accentuate the fact that Bulgaria is not in Eastern Europe, it is in South-eastern Europe, and as a result we are quite different to other [CEE] nations [...].

He goes further to point out a range of reasons that outline this divide: from differences in the climate, through the fact that 'we drink more like the French and Italian' to the fact that Bulgarians are much closer to Turks, Serbs and Macedonians in terms of mentality than Romanians and Lithuanians. Notably, all these reasons serve to counterbalance metonymical representations of 'Eastern Europeans'. Similarly, Emanuela emotionally exclaims: 'I hate it when people say I am Eastern European. I am from the Balkans!', stating that the difference between the two lies within the fact that Balkan people have 'more passion' and 'a great sense of humour'. This suggests the presence of a regional ethno-centrism, which is accentuated by dominant external stereotypes. Moreover, such an approach serves to not only to counterbalance negative discourses but it also helps young Bulgarians to make sense of a complex reality.

With regards to external stereotypes, another strategy to not only manage the effects of social categorisations but also to counterbalance them is the integrationist approach. Unlike the other two strategies, respondents who adopt this approach neither diminish their cultural background nor disassociate themselves from other, they accept both. Instead, they rely on diminishing stereotypes through openly talking about them in the form of jokes with friends and colleagues. This strategy allows participants such as Nayden, Ivan, Boris and Ralitsa to negotiate their place in the host society environment.

Finally, a number of participants employ proactive approaches that aim to not only promote the rich cultural heritage of Bulgaria but also to counterbalance both internal and external stereotypes. With regards to the latter, this strategy involves a conscious effort to demonstrate positive personal characteristics. A prominent example of this practise is sociology student Kamelia, who shares: '[…] I always explicitly say that I am Bulgarian. I almost view it as a cause. […] I try to be the best version of myself and of a Bulgarian that someone can meet'. Evidently, in her case, there is a conscious and purposeful effort to present herself positively. Moreover, for Kamelia, Maria, Simeon, Nelly and Maria this proactive approach involves being an 'Ambassador of Bulgaria' through sharing meals and national celebrations with their international friends. The practice of raising awareness of the cultural richness of Bulgarian traditions aims to counterbalance the overall negative British media rhetoric in relation to the country and its nationals. The process of othering in the host society has its emotional implications – shame – upon the experiences of my respondents. Consequently, highlighting one's nationality and focusing specifically on the positives serves as a way to promote a better image of the entire migrant group.

Finally, another proactive strategy, specifically directed toward internal stereotypes involves justifying migration as necessary step towards enriching one's personal skills, which will then enable return to the host society to make a difference. Young professional Boyan is the most prominent example. He keeps a diary where he writes down all ideas that he has come across or that have occurred to him, and spends time thinking about how they can be modified and implemented in Bulgaria. Similarly, Politics student Delyan contends: 'My goal is […] to get the best possible education and one day to apply it in such a way which will benefit my people'. Evidently, the improvement of the self is a necessary step in the achievement of making a difference. What makes an impression in Delyan's speech is the use of a possessive pronoun 'my' in relation to his fellow countrymen. This alludes not only to a strong sense of national belonging but also to an understanding of his educational choice almost as a cause – as a mission in the pursuit of counterbalancing internal stereotypes.

Overall, the respondents rely on a wide range of techniques that can be used either interchangeably or in conjunction with each other to react to double-sided othering. While the assimilationist, segregationist, integrationist and proactive strategies do not exhaust the list of possible ways that these young skilled Bulgarians in the UK employ to manage stereotypes, they nonetheless highlight some prominent tendencies.

'Between a rock and a hard place': implications on identity

The quest into understanding young highly skilled Bulgarians' experiences of internal and external national stereotypes reveals a complex puzzle of techniques and approaches that ultimately allow them to negotiate their place 'between a rock and a hard place'. These varied techniques not only renegotiate the power imbalance created by experiencing double-sided othering, but also affect the identities of the respondents.

The analysis of the four strategies reveals not only the multiplicity of identities that respondents draw on but also their situational character. Consequently, an assimilationist approach emerges as quite helpful in *avoiding* stereotypes and serves mostly as a prevention measure. As such, this strategy downplays national identity and draws on markers developed through a prolonged period of living, working and studying in Britain. In contrast, the proactive technique aims to *tackle directly* stereotypes, while the integrationist one *accepts and dismisses* them. In doing so, the first approach accentuates national identity, while the second one relies on one's skills to negotiate a place in the host society.

Furthermore, in the context of double-sided othering a certain particularistic tendency can be observed. The segregationist strategy is the approach that starkly highlights this trend, which is directed toward co-nationals and other CEE migrant groups. With regards to the first, Kalina and Ivan draw on their professional identity and their ability to negotiate their highly skilled status to differentiate themselves from low skilled compatriots. This suggests that Bulgarians in the UK are not a homogenous group and that as Moroşanu (2013a, 2013b) contends ethnic markers do not automatically lead to a sense of shared experiences and understanding. Furthermore, the segregationist strategy suggests that participants exhibit particularism, underpinned by ethno-centrism. By actively highlighting differences with other CEE nations, young Bulgarians point to the conclusion that 'Eastern European' is a rather problematic term that has negative connotations in the British context. Furthermore, the phrase is often viewed as a metonymical representation that erases specific socio-cultural and political factors that delineate national identities.

The thus discussed implications upon the respondents' identities highlight once again the importance of considering how internal and external stereotypes affect and questions migrants' choices. Hence, the exploration of double-sided othering, contextualised in light of the ongoing European crisis offers the chance to understand more deeply the experiences of migrants and their daily lives.

Conclusion

In a time of high levels of migration both within and outside the EU, combined with the effects of the ongoing economic crisis, fear and anxiety have questioned the unity of Europe. The sense of insecurity has permeated all levels of society from the supranational to the local – resulting in a multiplication and personalisation of the presence of a 'crisis'. In such a context, it has become increasingly important to achieve some sense of stability through clearly delineating and defining the boundaries of the Self through the image of the Other. Imminently, this has not only made the choice to migrate more problematic but it has also brought to the fore the powerful presence of processes of othering.

Consequently, this paper has aimed to explore young, highly skilled Bulgarians' migratory experiences in the context of the presence of dominant stereotypical discourses. By theoretically exploring such discourses and their relationship with stereotypes, power and identity, it has been argued that the notion of othering needs to be stretched further in order to take into account migrants' double embeddedness in both host and home society contexts. In that sense, the paper has conceptualised the idea of double-sided othering, arguing that it serves as a useful analytical framework that captures the temporal and spatial conditionality of simultaneously operating processes of internal and external stereotyping, which shape the contours of a discursive realm whereby power is constantly renegotiated and identities redefined.

Applying that analytical approach to a relatively less researched group of migrants in the UK, this article has focused on the case of young, highly skilled Bulgarians. By adopting a broad definition of the term highly skilled, the analysis has included both young professionals and university students who live, work and/ study in Britain. As such, the article has presented a snapshot of a specific group of people at a specific time. While this has not allowed generalisability, it has nonetheless highlighted some responses to and strategies of counterbalancing double-sided othering as well as its implications for the participants' sense of identity. Interestingly, the participants' accounts reveal more varied reactions to and experiences of external stereotypes than those which have occurred as a result of internal ones. This can be explained by the fact the participants in the study live in Britain and only go back to Bulgaria occasionally, which makes them more likely to be exposed to external, rather than internal stereotypes. Furthermore, while the participants initially reported the lack of effect of external stereotypes upon their daily lives, the further exploration of their experiences nonetheless revealed a more nuanced element of othering. This involved the presence of a strong perception and expectation of being subjected to discriminatory and/or condescending attitude over actual discrimination, which were highly dependent on location and the specificities of regional contexts. With regards to internal stereotypes, their effects were experienced either upon return or through interaction with family and friends. Regardless of the actual context and of the fact that such discourses of othering were automatically dismissed, their nature and characteristics left Bulgarian highly skilled migrants feeling out of place, thus also questioning their identities.

Furthermore, the exploration of the process of double-sided othering in the case of young, highly skilled Bulgarians in Britain has revealed that they employ four distinct strategies that aim to respond to and renegotiate the power imbalance created by stereotypes. While the assimilationist and segregationist techniques avoid the consequences of being othered, the integrationist and proactive approaches tackle it directly. Consequently, this process of reversing the power dynamics of double-sided othering affects the respondents' identities, highlighting a tendency towards particularism.

Finally, the paper has highlighted the necessity to treat catch-all labels such as 'Eastern European' critically. While migrants who come from that region imminently share many characteristics, they also have a lot of differences. Therefore, future research agendas should explore this further as well as the nature, characteristics and implications of the process of double-sided othering for other migrant groups.

Notes

1. DANS is the Bulgarian abbreviation of the State Agency for National Security, which closely resembles the English verb 'to dance'.
2. All participants are referred to by pseudonyms to preserve their anonymity.
3. As EU citizens, Bulgarian students for tuition fees purposes are treated as home students in the UK. However, the Student Awards Agency for Scotland pays the tuition fees for only Scottish residents and non-UK EU citizens. As the fee waiver does not apply to English students, this paradoxically results in giving Bulgarians more rights than the English. For more information, please see the Complete University Guide.

Acknowledgements

I would like to express my gratitude to Dr Aline Sierp and Dr Christian Karner for giving me the opportunity to contribute to this Special Issue and for their constructive criticism and support. I am also indebted to the Editor of *National Identities*, Professor David Kaplan, three anonymous peer reviewers, Emma Craddock and Helen Creswick for their helpful comments on earlier drafts. I wish to thank all my participants for their time and contribution to this research.

Disclosure statement

No potential conflict of interest was reported by the author.

References

Anderson, K. J. (2010). *Benign bigotry: The psychology of subtle prejudice*. Cambridge: Cambridge University Press.

Aull Davies, C. (2002). *Reflexive ethnography: A guide to searching selves and others*. London: Routledge.

Balibar, E. (2010). At the borders of citizenship: A democracy in translation? *European Journal of Social Theory, 13*(3), 315–322. doi:10.1177/1368431010371751

Barker, F. (2015). *Nationalism, identity, and the governance of diversity: Old politics, new arrivals*. Basingstoke: Palgrave Macmillan.

BBC. (2013). Bulgaria's government to resign, PM Boyko Borisov says. *BBC News Europe*. Retrieved from http://www.bbc.co.uk/news/world-europe-21516658

BBC. (2014a). Q&A: Bulgarian and Romanian immigration. *BBC News Politics*. Retrieved from http://www.bbc.co.uk/news/uk-politics-21523319

BBC. (2014b). David Cameron's EU speech: Full text. *BBC News Politics*. Retrieved from http://www.bbc.co.uk/news/uk-politics-30250299

Bozhidarov, D. (2012). Samo dva izhoda ot krizata- terminal 1 I terminal 2 [Only two exits from the crisis: Terminal 1 and terminal 2]. *Webcafe*. Retrieved from http://www.webcafe.bg/id_1342784288

Castells, M. (2004). *The power of identity*. Oxford: Blackwell Publishing.

Chongarova, I. (2010). *Bulgarskite studenti v London. Obrazovatelni strategii i migratsionni modeli: Sadarzhatelen otchet po proekt za sabatichna godina* [The Bulgarian students in London. Educational strategies and migration pattern: Study leave report]. Retrieved from http://files. slovo.uni-plovdiv.bg/clic/bulgarian-students-PRINT.pdf

Club Z. (2015). Nashite emigranti veche smeniha posokata. Veche ne otivat v Ispania I Italia [Our emigrants have changed direction. They no longer go to Spain and Italy]. *Club Z Politics*. Retrieved from http://clubz.bg/27478-nashite_emigranti_smeniha_posokata_veche_ne_otivat_v_ispaniq_ i_italiq

Csedő, K. (2008). Negotiating skills in the global city: Hungarian and Romanian professionals and graduates in London. *Journal for Ethnic and Migration Studies, 34*(5), 803–823. doi:10.1080/ 13691830802106093

Elliott, A. (2013). *Reinvention*. London: Routledge.

Datta, K. (2011). Last hired and first fired? The impact of the economic downturn on low-paid Bulgarian migrant workers in London. *Journal of International Development, 23*(4), 565–582. doi:10.1002/jid.1793

Elwood, S. A., & Martin, D. G. (2000). "Placing" interviews: Location and scales of power in qualitative research. *The Professional Geographer, 52*(4), 649–657. doi:10.1111/0033-0124.00253

Fox, J. E., Moroşanu, L., & Szilassy, E. (2012). The racialization of the New European migration to the UK. *Sociology, 46*(4), 680–695. doi:10.1177/0038038511425558

Fukuyama, F. (1992). *The end of history and the last man*. London: Hamish Hamilton.

Genova, E. (2015). To have both roots and wings: nested identities in the case of Bulgarian students in the UK. *Identities: Global Studies in Culture and Power*. doi:10.1080/1070289X.2015.1024125.

Gilroy, P. (2006). Multiculture in times of war. *Critical Quarterly, 48*(4), 27–45. doi:10.1111/j.1467-8705. 2006.00731.x

Iredale, R. (2001). The migration of professionals: Theories and typologies. *International Migration, 39* (5), 7–26. doi:10.1111/1468-2435.00169

Ivancheva, M. (2007). Strawberry fields forever? Romanian and Bulgarian student workers in the UK. *Focaal – European Journal of Anthropology, 49*, 110–117.

Jensen, S. Q. (2011). Othering, identity formation and agency. *Qualitative Studies, 2*(2), 63–78.

Maeva, M. (2010). Organizations and institutions of Bulgarian emigration in the UK. In M. Karamihova (Ed.), *European dimensions of culture and history on the Balkans* (pp. 276–291). Sofia: Paradigma.

Marcus, G. E. (1995). The emergence of multi-sited ethnography. *Annual Review of Anthropology, 24*, 95–117. doi:10.1146/annurev.an.24.100195.000523

Markova, E. (2010). Emigratsiata na bulgari vuv Velikobritania: London I Brighton, v *Tendentsii v Transgranichnata Migratsia na Rabotna Sila I Svobodnoto Dvizhenie na Hora- Efekti za Bulgaria* [Bulgarian emigration to Britain: London and Brighton. In A. Krasteva, G. Angelov, D. Ivanova, E. Markova, Z. Vankova, … T. Trifonova (Eds.), *Tendencies of the transnational migration of labour power and free movement of people-effects on Bulgaria*] (pp. 129–161). Sofia: Open Society Institute.

McGhee, D., Heath, S., & Trevena, P. (2012). Dignity, happiness and being able to live a 'normal' life in the UK – an examination of post-accession Polish migrants' transnational autobiographical fields. *Social Identities: Journal for the Study of Race, National and Culture, 18*(6), 711–727.

Moroşanu, L. (2013a). 'We all eat the same bread': The roots and limits of cosmopolitan bridging ties developed by Romanians in London. *Ethnic and Racial Studies, 36*(12), 2160–2181. doi:10.1080/ 01419870.2012.696668

Moroşanu, L. (2013b). Between fragmented ties and 'soul friendships': The cross-border social connections of young Romanians in London. *Journal of Ethnic and Migration Studies, 39*(3), 353–372. doi:10.1080/1369183X.2013.733858

Moroşanu, L., & Fox, J. E. (2013). 'No smoke without fire': Strategies of coping with stigmatised migrant identities. *Ethnicities, 13*(4), 438–456. doi:10.1177/1468796813483730

Nikolov, D. (2013, June 19). #neochakvanite [#theunexpected]. *Webcafe*. Retrieved from http://www. webcafe.bg/id_1245035277_#Neochakvanite

OECD. (2012). *International migration outlook 2012*. Paris: OECD Publishing.

Però, D. (2008). Political engagement of Latin Americans in the UK: Issues, strategies, and the public debate. *Focaal – European Journal of Anthropology, 51*, 73–90.

Pickering, M. (2001). *Stereotyping: The politics of representation*. Basingstoke: Palgrave.

Rolfe, H., Fic, T., Lalani, M., Roman, M., Prohaska, M., & Doudeva, L. (2013). *Potential impacts on the UK of future migration from Bulgaria and Romania*. Retrieved from the National Institute for Economic and Social Research (NIESR) website: http://www.niesr.ac.uk/publications/potential-impacts-uk-future-migration-bulgaria-and-romania#.UXMYUbU3v2o

Ryan, L. (2010). Becoming Polish in London: Negotiating ethnicity through migration. *Social Identities: Journal for the Study of Race, Nation and Culture, 16*(3), 359–376. doi:10.1080/13504630.2010.482425

Ryan, L., & Mulholland, J. (2014). Trading places: French highly skilled migrants negotiating mobility and emplacement in London. *Journal of Ethnic and Migration Studies, 40*(4), 584–600. doi:10.1080/1369183X.2013.787514

Salt, J. (1992). Migration processes among the highly skilled in Europe. *International Migration Review, 26*(2), 484–505. doi:10.2307/2547068

Seiter, E. (1986). Stereotypes and the media. *Journal of Communication, 36*, 14–26. doi:10.1111/j.1460-2466.1986.tb01420.x

The Complete University Guide. Retrieved from http://www.thecompleteuniversityguide.co.uk/university-tuition-fees/going-to-university-in-scotland/

Triandafyllidou, A. (2006). Nations, migrants and transnational identifications: An interactive approach to nationalism. In G. Delanty & K. Kumar (Eds.), *The SAGE handbook of nations and nationalism* (pp. 285–294). London: SAGE Publications.

UKBA. (2011). *Guidance for nationals of Bulgaria and Romania on obtaining permission to work in the UK* (BR 1 Guidance Notes, version 06/11). Retrieved from http://www.ukba.homeoffice.gov.uk/sitecontent/applicationforms/bulgariaromania/guidanceforbulgariaromania0408

Wolfeil, N. (2009). Student mobility from new to old member states in the European Union – changing patterns after 1st of May 2004? *CMR Working Papers, 42*(100), 1–39.

Appendix. Participant profiles

No.	Name	Sex	Age	Occupation	Length of stay in the UK	Level of education	BG hometown	UK location	Interview location
1	Emanuela	F	25	YP	2 years	Masters	Targovishte	East Midlands	Researcher's home
2	Paula	F	25	YP	4 years	Bachelors	Haskovo	London	Flight to BG
3	Kalina	F	25	YP	6 years	Masters	Bourgas	Southern England	Participant's home
4	Svetla	F	29	S	13 years	PhD	Rousse	East Midlands	Participant's home
5	Denitsa	F	24	S	5 years	Bachelors	Silistra	East Midlands	University café
6	Vasil	M	23	YP	4 years	Bachelors	Sofia	East Midlands	Café
7	Ivan	M	24	YP	5 years	Masters	Sofia	London	Café
8	Maria	F	20	S	2 years	Bachelors	Botevgrad	East Midlands	Skype
9	Hristian	M	25	S	4 months	Masters	Elhovo/ Sofia	Scotland	Skype
10	Leda	F	21	S	2.5 years	Bachelors	Plovdiv	Scotland	Pub
11	Kamelia	F	20	S	2 years	Bachelors	Stara Zagora	Scotland	Participant's home
12	Ignat	M	20	S	1.5 years	Bachelors	Sofia	Scotland	University café
13	Samuil	M	19	S	5 months	Bachelors	Rousse	Scotland	Participant's student hall
14	Yaroslava	F	23	S	4 years	Bachelors	Plovdiv	Scotland	University library
15	Marko	M	22	S	3 years	Bachelors	Rousse	Scotland	University library

(Continued)

Appendix. Continued.

No.	Name	Sex	Age	Occupation	Length of stay in the UK	Level of education	BG hometown	UK location	Interview location
16	Roza	F	21	S	2 years	Bachelors	Trudovets	Scotland	Participant's home
17	Karolina	F	21	S	2 years	Bachelors	Botevgrad	Scotland	Participant's home
18	Delyan	M	21	S	2 years	Bachelors	Sofia	Scotland	Skype
19	Simeon	M	24	S	4 years	PhD	Sofia/ Smolyan	Scotland	Skype
20	Nayden	M	20	S	2 years	Bachelors	Dimitrovgrad	Northern England	Participant's home
21	Kaloyan	M	28	S	4 years	PhD	Rousse	Northern England	University Student Union
22	Sava	M	25	YP	6 years	Bachelors	Sofia	Northern England	Pub
23	Stamen	M	24	S	4 years	PhD	Sofia	Scotland	Skype
24	Dessie	F	23	YP	3.5 years	Bachelors	Nikolaevo	London	Participant's home
25	Boris	M	23	YP	3.5 years	Bachelors	Pravets	London	Participant's workplace
26	Sabina	F	22	S	4 years	Bachelors	Dupnitsa	East Midlands	University café
27	Adrian	M	20	S	1.5 years	Bachelors	Rousse	East Midlands	University café
28	Kiril	M	19	S	5 months	Bachelors	Bourgas	East Midlands	University café
29	Natalia	F	24	YP	4 years	Bachelors	Sofia	London	Café
30	Bilyana	F	29	YP	7 years	Masters	Sofia	East Midlands	Café
31	Nikolay	M	27	YP	6 months	Bachelors	Kozlodui	East Midlands	Café
32	Teodora	F	32	YP	7 years	Masters	Knezha	London	Park
33	Boyan	M	23	YP	4 years	Bachelors	Stara Zagora	Southern England	Café
34	Ralitsa	F	23	YP	4 years	Bachelors	Sofia	London	Café
35	Maggie	F	29	YP	7 years	Masters	Sevlievo	Wales	Restaurant
36	Nelly	F	23	S	4 years	Bachelors	Sofia	Northern England	Café
37	Viktor	M	25	YP	11 years	Bachelors	Bourgas	Wales	Skype

- NB1: Status – 'S' stands for 'student', whereas 'YP' stands for young professional.
- NB2: Age and length of stay in the UK- the data provided is at the time of the interview.

3 A nation under attack

Perceptions of enmity and victimhood in the context of the Greek crisis

Zinovia Lialiouti and Giorgos Bithymitris

ABSTRACT

The economic crisis signifies a turning point for Greek national self-image. The present paper explores the ideological function of interpretative repertoires in relation to the reproduction and contestation of national identity. We focus on two basic repertoires: a victimizing and a self-blaming one. Even though connotations of victimhood are not homogenous, its association with an external enemy is very popular. This paper demonstrates that discourses of victimization are not unambiguous and solidified; they interact with self-blaming discursive patterns, thus leading to hybrid perceptions of the national self-image that are adjusted to particular political actors' strategies.

The interpretative repertoires and the mythscapes of the Greek crisis

The Greek crisis has had important ideological and political implications which had a profound influence on existing cleavages, party formations, as well as on popular attitudes (Teperoglou & Tsatsanis, 2014, pp. 222–242; Vasilopoulou, Halikiopoulou, & Exadaktylos, 2014, pp. 388–402). The form, the expression and the content of Greek nationalism as well as changes in the national self-image are important parts of these processes in the crisis context. A special chapter in this respect involves the interpretative uses of the past as a means of meaning attribution and politicizing the present (Boukala, 2014, pp. 483–499; Lialiouti & Bithymitris, 2014, pp. 249–268).

The debate about historical analogies highlights the importance of history as an interpretative framework and its connection with the negotiation of national identities (Karner, 2010, p. 387). Moreover, Critical Discourse Analysis (CDA) provides strong analytical tools in examining the role of discursive practices in the construction of collective identities contextualized within the complex set of social relations and power structures (De Fina, Schiffrin, & Bamberg, 2006; Howarth & Torfing, 2005; Wodak, de Cillia, Reisigl, & Liebhart, 2009). In addressing the issue of hegemony, CDA has also developed the concept of 'interpretative repertoires' which are defined as:

> … the building blocs speakers use for constructing versions of actions, cognitive processes and other phenomena. Any particular repertoire is constituted out of a restricted range of terms used in specific stylistic and grammatical fashion. These terms are generally derived

from one or more key metaphors and the presence of a repertoire will often be signaled by certain tropes or figures of speech. (Potter & Wetherell, 1987; Wetherell, 1998, pp. 387–412; Wetherell & Potter, 1988, pp. 168–183)

Condensing the relationship between language and power, 'interpretative repertoires' are here examined in the context of historically grounded, widely shared, though often contested-meanings (Marshall, 1994, p. 93), and they are seen to combine a cognitive function, as far as the attribution of meaning is concerned, with a political function (Karner, 2005b, pp. 411).

In what follows, we explore the ideological functions of interpretative repertoires in relation to the construction, reproduction and contestation of national identity and national self-image in – and through – public discourse in crisis-stricken Greece. Further, Van Dijk's conceptualization of ideological collectivities as 'communities of discourse' (Van Dijk, 2006, 115–140) promotes our analysis of national identity constructions in correspondence with the transformation and formulation of cleavages in the Greek crisis context. This involves the interpretations of patriotism and the conceptualization of schisms in the national community and of friend/foe concepts. A special chapter in our approach is the analysis of blame attribution processes focusing on the links with the hegemonic interpretive schemes in the Greek crisis debate and their normative implications. Wodak and Angouri have aptly argued on the normative content of blaming attribution patterns as well as on the importance of shared values that are involved in the process of explanation and justification (Wodak & Angouri, 2014, p. 418). Moreover, we explore the construction of 'mythscapes' in relation to recent transformations of national discourse. Duncan Bell has defined mythscapes as 'the temporally and spatially extended discursive realm in which the myths of the national are forged, transmitted, negotiated, and reconstructed constantly' (Bell, 2003, pp. 63–81). The concept of mythscape refers to 'ideologically heterogeneous and dynamic "discursive realms"' (Karner, 2010, p. 404).

Our starting premise is that the economic crisis (with the year 2009 as its conventional starting point) signifies a turning point for Greek national discourse and also a rupture in terms of national self-memory and memory practices. The present paper is part of an ongoing study of the consequences of the Greek economic crisis for the development of nationalism and the transformation of collective identities. Our empirical data is derived from a daily monitoring of political newspapers which represent almost the total of political–ideological spectrum: *Ta Nea, To Vima, Eleftherotypia* (Centre-Left), *Kathimerini* (Centre-Right), *Rizospastis* (Communist), *Dimokratia, Proto Thema* (populist Right), news portals (www.protagon.gr, www.realnews.gr, www.newpost.gr, www.newsbomb. gr.), as well as the websites of all Greek political parties from January 2010 to February 2014. By way of an introduction and contextualization, we argue that the period from the early 2000s until the end of 2008 could be approached as a period of national optimism succeeded by a period of widespread disillusionment. Two basic repertoires emerge here, premised on victimization and self-blame, respectively.

The earlier period of national optimism was directly linked to a then prevailing economic nationalism that had established a consensus among both political elites and popular audiences. The rise in living standards (increase of GDP per capita from 10.087$ in 1995 to 14.173 $ in 2005. Source: OECD) and the rise of consumerism had created a sense of relative prosperity and superiority compared to the neighbouring Balkan countries. This variety of economic nationalism was directly linked to a pro-Europeanism (Verney, 2011, pp. 51–80) as attested in Eurobarometer surveys at the time.[1] Its most tangible symbol was the substitution of the national currency, drachma, by the common European currency. The utilitarian aspect of Greek pro-Europeanism was summarized by Vernardakis in the following quote: 'Greek public opinion is thus pro-European to the extent that she anticipates (and to a significant extent attains) higher living, economic and consumption standards from its European membership' (Vernardakis, 2007, pp. 147–164).

This period was also characterized by the employment of distinct memory practices by politicians and in the mass media on the basis of a memory regime constructed on 'forgetfulness' as far as the country's past socio-economic conditions were concerned. The following statement by former Prime Minister Costas Simitis was a typical example: 'Today the image of a small and insecure Greece has come to an irrevocable end' (Simitis, 2000). It could be argued that this statement represents a rupture with defensive nationalism (the perception of Greece as a 'brotherless nation') – thus expressing 'a new-found self-confidence' – which had been an enduring feature of Greek political culture (Veremis & Koliopoulos, 2003, p. 19) as well as with the national stereotypes of poverty and backwardness compared to advanced capitalist societies of the 'West'.[2] In such discursive practices the concept of prosperity did not just describe a present and a future state of affairs, but it was also placed at the core of a hegemonic narration that modified previous memory practices. It is worth commenting at this point that Simitis' 'modernization movement' had rejected traditional, anti-western expressions of Greek nationalism and sought to distance itself from a Greek exceptionalism grounded in the purity of cultural identity. Nevertheless, Simitis exploited other aspects of nationalism and formulated a modernized nationalist discourse based on the goal of productive restructuring and competitiveness in the context of globalized capitalism. With slogans such as 'Greece comes first', he aspired to formulate a new patriotism with the goal of enhancing Greece's international competitiveness (Balabanidis, 2007, pp. 79–82).

This regime of forgetfulness and the consensus built on the expectation of prosperity had also an influence on perceptions of otherness, with the case of Albanian immigrants being the most typical example. The slogan raised against them, 'You shall never be Greek', with its emphatic denial of Greekness also reflected the inability of this particular 'other' to access certain living standards and consumption patterns that at the time seemed to separate Greeks from Albanians. The exclusivism in the national narratives during this period of optimism has undergone several shifts and transformations since the outbreak of the economic crisis in Greece. The interpretative repertoire of 'foreign occupation' can hardly be understood without bearing in mind its roots in the period just described.

We should also take into consideration the ideological developments that had taken place during the previous period, which dated back to the end of the Cold War and involved the landmark of the country's accession to the EMU, as well as a series of episodes of nationalism such as the Macedonian issue (Roudometof, 2002),[3] NATO's intervention in the Kossovo area (Lialiouti, 2011, pp. 127–155) and crises in Greek–Turkish relations, characterized by the tension between modernizing efforts and nationalistic tendencies. The goals of Westernization and Europeanization of Greek foreign policy as well as normalization of relations with Turkey were often challenged by prevailing anti-Western and defensive attitudes in public opinion and the political elites (Kazamias, 1997, pp. 71–94; Economides, 2005, pp. 471–491).

The interpretative repertoire of 'foreign occupation' and the mythscape of past prosperity

The emergence of the economic crisis and its rhetorical negotiation by Greek political elites has been a turning point as far as the discursive practices involving aspects of national identity are concerned. In early 2010 it became publicly known that Greece's public debt was no longer viable and the country risked with default. In April 2010, Prime Minister George Papandreou chose a small island on the Greek–Turkish borders – with the inevitable national connotations that the selection of this particular place entails – in order to announce the government's decision to appeal to the bailout mechanism that had been[4] created by the European Commission, the International Monetary Fund and the European Central Bank. Moreover, he argued that the country's economic problem was also a constraint to national sovereignty (www.youtube.com/watch?v= 4pC_d1M82uQ, viewed 25 May 2013). This interpretation of the economic crisis as a problem of national sovereignty was incorporated in the political communication strategies of all Greek parties following the country's loan agreements while for the government at the time the implications on an external enemy were a means of escaping political costs. The unpopular austerity policies that were implemented in this context were thus presented as foreign imposition (attributed to the IMF or to a German-led European Union) and the Greek government could appear as uninvolved actor obliged to conform to the terms of the loan agreements.

In Greek public discourse, the crisis triggered a passionate debate of the concepts of guilt, responsibility and victimization. Two basic interpretative schemes gained prominence in public debate, each of them associated with distinct aspects of national discourse.

The first interpretative scheme can be summarized in the concept of 'foreign occupation' and involves the construction of an external enemy who is blamed for the economic and social consequences of the crisis. A typical expression of this sort of reasoning is the anti-German discourse that uses memories and symbols of the Second World War, of Nazism and of Nazi occupation of Greece. This scheme involves elements of continuity with pre-existing stereotypes and belief systems concerning the perception of Germany as well as the historical expressions of Greek nationalism. However, the experience of the crisis was decisive in shaping these pre-existing stereotypes, concepts and memory practices into a coherent discursive construction (Lialiouti & Bithymitris, 2013, pp. 155–172).

Moreover, anti-German discourse became a vehicle for anti-capitalist and anti-globalization rhetoric, while in its right-wing uses certain elements of conspiracy theories were incorporated. In this respect, the anti-German discourse has structural, functional and ideological similarities with Greek anti-Americanism (Lialiouti, 2010) of the post-authoritarian period. Both the anti-American and the anti-German discourse are employed to denounce Greece's status of dependence; moreover, they treat 'resistance' of the Greek people towards the will of the country's powerful protectors/allies as an element of patriotism. An important unifying element has been the association of Nazism with US imperialism in the post-authoritarian period (1974–2009).

In terms of political communication, in January 2011, G. Papandreou announced his government's decision to appeal to the International Court of Justice in Hague on the issue of the compensations for the massacre in Distomo, invoking the national interest as well as the 'particular symbolism of the issue' (*Ethnos*, 12 January 2011). Kalavryta and Distomo (Greek villages where Nazi atrocities took place) dominated the printed and digital media agenda at the time. These places were represented as sites of martyrdom followed by emotional narrations and powerful images. In short, a mythscape of victimization was constructed. However, this discourse of victimization also included an element of a potential resistance movement.

Apart from the victimization aspect and the construction of an analogy with the present, these narrations on Nazi occupation also served as a means of restoring national pride emphasizing Germany's historical – both material and moral – debt towards Greece which was said to overshadow any present Greek debt as far as Germany is concerned. The following quote illustrates this belief on the German debt and associates it with Greek migration flows to Germany:

> Germany not only did not pay for the reparations and the occupational loan, but also received in the post-war period enormous help from Greece which had been destroyed from Nazi barbarity. The approximately one million workers that migrated from Greece to Germany were a huge capital … We gave her 10 trillion drachmas or 29 billion Euros of help! That's how the German miracle took place. With foreign workers. She owes us and we don't owe her. (*Eleftherotypia*, 2 March 2010)

This discursive practice became part of both right-ward and left-ward political culture in the context of the so-called anti-memorandum camp.[5] The instrumental use of the concept of German occupation took various forms in Greek politics such as the founding of the party of the so-called Independent Greeks in Kalavryta. Moreover the right-wing instrumentalism proved to be quite reflexive in incorporating conspiracy theories widely shared as interpretative elements of the Greek economic crisis. The neo-nazi Golden Dawn party thus articulated a variety of conspiracy theories 'explaining' the foreign enmity against the Greeks. The conspiracy of the big foreign powers against either Greece or Hellenism in general, was employed as a discursive pattern: 'All the foreign powers – Europe, Russia, and USA – conspired against Hellenism aiming at the expropriation of the energy resources of the Greek and Cypriot Exclusive Economic Zone' (Golden Dawn 2013). As it is stressed elsewhere, the flourishing of such constructs should be anticipated in a deep crisis context (Bale, 2007, pp. 50–51; Sapountzis and Condor, 2013, pp. 731–752).[6]

Not surprisingly, another aspect of this discourse is associated with the dramatic deterioration of socio-economic conditions. The symbolic consequence of this deterioration was the shuttering of the memory regime of forgetfulness that had emphasized the image of prosperity and reinstated in public discourse memories of collective poverty. Poverty came back as an organic part of national history; images and symbols from post-war Greece again became visible in mass communication channels (print and digital media, TV series etc.). The period of Occupation and its extreme poverty were and are now being remembered. It is in this context, that Alexis Tsipras, head of the major opposition party (SYRIZA), has stated that the winter of 2012–2013 was comparable to that of 1941 (http://www.tanea.gr/news/greece/article/4761805/?iid=2.[7] A central theme in SYRIZA's narration of the crisis (Tsakatika & Eleftheriou, 2013, pp. 81–99) is that Greece faces a 'humanitarian crisis' as a consequence of the austerity policies; that Greece is at present a 'colony of debt' (Tsipras, January 2014) and a 'devastated country'(Tsipras, 20 February 2014).

The other side to this 'return of poverty' as an element of national self-image is the resort to a fictitious memory, to a mythscape where prosperity, the ability to consume and the glamour of urban spaces, had been present, to a past that could have become present had it evolved linearly. A symptom of this mood was the reception of a photo (Figure 1) of Athens in the 1960s published for the first time[8] and widely reproduced by mass media and social media.

A columnist in a prestigious Sunday newspaper edition tried to explain the appeal of this photo in the following words:

> A photo made us nostalgic of a past that never existed ... Nostalgia is pain. It is pain because you know you cannot easily go back where you were. Nostalgia is also fraud ... there was no poverty, no oligarchies, no schemers, no treasons, there was nothing bad then ...

The columnist insists on the fact that the era in question also involved a 'generalized poverty that seemed nevertheless reasonable' (*To Vima*, 8 January 2013).

Summarizing, the interpretative repertoire of foreign occupation followed by strong victimization discursive practices (see also below), emerged as a hegemonic framework adopted mainly – though not exclusively – by the anti-memorandum camp. However, the abovementioned interpretations of the Greek crisis within the Greek public sphere, far from being unchallenged, have been constantly interacting with competing interpretative repertoires, such as those stressed below.

The interpretative repertoire of collective guilt: interactions and hybrid narratives

The second interpretative scheme of the Greek crisis is based on a perception of collective guilt that was captured in the emblematic phrase of Theodoros Pangalos – a well-known

Figure 1. "Stadiou Street, Athens, 1960s". Photograph by Costas Balafas. © Benaki Museum/ Photographic Archives.

Greek politician and Vice President of the government at that time – that could be loosely translated as 'we all did it together' (Pangalos, 2010). In September 2010 while the Parliament was discussing the prospect of shutting down public utilities and firing civil servants Pangalos argued that clientelistic relations and the misuse of public money were the source of the Greek problem. His phrase became the title of a book by Pangalos and also appeared on a website where a symbolic and ritualistic attribution of guilt was performed. The negotiation of guilt was at the centre of the book. According to the author its goal was to 'define the concept of mutual responsibility and of complicity of citizens in the party that had been going on. It describes … how the blame is allocated from the top to the bottom' (http://mazi-ta-fagame.gr/v1/?page_id=2491, viewed 5 September 2013). In his argumentation both politicians and their electorate were accomplices; politicians used the public sector as a means of buying off popular vote and the people tolerated this practice for personal gains.

In this sort of reasoning, blame is transferred from the external enemy to internal anomalies. Victimization is substituted by guilt and responsibility, thus legitimizing the need for the implementation of reforms. The crisis is perceived as the 'zero hour' of the Greek economic, political and social model. The following excerpts from two articles published by the prestigious conservative *Kathimerini* are typical examples:

> The hard thing to do, which requires guts and a great degree of self-awareness, is to say that eventually we are all to blame: the political system, the mass media, but also the generalized perception of what the Greeks should expect from the government … No one is 'innocent' … (*Kathimerini*, 17 February 2013)
>
> … the pressure does not come from some external factor, but from the bankruptcy of our own economic and political model … We are experiencing a crisis of identity on both the individual and social levels. We are still the victims of weak institutions, of the lack of self-discipline and the lawlessness that brought us to this point. (*Kathimerini*, 6 June 2010)

This discursive construction is also characterized by a different conception of temporality; it avoids references to the Occupation period and the war and it uses the post-authoritarian period (the so-called *Metapolitefsi*, since 1974) as its preferred period for constructing historical analogies. This interpretative scheme has become part of the centre-left, liberal, neo-liberal and conservative political discourse.

Nevertheless, both interpretative schemes embrace, with variations, the ultimate goal of national salvation. It is worth noting, however, that in the argumentation constructed upon these schemes one can observe the emergence of a divided national or political community, a picture of 'two Greeces', so to speak. In the case of the foreign occupation scheme, exclusion from the national 'body' is performed through the construction of a traitorous identity; the accused is considered to be a servile agent of foreigners (namely of the so-called 'troika' or the Germans) and in complete disagreement with the popular and national will. As a news website commented before a critical vote in the Parliament on the austerity measures:

> Perhaps the word "traitor" is too harsh, but how can you characterize someone who gives away national sovereignty to foreign powers with his vote? … Whoever MPs vote for Memorandum III will be enemies of their country and their people' (http://www.newsbomb.gr/politikh/story/250490/prodotis-opoios-ellinas-voyleytis-psifisei-ta-metra, viewed 30 January 2014)

In the scheme that prioritizes the concept of guilt combined with a critical perception of the Greek social and economic model, a distinction is drawn between a so-called 'productive Greece' which seeks to distance itself from the nation's problematic past and to prevail over 'the non-productive Greece'. This discursive pattern excludes from the national body and from the goal of national salvation the perceived non-productive parts of Greece, as attested in the following excerpt from a conservative newspaper:

> Only the productive Greece can be saved. The version of Greece that all those who were mentioned above suffocate. She consists of all those who work, produce, create. There are many people who can save this country, but they are sidelined by all the others, those who today weep that 'Greece wasn't saved' and what they mean is that their own failure wasn't saved. (*Kathimerini*, 1 December 2012)

What underlies this sort of discourse is the belief in a Greek exceptionalism – a sort of Greek 'malaise' – the notion that Greece is somehow excluded and differentiated from a western, idealized standard of normality. As a well-known columnist put it: 'ultimately the crisis, with all its victims and extremities, might turn us into a normal country' (*Kathimerini*, 9 January 2013).

On the other hand, prime-minister at the time Antonis Samaras after his party's secession from the anti-memorandum camp developed a pro-memorandum narrative involving nationalistic overtones. In this context, the state of affairs deriving from Greece's loan agreements is described as a parenthesis of 'humiliation' in the nation's glorious history, which ultimately will lead to national regeneration (Samaras, 26 October 2012).

However, the two interpretative schemes interact in public debate creating hybrid narrations that combine elements from both of them. Such a hybrid narrative scheme is the combination of the goal of national productive restructuring with the patriotic denouncement of the country's present dependence on others. This tendency is most evident in the following article by a Sunday newspaper entitled 'Only productivity and creativity can wash out the shame of bankruptcy'. In the article it was argued that:

> This process of complete dependence on the dosages [of the loans], on the debts and the 'goodness' of strangers can no longer be tolerated ... [Greece] should start acting dynamically so she can be freed as soon as possible from this hateful state of submission and dependence ... After all that has taken place during the three years of the crisis only an organized movement of production and creativity can wash out the shame of our great debt and bankruptcy. And for its inception and implementation all the combative and productive forces of the nation need to collaborate ... It's the only apt way to regain our country' s and our people's lost honour (http://www.tovima.gr/opinions/article/?aid=485210).

From a series of similar comments it becomes evident that national production and control over national economy are systematically associated with national pride. Loss or weakening of these elements leads to a perception of contested or threatened national identity which paves the way for seeking explanations based on a purported external enemy.

It is in this context that the concept of a plan or a plot against Greece – a trope that has often been associated with expressions of Greek nationalism – re-emerges in public discourse. Setting aside the most extreme, conspiratorial version of this interpretative repertoire,[9] we will focus on its inclusion in the bourgeois press that had supported the pro-memorandum camp.

In the following comment made by a columnist, the existence of a plot against Greece is addressed as a possibility, while economic independence is explicitly mentioned as an element of national identity:

Bankrupt banks and a bankrupt real economy will go under foreign control through the transfer of the decision making mechanism out of Greece. If certain people think that the concept of national sovereignty is void of meaning, they should know that none of the big countries has abandoned the systematic effort to safeguard a strong national identity which directly depends for its influence on the economic sphere. A Greece where young graduates, if they are lucky, will be working for 400 euros salaries in corporations controlled by foreign capitals will actually be a satellite country, a modern colony. Even if there never was a plan to disgrace Greece and to humiliate the Greeks, the emerging outcome looks like a plan. (*To Vima*, 9 September 2012)

Another hybrid scheme involving both topoi of victimization and guilt acknowledges the responsibilities and the mistakes of Greek society that led to the crisis, but perceives the response of the international community as unjust and cruel, as a sort of punishment that exceeds the errors committed. This scheme could be described as a 'guilty victim scheme'. It is in this mood that the news website *Protagon* chose the painting by Francisco Goya 'May 3, 1808' (Figure 2) to describe Greece's condition. While emotionally charged, the article stresses that this particular painting was chosen because the idealization of the victims is absent:

Here war has nothing to do with heroism. It's just brutal subjection. There are no festivities from the French, but also no effort to idealize the victims. Goya likes the victims. But he doesn't redeem them ... What we are watching is just an incident, a surrender, an inevitable fact. The submission of one country to another. Without shame, without defeatism, without triumphalism. This is how Greece surrenders to the rest of the Europeans. (*Protagon*, 26 October 2011)

Although comparing with the hegemonic repertoires of victimization, the latter interpretative framework seems like a residual category, a more detailed look at public attitudes and beliefs reveals a more complicated co-existence of the two blocks of discourse.

To elaborate further, the media's, political parties' and other organizations' use of symbols, notions and concepts that hark back to absolute evil in the Greek collective

Figure 2. Goya, F. (1814) "El 3 de mayo de 1808 en Madrid: los fusilamientos en la montaña del Príncipe Pío", Museo del Prado, Madrid. The inclusion of this image is inscribed within the "fair use" context for copyright material, as it is intended for nonprofit educational purposes.

memory represented by Hitler, Nazism, the third Reich, reflects a structure of anti-German sentiment and is deeply inscribed within the victimization community of discourse. As we can see in Figure 3, according to a poll conducted at February 2012, Germany denotes Hitler, the third Reich and Nazism for about one-third of Greek citizens.

The Global Attitudes Project conducted by the PEW Research Center and its findings concerning European unity also provide interesting empirical evidence of public beliefs in Greece premised on perceptions of Germany as an enemy. Figure 4 reveals the popularity of the perception of Germany, or the EU at large, as threats to Greeks' economic well-being.

In a similar vein, Figure 5 shows that Greeks are harshly critical of Germany, with 78% having an unfavourable view of the country.

Yet more interestingly, Figures 4 and 5 show that the interpretative repertoire emphasizing victimization does not exist in void but rather interacts with self-blaming patterns. In particular, the Greeks seem to conceive German power over Greek economy as a major threat for their economic well-being to a lesser extent comparing with the size of national debt or the power of banks. Moreover, to the question 'who is to blame for current economic problems', 42% of the Greeks answer in an apparent self-critical way ('ourselves'), while the respective percentage for the Spanish and the Italian respondents is 26% and 19% in respect.

To conclude, although the self-blaming interpretative repertoire is highly discernible during the first five years of the Greek crisis and interacts with the repertoire of victimization, *the analysis should not ignore the latter's structural components which are embedded in the national identity construction nor its hegemonic position within the Greek public sphere.* The case of the Merkel visit to Athens, sheds more light at this tentative assumption on hegemony.

The Merkel visit to Athens: a case of victimization interpretative repertoire?

Reactions to German Chancellor Angela Merkel's recent visit revealed the instrumental uses of deeper discursive structures. The visit took place in October 2012 – just a few

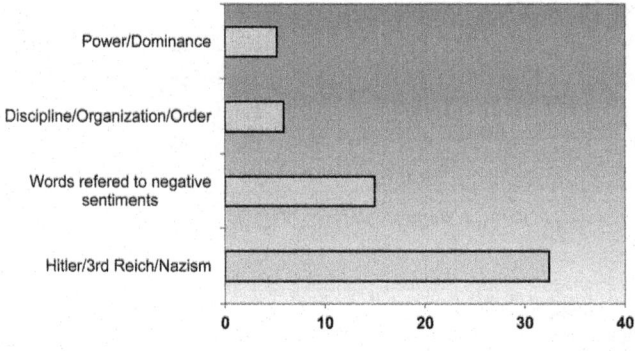

□ Thinking about Germany, which word or idea comes first in mind

Figure 3. Anti-German attitudes in Greek public opinion. Source: V-PRC, 2012 public accessed survey.

Major Threats to Economic Well-Being

% Major threat	Lack of jobs %	Size of national debt %	Rising prices %	Power of banks %	Trade unions %	Greece and Italy's econ problems %	German/EU power over our economy %	Economic problems in Europe %
Britain	87	72	67	65	24	54	--	--
France	89	80	74	68	21	64	--	--
Germany	70	77	56	78	10	71	--	--
Spain	97	83	74	80	32	--	47	--
Italy	95	81	89	74	30	--	39	--
Greece	97	97	93	88	40	--	83	--
Poland	84	78	79	58	21	56	40	--
Czech Rep.	84	82	62	56	18	58	46	--
MEDIAN	**88**	**81**	**74**	**71**	**23**	**58**	**46**	**--**
U.S.	82	71	64	52	26	--	--	41

PEW RESEARCH CENTER Q41a-h.

Figure 4. Pew Research Centre (2012). Reproduced with permission from PEW Research center on 2 April 2014.

days before the National Holiday on October 28th (i.e. a day of World War II remembrance) – and triggered the emergence of a resistance discourse against the perceived German threat. The President of the party of Independent Greeks suggested in his public statements that all Greeks should hang a Greek flag on their balconies on the day of the visit in order to declare that 'Greece is a sovereign state and will not negotiate her national sovereignty' (http://anexartitoiellines.gr/post.php?post_id=1122, viewed 18 July 2013).

Part of the media represented the German Chancellor as an occupier and the Greek government as subordinate to the creditors' will. Two days before Merkel's visit, the

Who's to Blame for Current Economic Problems?

	Our gov't %	Banks, financial institutions %	U.S. %	EU %	Our-selves %
Czech Rep.	91	27	5	39	21
Poland	90	39	5	28	15
Greece	87	39	4	19	42
Italy	84	58	2	15	19
Germany	70	74	12	25	9
Britain	67	69	10	16	19
Spain	59	78	8	19	26
France	59	74	10	37	18

Asked only of people who said economy was "bad" in Q14.

Total adds to more than 100% because of multiple responses.

"Who is most to blame for (survey country's) current economic problems? Is it..." & "Who is second most to blame for (survey country's) current economic problems?"

PEW RESEARCH CENTER Q16 & Q17.

Figure 5. Pew Research Centre (2012). Reproduced with permission from PEW Research center on 28 March 2014.

front page of *Proto Thema*, a populist Sunday newspaper with the biggest circulation figures among Greek papers, depicted a frightening portrait of Merkel pointing her finger in a menacing manner, while the infamous Nazi greeting 'HEIL' had been chosen as background. Similar connotations were employed by the rest of the populist oppositional press. *Free Sunday*, for instance, chose to publish a collage depicting Angela Merkel smiling while in the background a closed store with a 'to let' notice could be discerned. Even pro-governmental newspapers hosted opinion pieces with references to victimization, including the following argument by a columnist in a mainstream centre-left newspaper who protests against the behaviour of German tourists in Greece:

> The Germans are coming to their new feuds already as conquerors. Who? The great grand-children of Hitler [. .]Enough with the self-blaming apology. They are those who should apologise, not us [. .] And when they are scolding us, we answer that we do not discuss with Nazi descendants. (*To Vima*, 7 October 2012)

Although this apparent use of history for the identification of the Germans as enemies is far more familiar to populist right, we should not ignore its pervasiveness to centre-left media too. A few days later an acknowledged journalist writing for another mainstream centre-left newspaper made the following argument:

> [Is this] a co-operation between equal parties? It certainly is not. But as far as I am concerned Greece has gone bankrupt. Not occupied [. .] Because if this occupying process does not come to a halt, Greece will not change either'. (*Ta Nea*, 29 October 2012)

Furthermore, it is worth commenting on the attitude of the President of the Hellenic Republic at the time – the 89-year-old Carolos Papoulias – who just a few days after Merkel's visit made the following statement expressing his opposition to the austerity measures and to external pressures: 'I have said it to Mrs Merkel. If you want to impose more measures then you'd better consider the option of choosing another people' (Papoulias, 2012). Carolos Papoulias is a centre-left politician who used to emphasize his participation in the National Resistance (1940–1944) as an important element of his political identity. The interesting discursive feature in this reasoning is the combination of a foreign, historically grounded threat with the rejection of a perceived socio-economic model which seems to be promoted by Germany. This double interpretation of the German threat is also common in the leftist discourse of the opposition.

As far as the anti-memorandum camp and its leaders were concerned, blame was attributed equally to Germany and the Greek government, which is mostly perceived as a subordinate tool. The leader of the major opposition party, Alexis Tsipras warned a few days before Angela Merkel's visit to Athens:

> Mrs Merkel arrives hastily in Athens on Tuesday to support the crumbling government … She is not coming to support Greece, having herself – with her insistence on the Memorandum's austerity – led us over the cliff. She comes to save the corrupted, infamous and subordinate political system. (Tsipras, 7 October 2012)

It would be fair to argue that the main target of his critique was not the German Chancellor, but the coalition government and the austerity policies. Nevertheless, we once again see elements of the interpretative repertoire premised on purported victimization by the German government.

The populist and the centre-right press were also critical of the likelihood of a 'surrendering' (*Real News*, 8 October 2012). In a similar vein, though with a much more exclusivist and nationalist rhetoric, the extreme right, neo-Nazi party of Golden Dawn also focused on the 'surrendering of Greece to our country's rulers' (Golden Dawn, 2012). Nevertheless by then the intensity of such critiques had been mitigated in comparison to the mass demonstrations against the memorandum and the Troika just a few months earlier; thus, we should not underestimate the re-alignment processes that took place after the elections of June 2012.

The left-leaning press targeted its efforts on attributing an oppositional character to the 'anti-Merkel' demonstrations, although with some variations in the personification of the protest: the newspaper of the Greek Communist Party omitted any reference to Merkel, focusing on the need of a popular demonstration against government's austerity measures and state repression. As the General Secretary of the Greek Communist Party, Aleka Papariga, had remarked a few days before Merkel's visit to Athens,

> we (the communists) are not eager to play the game of those who reduce the EU problem to a Merkel problem, or if you prefer to a Holland – Merkel controversy, or to a South-North division. Mrs Merkel is the Chancellor of a leading capitalist country in Europe'. (Papariga, 9 October 2012)

Actually the Communist Party of Greece opted for a class-oriented discursive strategy through which the blame for austerity was attributed to the choices made mainly by the domestic bourgeois social class, but this is a rather marginal positioning within the Left, at least at the time of Merkel visit.

With the exception of the aforementioned traditional anti-capitalist discourse, the balance between class-oriented rhetoric and nationalist rhetoric was difficult to maintain and hybrid forms of discourse appeared in many cases of political mobilization orchestrated by trade unions and other social protest actors. The country's union confederations called for massive protests on the day of the Chancellor's arrival. In such rhetoric, the denouncement of neo-liberalism was articulated with anti-German stereotypes and latent euro-scepticism. In its declaration the Civil Servant's Confederation targeted the punitive policy of the EU towards Greece and urged the people to react to the 'neoliberal policy that is being implemented at the national and the European level on the orders of Mrs Merkel and the European leaders' (http://www.adedy.gr/adedy/site/home/ws/primary+menu/deltia/2012/october/5102012-2.csp, viewed 20 February 2014).

In the same vein, the journalists' union (POESY) referred to the Chancellor as the 'Memorandum's architect' and argued that 'her visit is part of the broader plan to blackmail the Geek people, but also the other European peoples as well, in order to accept the new projects for social genocide'

(http://www.poesy.gr/index.php?option=com_content&view=article&id=911:2012–10-06-14-06-38, viewed 20 February 2014).

Even though the leaderships of trade unions and the Left avoided employing straightforward anti-German rhetorical vehicles, as they pointed their critique mostly towards the government, the demonstrations did not lack victimization discursive practices and foreign enemy stereotyping. As we can see in Figures 6–8, some blocks of demonstrators were holding pickets and banners referring to the third Reich, Nazism and similar symbols.

Figure 6. 'No to the 4th Reich'. Photo taken by the authors on 9 October 2012.

Figure 7. 'Sabotage German products. RESIST THE 4th REICH. Buying Greek products, we prevent (our) wages and pensions from being cut'. (Photo taken by the authors 9 October 2012. Our translation). Photo taken by the authors on 9 October 2012.

Figure 8. Banner with 'Guernica' and the slogan 'No to the Memorandum of pauperization'. Photo taken by the authors on 9 October 2012.

While we were observing those protests, it was made apparent to us that in most cases the above connotations had a rank-and-file character, meaning that those indicative dramaturgies have been designed, directed and performed at a grassroots level.

On the other hand, the pro-memorandum camp, namely the tri-partite governmental parties, represented the Merkel visit as a vote of confidence in favour of Greece and its prospects within the Eurozone. Self-blaming interpretative repertoires were here employed in order to stigmatize Greek 'self-catastrophic tendencies' that were also ascribed to the so-called irresponsible and violent practices during the demonstrations. As far as it concerns the penetrative function of the self-blaming repertoire, at the case of the Merkel visit this seems to be rather weak, as the hegemony of the 'foreign occupation' schemes had not been critically challenged, even in mainstream media.

Conclusions

The literature on the interaction between crises and national identity issues has established that they tend to transform 'previously (largely) taken-for-granted cultural meaning[s] into ideologically varied politicized opinions' (Karner, 2005a, p. 222). The cleavage between the pro- and anti-Memorandum camps is just one aspect of the ideological processes taking place in Greece during the crisis. However, this cleavage involves two distinct 'communities of discourse' who fight for hegemony and employ distinct and competing interpretative repertoires. Through this process the negotiation of national identity and national self-image is performed. Even though the interpretative repertoires presented here and the mythscapes constructed appear as mutually contradictory in public discourse, they also interact and shape hybrid discursive constructions. Despite the important ideological differences between the two discursive constructions, it is worth noting that they both acknowledge the nation as an uncontested and principal point of reference, while they both reproduce the perception of Greek exceptionalism, though in different modes. This paper has demonstrated that although the victimization interpretative repertoire holds a hegemonic position during the period under scrutiny, it is not unambiguous and solidified; despite its obvious penetrative power indicated first and foremost at cases of political mobilization such as the Merkel visit, it co-exists and interacts with the self-blaming repertoire, thus also leading to hybrid perceptions that are adjusted to political actors' argumentative strategies and needs. However, the victimization interpretative repertoire is far more grounded in popular belief systems and only gradually the hybrid schemes come to the fore. In any case, in the current context and certainly since the 2012 elections, Greek political-, business- and media elites seem to have tried to moderate or control anti-German attitudes. The dramatic political developments in 2015 and the 'great turn' of the previously anti-memorandum governmental coalition of SYRIZA-ANEL towards more consensual discursive patterns adjusted to the new status of communication with the creditors, highlights a shift towards a meta-hegemonic period in Greek political discourse, where hybrid narrations start dominating across the political spectrum.

Yet, attention should still be drawn to the structure and the content of the anti-German discourse. Setting aside its cultural and historical connotations we should not ignore the fact that in the current crisis context it constitutes a specific mode of expressing popular discomfort. The sources of this discomfort are the worsening of socio-economic conditions on one hand, and the growing limitations of national sovereignty in light of supra-national decision-making processes, on the other. An open research question in this respect is the links between the development of anti-German discourse and the emergence of Greek Euro-scepticism in the crisis context.

Notes

1. For example, in the 2001 Eurobarometer survey (EB 55, spring 2001) support for the single currency in Greece scored 72% compared to 59% EU average. The most popular answers the Greeks gave to the question «What does the EU mean to you personally?» were 'freedom of movement' (49%), 'the Euro' (44%) and peace (43%). Available at http://ec.europa.eu/public_opinion/archives/eb/eb55/eb55_en.htm (viewed 25 February 2014).

   In the following year (EB 57, spring 2002), support for the single currency rose to 80% (EU average: 67%). Available at http://ec.europa.eu/public_opinion/archives/eb/eb57/eb57_en.htm (viewed 25 February 2014). Even though support for the Euro dropped in the following years after Greece's accession to the EMU – reaching a low point in 2005 (49%) (EB 63, spring 2005) – it remained at high levels. Available at http://ec.europa.eu/public_opinion/archives/eb/eb63/eb63_en.htm (viewed 25 February 2014).

2. It is also worth considering the opposing conceptualization between Simitis' phrase and the slogan of 'small but honest Greece' which was raised against Venizelos' expansionist policy in Asia Minor at the beginning of the twentieth century by his political opponents. See Smith (1998, p. 153). The slogan exceeded this specific context and was incorporated in the Greek political and everyday discourse as an element of national self-image.

3. In the context of post-1989 developments in the Balkan region, the People's Republic of Macedonia (Skopje) declared its independence from the Yugoslav Federation in 1991. This triggered an intense diplomatic conflict with Greece who refused to recognize the new state insofar as it used the term 'Macedonia'. Greece perceived the creation of the new state in its Northern borders as a security threat but also as a threat to its cultural and national identity. After a series of diplomatic battles an interim agreement was signed by Greece and the Former

Yugoslavic Republic of Macedonia (FYROM) in 1995. Despite the attainment of a compromise between the two countries, the issue has not been completely resolved to this day.

4. After a series of negotiations, the Eurozone countries and the IMF agreed on a bailout agreement and Greece undertook the obligation to implement harsh austerity policies and to carry out structural reforms (May 2010). However, the deep recession of the Greek economy that followed led to a second bailout loan and to a restructuring of the Greek debt (October 2011). The second bailout plan extends from 2012 to 2014. The terms of the bailout agreements provoked a series of political crises, as a result of which Papandreou was forced to resign in November 2011 and a coalition government was formed under Loukas Papadimos. It took two parliamentary elections in 2012 before a new coalition government was formed in June 2012.

5. The bailout agreements were coined the term 'memoranda' in the Greek public debate. Thus, those opposed to the agreements formed the so-called 'anti-memorandum camp', while their defenders constitute the 'pro-memorandum' bloc.

6. Jeffrey M. Bale explains in a very convincing way why conspiracy theories thrive among the most vulnerable and powerless social strata:

> [...] conspiracy theories help to make complex patterns of cause and effect in human affairs more comprehensible by means of reductionism and oversimplification. Second, they purport to identify the underlying source of misery and injustice in the world, thereby accounting for current crises and upheavals and explaining why bad things are happening to good people or vice versa. Third, by personifying that source they paradoxically help people to reaffirm their own potential ability to control the course of future historical developments [...] In short, a belief in conspiracy theories helps people to make sense out of a confusing, inhospitable reality, rationalize their present difficulties and partially assuage their feelings of powerlessness'. (Bale, 2007, pp. 50–51)

See also, Sapountzis and Condor (2013).

7. This argument was made in the context of an article by Alexis Tsipras published by the German newspaper *Neues Deutschland*. Parts of the article were translated and reproduced by the Greek media on 21 October 2012. Available at http://www.tanea.gr/news/greece/article/4761805/?iid=2 (viewed 1 August 2013).

8. The photo had been taken by the famous Greek photographer Costas Balafas (1920–2011) and had not been published during his lifetime. Balafas had donated his archive to the Benaki Museum. In December 2012 the Museum uploaded the picture in facebook and twitter.

9. A powerful, though not isolated, conspiracy theory was disseminated by the neo-nazi party Golden Dawn in the aftermath of the imprisonment of some of its MPs and leading executives accused of criminal activities. According to the official website of the party: 'Zionists asked for the political persecution of the Golden Dawn and their miserable servant the prime minister Antonis Samaras followed the orders'. Available at http://www.xryshaygh.com/index.php/enimerosi/view/apothewsh-samara-apo-tous-ebraious-entoleis-tou-gia-tis-politikes-diwjeis-t (viewed 15 February 2014).

References

Balabanidis, Y. (2007). *"For a strong society, for a strong Greece". A critical reading of the modernizing project (1996–2004). Politics and ideology* (Master Dissertation). Panteion University of Social and Political Sciences, Athens.

Bale, J. M. (2007). Political paranoia v. political realism: On distinguishing between bogus conspiracy theories and genuine conspiratorial politics. *Patterns of Prejudice, 41*(1), 45–60.

Bell, D. (2003). Mythscapes: Memory, mythology, and national identity. *The British Journal of Sociology, 54*(1), 63–81.

Boukala, S. (2014). Waiting for democracy: Political crisis and the discursive (re)invention of the 'national enemy' in times of 'Grecovery'. *Discourse and Society, 25*(4), 483–499.

De Fina, A., Schiffrin, D., & Bamberg, M. (Eds.). (2006). *Discourse and identity*. Cambridge: Cambridge University Press.

Economides, S. (2005). The Europeanisation of Greek foreign policy. *West European Politics, 28*(2), 471–491.

Ethnos. (2011, January 12). Retrieved May 12, 2013, from www.ethnos.gr/article.asp?catid=22767&subid=2&pubid=50314948

Golden Dawn. (2012, October 6). Retrieved July 10, 2013, from www.protothema.gr/politics/article/227964/sxolio-xryshs-ayghs-gia-episkepsh-merkel-sthn-athhna/

Howarth, D., & Torfing, J. (Eds.). (2005). *Discourse theory in European politics: Identity, policy and governance*. Basingstoke: Palgrave Macmillan.

Karner, C. (2005a). National DOXA, crises and ideological contestation in contemporary Austria. *Nationalism and Ethnic Politics, 11*(2), 221–263.

Karner, C. (2005b). The "Habsurg dilemma" today: Competing discourses of national identity in contemporary Austria. *National Identities, 7*(4), 409–432.

Karner, C. (2010). The uses of the past and European integration: Austria between Lisbon, Ireland, and EURO 08. *Identities: Global Studies in Culture and Power, 17*(4), 387–410.

Kazamias, A. (1997). The quest for modernization in Greek foreign policy and its limitations. *Mediterranean Politics, 2*(2), 71–94.

Lialiouti, Z. (2010). *Greek anti-Americanism, 1947–1989* (PhD thesis). Panteion University of Political and Social Sciences, Athens.

Lialiouti, Z. (2011). Greek anti-Americanism and the war in Kosovo. *National Identities, 13*(2), 127–155.

Lialiouti, Z., & Bithymitris, G. (2013). The Nazis strike again: The concept of the German enemy, party strategies and mass perceptions through the prism of the Greek economic crisis. In C. Karner & B. Mertens (Eds.), *The use and abuse of memory: Interpreting World War II in contemporary European politics* (pp. 155–172). New Brusnwick, NJ: Transaction.

Lialiouti, Z., & Bithymitris, G. (2014). Implications of the Greek crisis: Nationalism, enemy stereotypes and the European Union. In B. Stefanova (Ed.), *The European Union beyond the crisis: Evolving governance, contested policies, disenchanted publics* (pp. 249–268). New York, NY: Lexington Books, Lanham, Boulder.

Marshall, H. (1994). Discourse analysis in the occupational context. In C. Cassell & G. Seymour (Eds.), *Qualitative methods in organizational research: A practical guide* (pp. 91–106). London: Sage.

Pangalos, T. (2010). *Speech*. Retrieved June 10, 2013, from www.enet.gr/?i=news.el.article&id=205326

Papariga, A. (2012, October 9). *Press conference on the political developments*. Retrieved May 30, 2013, from www.rizospastis.gr/page.do?publDate=9/10/2012&id=14240&pageNo=6&direction=1

Papoulias, K. (2012). *Statement*. Retrieved July 18, 2013, from www.tovima.gr/politics/article/?aid=479759

Pew Research – Global Attitude Project 'European Unity on the rocks: Greeks and Germans at polar opposites' (2012, May 29). Retrieved June 10, 2013, from http://www.pewglobal.org/2012/05/29/european-unity-on-the-rocks/

Potter, J., & Wetherell, M. (1987). *Discourse and social psychology*. London: Sage.

Protagon.gr. (2011, October 26). Retrieved September 5, 2013, from http://www.protagon.gr/?i=protagon.el.article&id=9717

Real News (2012, October 8). Retrieved July 27, 2013, from www.real.gr/DefaultArthro.aspx?page=blogitem&eid=18&id=178410

Roudometof, V. (2002). *Collective memory, national identity and ethnic conflict: Greece, Bulgaria and the Macedonian question*. London: Praeger Westport.

Samaras, A. (2012). *Speech*. Retrieved September 5, 2013, from http://www.primeminister.gov.gr/2012/10/26/9806

Sapountzis, A., & Condor, S. (2013). Conspiracy accounts as intergroup theories: Challenging dominant understandings of social power and political legitimacy. *Political Psychology, 34*(5), 731–752.

Simitis, C. (2000). *Speech*. Retrieved March 10, 2013, from www.costas-simitis.gr/content/75

Smith, M. L. (1998). *Ionian vision: Greece in Asia Minor, 1919–1920*. London: Hurst.

Teperoglou, E., & Tsatsanis, E. (2014). Dealignment, de-legitimation and the implosion of the two-party system in Greece: The earthquake election of 6 May 2012. *Journal of Elections, Public Opinion & Parties, 24*(2), 222–242.

Tsakatika, M., & Eleftheriou, C. (2013). The radical Left's turn towards civil society in Greece: One strategy, two paths. *South European Society and Politics, 18*(1), 81–99.

Tsipras, A. (2012). *Speech*. Retrieved July 21, 2013, from www.naftemporiki.gr/story/362990

Tsipras: the government has provoked a humanitarian crisis. *TaNea.gr*. (2013, April 28). Retrieved January 11, 2014, from http://www.tanea.gr/news/politics/article/5014846/tsipras-h-kybernhsh-exei-epiferei-anthrwpistikhkrish-sth-xwra/

Tsipras, A. (2014). *Statement*. Retrieved February 25, 2014, from http://www.protothema.gr/politics/article/355071/tsipras-katestrammeni-hora-i-ellada-/

Traditional bustle. (2012). Inewsgr.com. Retrieved November 25, 2012, from http://www.inewsgr.com/94/paradosiaka-epeisodia.htm

Van Dijk, T. A. (2006). Ideology and discourse analysis. *Journal of Political Ideologies, 11*(2), 115–140.

Vasilopoulou, S., Halikiopoulou, D., & Exadaktylos, T. (2014). Greece in crisis: Austerity, populism and the politics of blame. *Journal of Common Market Studies, 52*(2), 388–402.

Veremis, Th., & Koliopoulos, J. (2003). The evolving content of the Greek nation. In T. Couloumbis, T. Kariotis, & F. Bellou (Eds.), *Greece in the twentieth century* (pp. 13–30). Oxon: Frank Cass.

Vernardakis, C. (2007). Evropaismos ke evroskeptikismos stin Ellada' [Pro-Europeanism and Euroscepticism in Greece]. In C. Vernardakis (Ed.), *He koine Gnomi stin Ellada 2005–2006* [Public opinion in Greece 2005–2006] (pp. 147–164). Athens: Savvalas.

Verney, S. (2011). An exceptional case? Party and popular euroscepticism in Greece, 1959–2009. *South European Society & Politics, 16*(1), 51–80.

V-PRC. 'The image of Germany and the German politics in Greek public opinion' – survey commissioned by the magazine Epikaira. Retrieved February 20, 2014, from http://www.vprc.gr/article.php?id=1144

Wetherell, M. (1998). Positioning and interpreting repertoires: Conversation analysis and post-structuralism in dialogue. *Discourse and Society, 9*(3), 387–412.

Wetherell, M., & Potter, J. (1998). Discourse analysis and the identification of interpretative repertoires. In C. Antaki (Ed.), *Analysing everyday explanation* (pp. 168–183). London: Sage.

Wodak, R., & Angouri, J. (2014). From grexit to grecovery: Euro/crisis discourses. *Discourse and Society, 25*(4), 417–423.

Wodak, R., de Cillia, R., Reisigl, M., & Liebhart, K. (2009). *The discursive construction of national identity* (A. Hirsch, R. Mitten, & J.W. Unger, Trans.). Edinburg: Edinburg University Press.

4 Feeling the pulse of the Greek debt crisis

Affect on the web of blame

Tereza Capelos and Theofanis Exadaktylos

ABSTRACT

This article examines the affective content of Greek media representations of the debt crisis, from 2009 to 2012. We analyze the content of opinion pieces from journalists, experts and public intellectuals published in Greek newspapers, and identify their affective tone towards political actors and institutions. We focus on anger, fear and hope, and identify blame attribution frames, which underpin the public's trust and confidence in domestic and European Union institutions. This article contributes to the systematic understanding of the impact of the debt crisis as a traumatic event on public opinion, and considers its implications for attitudes towards European integration.

Introduction

In this article we examine the affective content of newspaper opinion pieces authored by Greek citizens and elites focusing on political actors and institutions during the debt crisis. The Greek sovereign debt crisis and economic breakdown, generated due to pathologies of the Greek political system (clientelism, populism, weak democratic institutions and civil society), and triggered by the global economic crisis, has led to dramatic changes in the dynamics of the Greek political and social reality and received extensive media coverage at home and internationally (Featherstone, 2011; Mitsopoulos & Pelagidis, 2011; Mouzelis & Pagoulatos, 2002; Pappas, 2013; Tzogopoulos, 2013; Vasilopoulou & Halikiopoulou, 2013). References to 'the sinking Euro', 'lazy Greeks', 'hard-working Germans' and 'detached Brits' have frequently been hosted in headlines, news reports and editorial commentary in newspapers and magazines across international media outlets from 2009 onwards (e.g. Der Spiegel, 2011; EU Observer, 2011; Forbes, 2011; The Economist, 2011).

The impact of this crisis on citizens and political elites has captured the attention of several studies, some of which use public opinion data, and others that code the content of relevant political communication channels. For example, Karyotis (2014) examines public opinion perceptions of austerity policies, while Dinas and Rori (2013) use survey data to measure the impact of the crisis on voting behavior. Chalari (2014) examines subjective experiences and evaluations of citizens during the crisis employing interview data.

Capelos and Exadaktylos (2015), and also Tzogopoulos (2013), study media representations of the crisis and focus on identifying coverage patterns and the stereotypes and preconceptions media reports adopt, while Exadaktylos and Zahariadis (2014) discuss the crisis implications for political trust.

The above studies provide valuable insights at the individual and aggregate levels of analysis and help understand on one hand how citizens' political attitudes have been shaped by the crisis, and on the other hand what was the content of Greek media during the reporting of events. Our article sits between these two levels, focusing on the intermediate-level dynamics taking place between the individual and the aggregate, where individual opinions are circulated in the public domain via mass media, often setting the tone of public discussions among engaged citizens and elites. Looking at opinion pieces we come across elements of the public debate and discussion about the crisis that might influence public opinion in the aggregate sense. Shoemaker and Reese (1996) propose that similar approaches help us understand political attitudes and shed light on the media role in society. The analysis of widely disseminated individual opinion pieces can point to the protagonists of the crisis, the concerns that surface at particular points in time, the evaluation of proposed solutions, and the affective pulse of public reactions, adding value to our understanding of the crisis and complementing the findings of standard surveys, interviews, as well as political communication studies that map the content of standard news items like headlines and news reports.

Capturing the affective pulse of the crisis is one of our central aims. A 'crisis' signifies the emotional reaction to a problematic, disruptive and painful situation (Caplan, 1974), but during the Greek crisis the affective content of citizens' and elites' considerations has largely remained understudied. Our article addresses this gap by offering a rigorous content analysis that identifies the emotions detected in opinion pieces, particularly anger, fear and hope. We discuss our findings drawing insights from political psychology and political economy debates that focus on how elites and citizens reach their judgments in times of crisis.

As we will show, citizens and elites engage not only cognitively but also emotionally with the crisis and their protagonists. Their level of emotional engagement can be drawing on individual or social subjective experiences expressed in the singular ('I feel'), or collective experiences expressed in the plural ('we feel') as shared emotions in actual or imagined crowds and communities (von Scheve & Salmela, 2014). Understanding how the key emotions of anger, fear and hope evolved over time in the experiences of individuals and how they featured in Greek media coverage since 2009 can help us study more effectively the emotions expressed collectively as anger, frustration, and even rage in demonstrations, rallies, and other ritualized activities. These collective emotions which are often disseminated via social and mass media could have significant implications for the future of democratic values in Greece, and also trust in its domestic political institutions and leaders. The intense crisis context also fueled fears, angry protests and uncertainty in many European countries outside Greece, making this study relevant for understanding trust in the European Union (EU) and international institutions more broadly. As such, our work extends research on the Greek financial crisis on two fronts: it sits at the intermediate political communication space of opinion pieces provided by citizens and political elites in reaction to the events and news that covered them, and it places particular focus on the affective content of the crisis experiences, highlighting its psychological and political impact.

Why emotions matter

The affective side of political judgments is as valuable to the understanding of public opinion formation as their cognitive components. Emotions condition the way citizens think and act about politics, and it is impossible to completely disentangle them from cognitions (Marcus, 2000; Ottati & Wyer, 1993). As Eagly and Chaiken (1993) point out, there is a symbiotic relationship between cognition and emotion: citizens often rationalize their emotions and their reasoning about politics generates further emotional reactions. Emotions have been shown to increase interest in politics (Graber, 1990; Marcus, 2000), override self-interest, promote altruism (Sears, 1993), affect perceptions of blame and policy evaluations (Capelos, 2010, 2013) and stimulate participation (Sniderman, Brody, & Tetlock, 1991).

Certain political phenomena such as natural disasters, scandals and crises offer particularly interesting opportunities to study emotionality arising at the individual and societal level. Studies of individual affective experiences show that as citizens and political elites engage with a crisis, they have emotional reactions ranging from fear to anger to hope or empathy, which in turn stimulate political reasoning and action (Damasio, 1994; Marcus, Neuman, & MacKuen, 2000). According to Lazarus (1993) a crisis involves discrete emotional reactions that are basic (anger, disgust, fear, anxiety, sadness) and social (shame, guilt, envy, jealousy). These emotions stimulate mental and physiological readiness and motivation to action for the individuals that experience them (Frijda, 2004). Gut-feelings – whether an event 'feels right' or 'feels wrong' – or intuitions also serve to generate political reactions among citizens often compensating for factual information that would promote abstract reasoning (Wilson, Dunn, Kraft, & Lisle, 1989). Similarly to emotions, these decision-making pathways are not 'purely rational' but they are quick in establishing reactions to events, yet we know very little about them (Sniderman et al., 1991).

Political psychologists study individual emotional reactions of anger, fear and hope due to their distinct effects on political thinking and decision-making. Anger is associated with lack of careful cognitive processing, rushed action, lack of attention to new information and extensive use of habitual forms of decision-making such as stereotypes. Anxiety in its mild forms is associated with investigative attention to new information in order to minimize the stress caused by a new situation, while as it escalates to fear, it is associated with the 'flight' mechanism, lack of action, and risk-adverse political preferences. Hope and enthusiasm are positive emotions that promote the use of habitual decision-making and stimulate engagement and action (Capelos, 2011). Overall, studies concur that cognition, affect, motivation and action are interrelated (Ekman, 2004). Anxious citizens do not navigate the political space the same way as citizens who are angry, hopeful, ashamed or proud. Their decision-making and also their appreciation of political events and cognitive understanding of developments as they unfold is conditioned by their emotionality.

At a societal level, individuals can also have collective emotions, the feelings of shared pride, grief, disappointment or elation, which provide a sense of unity and collective experience, even to those not in physical proximity to the particular event that facilitated their occurrence. Naturally, these two levels of emotionality are interactive. Classic studies in the psychology of crowds treated collective emotions as contagious, seen as overriding individuals' thoughts and feelings (Le Bon, 1896; McDougall, 1920), and manipulative (Canetti, 1960) while others saw their origin in imitation (von Scheve & Salmela, 2014). Durkheim (1912/1995) pointed to the collective effervescence of group rituals and community events emphasizing their power in coloring individuals' beliefs and values with affective meaning. The relationship between collective emotions and the cultural aspects of individual emotions has recently inspired cross-disciplinary studies in sociology, political science, history and psychology. Related concepts such as inter-group emotions, emotional climates, emotional communities are used to capture the contagion and interconnectivity of the two levels of emotional experience where the 'us', 'them' and 'I' meet, and new studies in political neuroscience identify the physiological links between individual and collective emotions (Lamm & Silani, 2014).

To appreciate how a crisis affects the political landscape of a country, we cannot sidestep the role of emotionality, both individual and collective. Stereotypes, biases, policy preferences, action readiness or inactivity, cynicism or engagement, have their root at the interaction of cognition and emotion (Frijda, Kuipers, & Ter Schure, 1989). With this in mind we focus here on the affective pulse of the Greek crisis, focusing on the types of emotional reactions experienced by citizens and elites and expressed via mass media.

Mediated emotionality in crises

Mass media is critical to the generation and dissemination of individual, social and collective emotions. As broadcast and social media cover a crisis, they also document and capture emotionality via their narrative and presentation of stories to individuals who are not physically co-present. Graber notes that news broadcasts host emotions which explain trends in public opinion, place mass political actions in context, and highlight decision-making preferences adopted by political elites (Graber, 2010). It is the communication of individual and social emotions in the public social space that turns the individual or social feelings of one person to collective affective experiences that stimulate cohesion, identification or alienation towards political actors and institutions.

The role of media in times of crises has received attention from political communication scholars. Citizens rely on media to gain information about current developments of the crisis, identify potential solutions to problems, and also form opinions, stimulate their sense of political efficacy, and alleviate their stress originating from the complexity of the situation (Graber, 2009; Zaller, 1992). While most citizens prefer to use broadcast media to stay informed about politics during non-crisis periods, the readership of newspapers increases during crises, because they provide details, in-depth analysis and commentary not available in television broadcast (Graber, 2001). Familiar media sources, like one's preferred newspaper, offer a safe information environment and host interpretations of the event by media and political elites which turn complex social and political issues into coherent stories (Nimmo & Combs, 1985; Singer & Endreny, 1993; Walters, Wilkins, & Walters, 1989).

Opinion pieces complement the content of news items as they provide citizens with an idea of how experts, public intellectuals and sophisticated citizens cope with the crisis at a particular point in time, and allow them to solidify their own ideas and policy preferences. Opinion pieces provide a snapshot of public agendas and offer public opinion scholars that study crises the opportunity to compare them to media agendas. As Rogers and Dearing (1988) highlight, there are often differences between public agendas that reflect citizens' perceptions of what is important and set the standards on the basis of which governments are often judged, media agendas that reflect the most extensively covered media content, and policy, or political, agendas that reflect decisions and actions of political elites.

Public, media and political agendas might be different but they are not independent of each other. Public perceptions of what is important are often determined by media agendas, so it is worth documenting and studying them in conjunction. As Wright (1986) notes, what citizens view as important is also affected by conversations with others regarding social and political issues. McLeod, Becker, and Byrnes (1974) also note that content presented in mass media has greater effect in shaping perceptions among individuals who engage in interpersonal communication about the topics in the media agenda. This is particularly relevant for our study since opinion pieces offer opportunities for citizens to engage and exchange opinions about the crisis, providing a context that influences how people think about the crisis and who is to blame. So although we are not making any inference claims about how audiences interpret messages that appear in opinion pieces, or suggest that the analysis of opinion pieces offers direct insight into audience perceptions, we argue that we contribute to an integrated approach of understanding the media and public debate content of the financial crisis. By focusing on opinion pieces, our study facilitates a better understanding of the emotional temperature of the crisis as expressed by these particular media users, which enter the public mediated sphere via their opinion pieces.

An additional complication is that media content is not homogeneous during a crisis. In the early stages, when the crisis is announced, media provide mainly information about the facts, and speculation about the causes of the event. Details and accounts of the crisis hosted in opinion pieces and elsewhere in print and broadcast media allow citizens to feel part of a 'community of suffering', seeing that their fears, worries and, often, misfortune is shared. As the crisis evolves, newspapers and news broadcasts attempt to place the situation in perspective, and provide a coherent story. Experts and intellectuals go beyond the facts and often provide colorful attributions of responsibility and emotionally arousing interpretations. And when the crisis remains in the media and public agenda for some time, we often see media and public officials attempting to place the issue into a long-term perspective and offer suggestions on how to cope with the aftermath or the prolonged nature of the crisis (Graber, 2010).

Emotions in the Greek financial crisis

In a study that sets the stage for the exploration of emotionality in the Greek media during the crisis, Davou and Demertzis (2013) mapped the collective emotions available in news headlines featured in the Greek public sphere during the financial crisis. They highlight the negative and but also action-limiting nature of these emotions, expressed as collective anxiety, fear, shame and very often despair. In our study of opinion pieces in the Greek press we extend this work by providing an overview of the individual, social and collective emotions prominent in the public sphere during the same period. The novelty of our work is three-fold. We aim to systematically capture the affective content of political communication messages at individual, social and collective levels. We identify their transformation or continuation over time. And we explain how they fit in a pattern of social affectivity during the crisis. Going beyond what is being said about the political events and actors marking the crisis, to what is being said *about their emotional footprint* allows us to get closer to the understanding of how elites and citizens experienced the changing political reality in hard times, and attempted to manage it in their hearts and minds.

The media coverage of the Greek debt crisis in news headlines was broadly classified in three stages by Davou and Demertzis (2013). Their research shows that in its early phase (December 2009–May 2010) the crisis was presented in print media outlets (with affiliations across the political spectrum) as the worst development in Greek history since the 1949 civil war, and headlines stressed the shock and traumatic nature of the crisis. In its second phase (June 2010–December 2011), media headlines captured the anger and frustration of the public which was expressed in public demonstrations and protests. During its third phase (from early 2012 onwards), Greece experienced a growing recession and citizens witnessed the inability of the political system to deal with the crisis. News headlines reflected the lack of hope, sense of helplessness and meaninglessness, but also a sense of gained efficacy after the results of the general elections (for examples of that, please refer to Table 1, column 'Headlines'). It is interesting to observe in their study that the crisis overrides political affiliation and headlines engage in a broader debate of blame attribution in trying to assess the extent of the implications of the crisis for the political system.

The protagonists of the crisis and who's to blame

Political actors and institutions that facilitate or constrain political action are featured heavily in media descriptions of events and discussions of praise or blame. Stories about a crisis often involve critical references to ministers, MPs, leaders of political parties, or parliamentary procedures, central banks and credit agencies or courts, financial markets, particular states, international organizations. As these agents are at the heart of important political developments, they become the focal point of media and public dialogues. We are interested here in the frequency and the affective tone of the representations of these agents as they carry significant weight in understanding how citizens understand and respond to crises.

Blame in times of crises is spread across a number of different political actors, who often attempt to shift and diffuse it (Capelos & Wurtzer, 2009; Kinder & Sanders, 1990; Lasorsa & Reese, 1990; Weaver, 1986). Vasilopoulou, Halikiopoulou, and Exadaktylos (2014) studied parliamentary debates between Greek party leaders during the crisis, and found that blame was shifted around to multiple targets such as the party of government (Panelinio Socialistiko Kinima - PASOK), the prime minister and its ministers; the main opposition party (Nea Dimokratia – ND), its leader and MPs; external elites and actors such as the EU, the USA, the International Monetary Fund or specific EU member states; interest groups such as banks, industries, corporations or rating agencies. In our analysis, we identify the main agents of the crisis as they appear in opinion pieces and briefly consider the relevant blame frames over the same period.

Prior to the crisis, the Greek political system was mainly a two-party system with government rotating between the Greek Socialists (PASOK) and the Greek Conservatives (ND). There were other political parties in parliament but none with significant power (Pappas, 2013). In the recent years, the crisis served as a catalyst to the redefinition of the political system, with the collapse of PASOK's electoral influence, the emergence of the radical left party Synaspismos Rizospastikis Aristeras as a contender to power, the creation of coalition governments since 2012, and the rise of the extreme right party of Golden Dawn in parliament (Vasilopoulou & Halikiopoulou, 2013). By extrapolating our results in this content

Table 1. Timeline of emotionality, protagonists of blame and newspaper headlines.

Dates	Emotions	Public agenda focus	Protagonists of blame	Headlines
December 2009	'alert', 'anxiety', 'uncertainly', 'hesitation'	Government (29%) EU actors (25%) Media (27%) Foreign investors and markets (50%)	Government (23%) Interest groups (23%)	'Nightmarish Report on Social Security' (Typos tis Kiriakis) 'The market suffocates' (I Chora)
May 2010	'uncertainty', 'alarm', 'anxiety', 'anger', 'rage', 'despair', 'disappointment', 'pessimism', 'misery', 'hope', 'courage', 'excitement'	Political parties (21%) Media (27%)	Political system (21%) Opposition (29%) Interest groups (23%)	'Hunger and misery for salaried employees and pensioners' (Avriani) 'People at the Guillotine' (24 Hours) 'In vain Sacrifice' (I Vradyni) 'Suffocation for five stony years' (Ethnos)
June 2010	'anger', 'frustration', 'revenge', 'anxiety', 'nervousness', 'fear', 'pessimism', 'depression' 'despair'	Government (21%) Political leaders (28%)	Government (23%) Political system (25%) External actors (30%)	'Blood and Tears for 100 bns' (Ta Nea) 'Four-year Tax Nightmare' (Eleftherotypia) 'Coup de Grace to Salaried Employees and Pensioners'(I Vradyni) 'Massacre against the Greek People' (Rizospastis) 'Panic' (Democratia)
November 2011	'anger', 'rage', 'fury', 'uncertainty', 'anxiety', 'fear', , humiliation', 'hope', 'excitement'	Government (29%) Political leaders (28%) Political parties (32%) EU actors (25%) Political elites (18%) Foreign investors and markets (25%)	Government (23%) Opposition (29%) Domestic & external actors (36%)	'Gate of Hell' (Democratia) 'Prince of Chaos' (Eleftherotypia) 'Political Thriller (Aggelioforos) 'Earthquake in Europe' (Avriani) 'Blackmail' (Eleftheros Typos)
May 2012	'ambivalence', 'guilt', 'anger', 'hate', 'anxiety' 'threat', 'worry', 'fear', 'panic', 'terror', 'hope for survival', 'hope for a better Greece'	Political parties (37%) Interest groups (33%) Political elites (27%)	Political system (29%) Interest groups (23%) Domestic & external actors (36%)	'People's Rage: Change the Memorandum' (Eleftheros Typos) 'Thriller' (I Vradyni) 'Black Dawn' (Ethnos)
June 2012	'pressure', 'humiliation', 'insecurity', 'anxiety', 'fear' 'desperation', 'disgust', 'hate', 'rage', 'terror', 'hope', 'determination'	External actors (27%) Domestic & external actors (23%) Political elites (27%)	External actors (27%) Domestic & external actors (23%)	'The Collaborators of Troika Kill Cancer-Patients' (Avriani) 'Drama' (Democratia)

Note: Percentages in public agenda focus and protagonists of blame columns represent frequency of mentions within each specific category. Selection of headlines from Davou and Demertzis (2013).

analysis exercise to reflect the outcome of Greek elections, we can also draw some links between the emotional footprint of the crisis and its influence on the political behavior of the electorate in the elections following the collapse of PASOK's government and the emergence of populist parties within Greek parliament.

Methodology and data

Our aim was to capture individual and collective sentiments expressed through the statements of public opinion shapers and prominent public figures, in order to complement public opinion studies that use survey and interview data. We conducted a manual content analysis of opinion pieces published in the online edition of the Greek newspaper *To Vima* from December 2009 to June 2012. This way our work unpicks emotionality at the starting point of the public dialogue that developed within the crisis. Content analysis of stories appearing within this wide timeframe allowed us to trace the evolution of the public debate and pinpoint the insertion of particular elements within the content of blame and emotions that can influence trust and confidence in public actors.

Selection of newspaper

We selected *To Vima* because of its moderate centrist political affiliation and because it is one of the biggest – formerly broadsheet – newspapers in Greece in terms of circulation (European Journalism Centre, 2015). It is considered independent and hosts opinions and experts from the wider political ideological spectrum with a large variance of opinions.

Using *To Vima* as our sample base was the best available approach. This newspaper sits ideologically in the middle of the political spectrum, its online edition is identical to its print edition, and its website offers a complete and extensive newspaper archive for opinion pieces and expert commentary that is easily searchable. A quick skim through *The Vima* headlines over the specified period allowed us to conclude that its inclusive nature and balance matches the headlines from other print media outlets identified by Davou and Demertzis (2013). The online edition of the newspaper had roughly 4.5 million monthly visits during our time period (SimilarWeb Analytics, 2015).

Alternative sources were eliminated for a variety of reasons: the online version of Kathimerini (www.kathimerini.gr) which provided similarly convenient search functions were not preferred because the newspaper represents a conservative political line (Molokotos-Liederman, 2007). The search functions of Ta Nea (www.tanea.gr), Eleftherotipia (www.enet.gr; no longer operational) and Ethnos (www.ethnos.gr) which are center-leaning newspapers (Lialiouti, 2016) offer only limited search options that do not allow the specification of commentaries and opinion pieces, and their online editions do not contain all content from the printed version. In addition, for the time period at stake other newspapers did not host a large number of opinion pieces but included mostly editorials and commentary from their own columnists. For the reasons noted above, while we recognize the limited range of our sample, we believe that our study provides a solid starting point for further analysis of opinion pieces in Greek newspapers.

A search of the newspaper's online index using the keyword 'German*' ('Γερμαν*') between December 2009 and July 2012 yielded a large number of hits which were then assessed for relevance to the Greek debt crisis. We used this search term because Germany was identified by opinion polls and other academic studies as the 'enemy country' in Greek perceptions of the crisis, and references to Germany were likely to contain references to the crisis and affective content. Permanent editorial columns, reproductions of foreign source articles and irrelevant material were excluded from the coding.

Sampling

Instead of a census (selecting all units) we sampled around six time points, expanding on the three stages of the Greek crisis analyzed by Davou and Demertzis (2013): December 2009, May 2010, June 2010, November 2011, May 2012 and June 2012. We identified these six points on the basis of important pieces of controversial legislation being brought forward to Parliament, the crucial decisions made at the EU level, the specific actions by the government and other public actors, and the animated civil society mass reactions. We expected interesting variations in the emotional content of opinion pieces to be clustered around these dates following the public pulse for political analysis of ongoing events.

The first three instances include the unraveling of the crisis in Greece (December 2009), the signing of the first bailout agreement (Memorandum of Understanding) in May 2010, and the protests and public demonstrations that followed (June 2010). December 2009 marks a month when the international credit rating agencies began downgrading the lending credibility of the country following the announcements of the extensive public debt and deficit (see e.g. Almunia, 2009). The first bailout agreement marks a significant event as it demarcates effectively the beginning of austerity in Greece as well as the emergence of a pro-bailout/anti-bailout cleavage. The first tough austerity measures of the memorandum led to considerable reaction by the Greek public independent of political affiliation in June 2010 (Vasilopoulou et al., 2014). During this time we anticipate a concentration of opinion pieces on perceptions of the crisis, rather than solutions. We anticipate generalized statements about corruption, patronage, easy money and state benefits. During this time we also expect to find a strong demarcation of 'them' versus 'us' in the way media stories discuss the events, which can have implications for public policy-making. In the context of the other three occasions (November 2011, May 2012 and June 2012) external pressures for reform are expected to receive more coverage. The Greek threat to hold a referendum over the sovereign debt bailout took place in November 2011, followed by debates about scenarios for a potential EU exit. This is the first time that we have a 'Grexit' scenario being discussed in the public domain (Vasilopoulou & Halikiopoulou, 2013). In light of this threat, the consecutive elections that took place in May and June 2012 marked the end of a two-party system in Greece and the shrinking of the popular base of PASOK, thus signifying an important turn in the Greek political system. During this period we expect external perceptions of domestic political elites to penetrate the political debate reflecting priorities beyond policy implementation – including moves towards saving face in respect to international partners.

For each time point we used all the relevant pieces appearing in the first and third week of each month, from Monday to the following Monday. Selecting by week, rather than using the full universe of pieces for each month allowed us to work with an economic sample which at the same time allows for sufficient breadth. This sampling method is considered to provide optimum results (Riffe, Lacy, & Fico, 1998). This resulted in a strati-fied composite sample of 69 opinion pieces (44,388 words in total), with most being around 437 words and ranging from 7 to 1759 words. Because automatic coding systems do not work with Greek language text, and computer translations are not reliable for capturing emotionality, charged language, and the context of particular content, the articles were coded manually to identify emotion words that expressed individual, social and collective emotions, as well as the political actors and institutions featured heavily in the presentation of the crisis and the assignment of blame, per each time point. We designed an electronic coding sheet where data was entered directly into the computer system, two coders engaged in pre-coding training, pilot-coded six articles (one from each time point) to ensure consistency in coding approach, and re-briefed regularly to ensure clarity and consistency in instructions and coding decisions. Our codebook contains a list of variables measuring the opinion piece prominence (page number), size (length of entry in words) and tonal qualities of the article overall (positive, negative or neutral). Overall tone was assessed on the basis of the total number of positive and negative refer-ences within each piece. For example, references to pride were considered positive and irony was considered negative. When an opinion piece contained a large proportion of positive over negative references, it was coded as positive. When it contained a large pro-portion of negative over positive references it was coded as negative and when the number of positive and negative mentions was balanced, it was coded as mixed.

Turning to specific emotional language we used six broad emotion categories to capture expressed emotionality (without making here a distinction of whether it was indi-vidual, social or collective): anger (also containing references to rage, fury, disgust, frustra-tion), anxiety (references to fear, worry, alarm, threat, panic, terror, nervousness, pressure), disappointment (references to depression, misery, sadness, despair, pessimism, despera-tion), uncertainty (references to ambivalence and hesitation), shame (also humiliation, guilt) and hope (references to courage, excitement, determination).

We were also interested in the presentation and protagonists of the crisis. To assess whether the opinion pieces had a domestic (Greece only) or international focus, we kept track of the number of references to Greece, Germany, France, Spain and other countries. To get a picture of which actors occupy the central stage in public debate, we kept an account of the types (individuals, organizations) and names of political actors mentioned, which we then classified in domestic political leaders, domestic political parties, govern-ment, EU actors, political elites broadly, interest and social groups, press and the media, and finally foreign investors and markets. We also recorded blame attributions towards pol-itical agents, adopting a truncated version of the typology of Vasilopoulou et al. (2014). Instead of the original nine classifications of party of government; main opposition party; both of the above; lesser opposition; external elites; specific interest groups; all parties in the system; party of government and main opposition party and external elites combined; party of government and main opposition party combined with specific interest groups (p. 393), we used the following broader and truncated categories: the political system in general, the government, the opposition, interest groups, domestic and external insti-tutions. Quantitative analysis was then carried out on the collected data.

We are confident that the above steps provide us with useful data that allow us to map the emotional content and framing with regards to the actors operating within the time period, while ensuring validity and replicability. Our methodological thoroughness allows for a high level of generalizability, although do not have the ambition to offer a full account of the Greek debt crisis, make deterministic assertions regarding the emotional framing and the outcomes of the crisis, or engage in investigating motivations or political agendas.

Analysis and findings: unweaving the web of passions and blame

The tone of the opinion pieces we analyzed was mostly mixed (61%), containing both positive and negative references and arguments. About 30% of the opinion pieces were pessimistic and 9% were optimistic that the crisis would be favorably resolved. Turning to the specific emotional content of the opinion pieces, we found that the discussion of the Greek debt crisis is loaded with emotion words denoting mainly anxiety (39%) and anger (36%) expressed at various levels, from moderate to high. In addition we identified expressed shame (15%); disappointment (7%); uncertainty (4%), but also modest hope (16%).

Emotion words pointing to anxiety and fear appeared at a slowly increasing rate throughout the period we examined, starting with 11% during December 2009 and May 2010, and continued at 19% during June 2012, where fear-related references reached 22%. This is in line with emotional reactions of the public during this time period when anxiety regarding the Greek debt was most prominent (Davou & Demertzis, 2013). Fear of the unknown is featured in opinion pieces, especially in relation to the future of the country in the EU and in the run-up to the two elections.

Interestingly, emotional reactions that point to anger started a bit later, in May 2010, and escalated faster, often reaching levels of fury and rage, during June 2010 (32%) and November 2011 (36%). This can be linked to the first attempt to implement austerity measures affecting previously favored social groups spreading to other targeted populations, which in turn led to the protests of May 2010. Following the violent protests and the death of three people in the burning building of a bank in June 2010 marked a turn of anger to fury and rage, towards the handling of the incident by the government, and fueled by smaller opposition parties. By November 2011, rage was pointed towards the Prime Minister and PASOK's actions, and the public called for his resignation.

Uncertainly and ambivalence concentrated in December 2009 (67%) and November 2011 (33%) when we also see the majority of shame-related references (50%). This can be attributed to the damaged image of the country internationally and linked to the imported stereotypical discourse that we mentioned above. Disappointment, sadness or expressed depression, appeared also in the early stages, particularly during May 2010 (60%). Traces of uplifting emotions like hope were found from May 2010 (18%) and November 2011 (9%) onwards, and reached their height in May 2012 (46%). These moments in time were marked by pockets of breathing space provided by the bailout money (May 2010), the renewed hope in a cooperation government (November 2011) and the optimism for a wider coalition of political forces in May 2012. By June 2012 however, hope references dropped to 27%. While this is a serious drop, it shows the preservation of some optimism following the agreement on a coalition government across three political parties and the promise for renegotiation of the bailout terms and the easing of austerity measures. We visually present the above in Figure 1.

We get a fuller appreciation of the content of emotional reactions when we review emotion terms as they appeared every month. In December 2009 we see references to affective reactions of being 'alert', and feeling 'anxiety', 'uncertainly' and 'hesitation'. By May 2010, the emotions expressed were 'uncertainty', 'alarm', 'anxiety', 'anger', 'rage', 'despair', 'disappointment', 'pessimism', 'misery', but also occasionally 'hope', 'courage' and 'excitement'. In June 2010 we came across emotional reactions pointing to 'anger', 'frustration', 'revenge', 'anxiety ', 'nervousness', 'fear', 'pessimism', 'depression' and 'despair'. November 2011 was equally marked by 'anger', 'rage', 'fury', 'uncertainty', 'anxiety', 'fear' and ' humiliation', but also featured attempts of social and political detachment expressed as 'cynicism', counterbalanced by traces of 'hope' and 'excitement'. May 2012 brought 'ambivalence', 'guilt', 'anger', 'hate', 'anxiety', 'threat', 'worry', 'fear', 'panic', 'terror' but also 'hope for survival' and 'hope for a better Greece'. The following month, June 2012, feeling 'pressure', 'humiliation', 'insecurity' and 'anxiety', 'fear' that became 'desperation', 'disgust', 'hate', 'rage' and 'terror' were occasionally interrupted and infused by positive emotions of 'hope' and 'determination'. These emotional reactions follow the political developments and demonstrate that public discourse rides the spirit of the times.

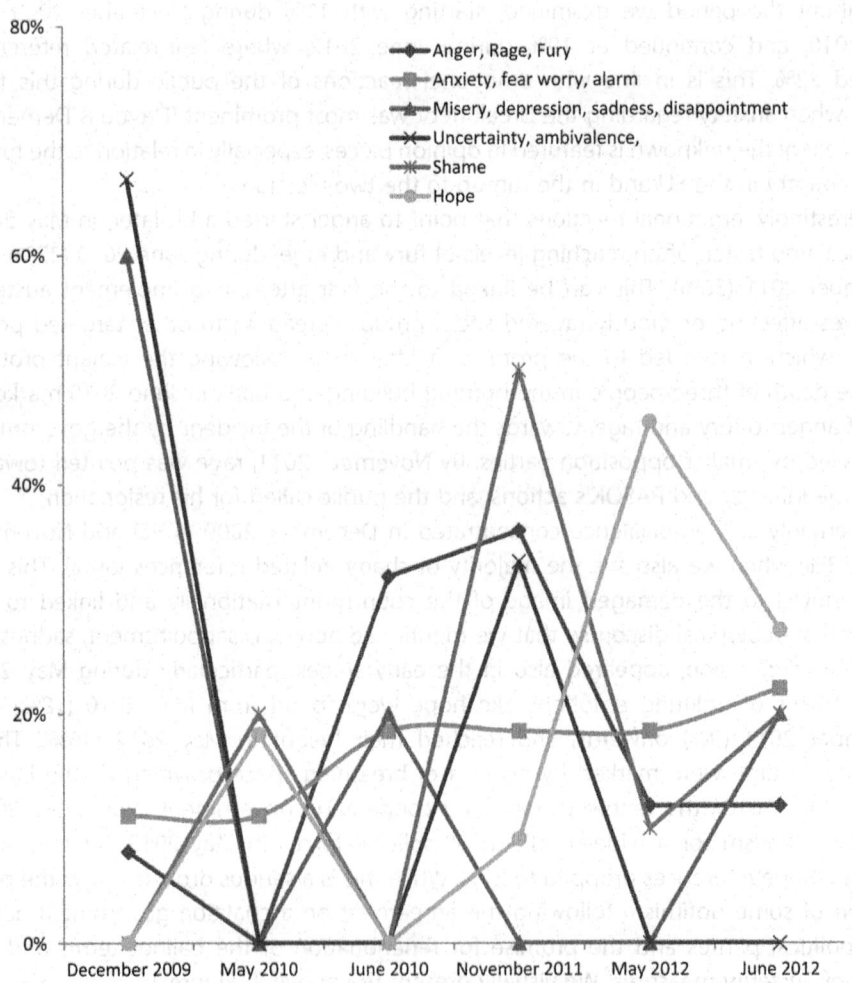

Figure 1. Variations of emotional reactions during the Greek debt crisis.
Notes: Cross-tabulation analysis. Data points represent % of emotion words appearing each month.

An analysis of the affective echo of the Greek debt crisis cannot omit a review of the multiple political and social, national and international actors and institutions featured in the opinion pieces. Interestingly, only 9% of the cases examine the Greek debt crisis as a national-only matter and the majority of articles feature references to Germany, France, Spain, Italy and other countries. Interestingly, 16% of the articles focused exclusively on Germany, in line with the argument made by Bee and Chrona (2013) that the bailout agreement was perceived as a German-style occupation in Greece and the protests of June 2010 placed Germany in center-stage for the Greek predicament. France was also mentioned, but mainly in the later stages of the crisis, following the election of François Hollande as French president. He was perceived as someone who could control the advent of German austerity in Europe, thus renewing hope according to the opinion pieces. Spain, Italy, Portugal, Ireland, the USA are also occasionally mentioned.

Turning to the focus of the opinion pieces we see that it was not monotonous or single-focused. Rather, most opinion pieces included references to a number of social and political actors and institutions. For example, mentions of domestic political leaders appeared 38% of the time, domestic political parties were discussed 28% of the time, and the government was mentioned 20% of the time. EU actors (17%), Interest and Social groups (17%), Political Elites (16%), Press and Media (16%), Foreign Investors and Markets (12%) were also mentioned.

The focus on specific actors is not homogenous across the six time points. In fact, the majority of references to *political leaders* were in June 2010 and November 2011 (both at 28%). During these times, public opinion was demanding for the leaders of the two major parties in Greek parliament (PASOK and ND) to reach some sort of compromise regarding the implementation of the bailout measures (June 2010) and the consolidation of a cooperation government in November 2011. References to *political parties* appeared in 21% of the coded articles in May 2010 when the bailout agreement was ratified, and increased to 32% by November 2011 during the formation of a cooperation government. References to parties peaked in May 2012, appearing in 37% of the articles, as the first round of national elections took place. The majority of references to *Government* appear in December 2009 and November 2011 (both 29%) and also June 2010 (21%) following the social unrest and violent protests against the bailout agreement. Emphasis on *EU actors* was at its highest in December 2009 and November 2011 (25%) as public and media attention was placed on the EU to resolve the Greek debt crisis by agreeing on a bailout (December 2009) and then dealing with the prospect of a referendum for the second bailout agreement in Cannes (November 2011). References to *interest and other social groups* gradually increased as the crisis unfolded. It peaked at 33% in May 2012, reflecting the protests that took place and the attempts of political parties to capitalize on the vulnerability of affected by the crisis citizens seeking political gains (Davou & Demertzis, 2013). *Political elites* were featured mostly in November 2011 (18%) and peaked in May and June 2012 (both at 27%) reflecting the deliberations to form a coalition government. The role of the *media* was most prominently discussed during the first phase of the crisis, reaching 27% in December 2009 and May 2010, focusing on the reporting style of media organizations (both domestic and international), their responsibility in informing their audiences and framing the crisis. Foreign investors and markets were mostly discussed in December 2009 (50%) and then November 2011 (25%), reflecting lack of confidence in the Greek program and/or proposed European resolution.

Finally we were interested in examining blame-shifting strategies in the context of the crisis. As we show on Figure 2, blame attribution is spread across several actors: the political system, the government, interest groups, and domestic and external institutions received blame between 30% and 35% of the time. The opposition was blamed less frequently, about 20% of the time. In addition, blame was not evenly spread over time. Characteristically, the government was blamed the most in December 2009, June 2010 and November 2011, while the opposition was mainly blamed in May 2010 and November 2011. The government was held accountable for requesting the bailout and responding to protest, while the opposition was held accountable for its unwillingness to take responsibility for the bailout ratification and negotiating the terms of participating in a cooperation government. The political system in general received the majority of its blame references in May 2012 reflecting its inability to act due to its high fragmentation.

The timeline of combined information on emotionality references, public agenda focus, protagonists of blame from our study are listed in Table 1, matched with the newspaper headlines from Davou and Demertzis (2013), allowing for a clearer picture of the emotional footprint of the crisis on Greek society. The second column highlights the tense emotional content of opinion pieces; columns three and four point to the political actors and agents falling in and out of blame focus as time progressed; and column five presents a selection of headlines as listed in Davou and Demertzis (2013).

Three important observations can be made here. First, the emotions accounted for in the opinion pieces track closely the affective content of newspaper headlines, pointing to the interactive nature of public and media agendas. Second, agents and actors with most mentions in each month are often the ones that receive public blame, showing how developments and events during the crisis weave a complex pattern of responsibility in public perceptions. Third, the debates in opinion pieces appear to be multi-focused, pointing to the complexity of the issue and its appreciation by those who engage in political discussions.

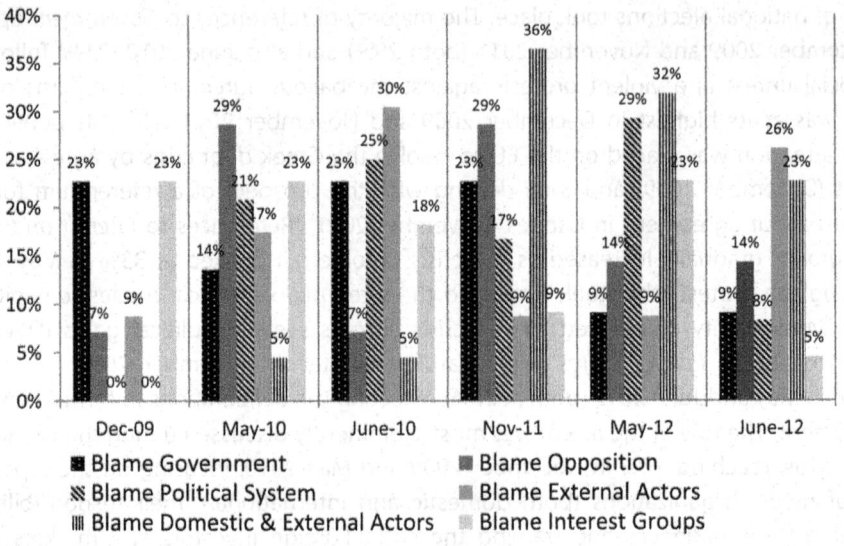

Figure 2. Blame attribution dynamics during the Greek debt crisis.
Note: Data points represent % blame per actor in opinion pieces for each time point.

Conclusions

The analysis of the emotional content of opinion pieces in the context of the financial crisis provides valuable insights on how opinion shapers, public intellectuals and citizens discussed and responded to the unfolding events, and complements public opinion and media content studies of the crisis. Negative perceptions of the crisis were associated with anger, fear and also hope at its different stages, following closely particular political developments. These emotional reactions were in line with the general sentiment captured by the analysis of newspaper headlines of Davou and Demertzis (2013). The commentary featured in opinion pieces highlighted the human impact and societal implications of the crisis, and involved a number of political actors and institutions. Attributions of blame rested more heavily on government and prominent international actors rather than the opposition. Vasilopoulou et al. (2014) in their analysis of parliamentary rhetoric found that when politicians shifted blame, government and opposition were equally targeted. Here we see that the focus of public attention and appetite for justice zoom in on the power holders, the incumbents and international actors that feature prominently in the media. This can be explained by the avenging or retributive nature of opinion pieces that criticized the structural side of the Greek debt crisis, focusing on the power holders (Capelos & Exadaktylos, 2015). On the other hand, political leaders' speeches in the same period demonstrated strong exclusivity as they effectively adopted a partisan approach of blame-shifting (Vasilopoulou et al., 2014). This is an important finding as it illustrates that the political opposition in Greece was not identified consistently as a front-stage player.

At the juncture of emotions and cognition lies the feeling of institutional, political and social trust. In the case of the Greek debt crisis, citizens' already low trust towards the national government as well as financial and political institutions of the EU and its future has been put to a hard test (Davou & Demertzis, 2013). The financial hardships, newly introduced taxation and the implementation of more and harsher austerity measures are the obvious suspects. Outlying the affective 'footprint' of the crisis allows us to think more about how trust towards internal and external actors and institutions can be restored (Hetherington, 2004). Anger, fear and hope affect appraisals and have different behavioral consequences. Initiatives to stimulate trust towards formal and informal political institutions both at the domestic and the European level will fail unless they understand and successfully address citizens' emotionality.

An extension of this research involves the analysis of citizens' reactions and comments to the opinion pieces we coded. Online opinions allow readers to offer their own response and express their views, thus providing an open forum for public debate and potentially stimulate political learning and engagement. Coding the content of this communication feedback loop could provide us with valuable insights into a parallel discourse path: the way ordinary citizens engage with the causes, consequences, and key players of the financial crisis, as well as the media presentation of the events. This, in turn could help us understand even better the multi-dimensional character of public attitudes towards the proposed and implemented strategies and measures to tackle the crisis.

An equally interesting project to build on the present study would involve the systematic analysis of the affective content of public opinion polls, political rhetoric, media headlines, opinion pieces, blogs and other online communication forums in the Greek public arena. Comparing media, political and public agendas would offer public opinion scholars that study the financial crisis a fuller appreciation of the public dialogue that different agents deploy in difficult times. Concentrating on their affective content would allow us insight into the long lasting effects of the crisis. Borrowing the famous words of Maya Angelou, people can forget what you said and did, but will never forget how you made them feel (Kelly, 2003).

References

Almunia, J. (2009, December 8). *Statement by commissioner almunia on Greece*. European Commission, MEMO/09/541. Retrieved from http://europa.eu/rapid/press-release_MEMO-09-541_en.htm

Bee, C., & Chrona, S. (2013). *The public sphere in the Euro-crisis: Media and policy agendas in Greece, Italy and Turkey*. Working paper presented at the 7th ECPR General Conference, Science Po, Bordeaux.

Canetti, E. (1960). *Masse und Macht*. Hamburg: Claassen.

Capelos, T. (2010). Feeling the issue: How citizens' affective reactions and leadership perceptions shape policy evaluations. *Journal of Political Marketing, 9*, 9–33.

Capelos, T. (2011). Emotions in politics. In George T. Kurian (Ed.), *Encyclopedia of political science (EPS)* (pp. 500–502). Washington, DC: CQ Press.

Capelos, T. (2013). Understanding anxiety and aversion: The origins and consequences of affectivity in political campaigns. In N. Demertzis (Ed.), *Emotions in politics: The affect dimension in political tension* (pp. 39–59). Basingstoke: Palgrave Macmillan.

Capelos, T., & Exadaktylos, T. (2015). The good, the bad, and the ugly: Stereotypical representations of the Greek debt crisis. In G. Karyotis & R. Gerodimos (Eds.), *The politics of extreme austerity: Greece beyond the crisis* (pp. 46–70). Basingstoke: Palgrave Macmillan.

Capelos, T., & Wurtzer, H. (2009). United Nations scandals and media coverage. *Journal of Contingencies and Crisis Management, 17*, 75–94.

Caplan, G. (1974). *Support systems and community mental health: Lectures on concept development*. New York: Behavioral Publications.

Chalari, A. (2014). Re-organizing everyday Greek social reality: Subjective experiences of the Greek crisis. In G. Karyotis & R. Gerodimos (Eds.), *The politics of extreme austerity: Greece beyond the crisis* (pp. 160–176). Basingstoke: Palgrave Macmillan.

Damasio, A. (1994). *Descartes' error: emotion, reason and the human brain*. New York: Vintage.

Davou, B., & Demertzis, N. (2013). Feeling the Greek financial crisis. In N. Demertzis (Ed.), *Emotions in politics: The affect dimension in political tension* (pp. 93–123). Basingstoke: Palgrave Macmillan.

Der Spiegel. (2011, May 18). *German chancellor on the offensive: Merkel blasts Greece over retirement age, vacation* (Online international ed.). Retrieved from http://www.spiegel.de/international/europe/german-chancellor-on-the-offensive-merkel-blasts-greece-over-retirement-age-vacation-a-763294.html

Dinas, E., & Rori, L. (2013). The 2012 Greek parliamentary elections: Fear and loathing in the polls. *West European Politics, 36*(1), 270–282.

Durkheim, É. (1912/1995). *The elementary forms of religious life.* (K. E. Fields, Trans.). New York: Free Press (Simon & Schuster).

Eagly, A. H., & Chaiken, S. (1993). *The psychology of attitudes.* Fort Worth, TX: Harcourt Brace Jovanovich.

Ekman, P. (2004). What we become emotional about. In A. Manstead, N. Fridja, & A. Fischer (Eds.), *Feelings and emotions: The Amsterdam symposium* (pp. 119–135). Cambridge: Cambridge University Press.

EU Observer. (2011, May 19). *Merkel under fire for 'lazy Greeks' comment* (Online ed.). Retrieved from http://euobserver.com/political/32363

European Journalism Centre. (2015). *Greece – media landscape.* Retrieved August 4, 2015, from http://ejc.net/media_landscapes/greece

Exadaktylos, T., & Zahariadis, N. (2014). Quid pro quo: Political trust and policy implementation in Greece during the age of Austerity. *Politics & Policy, 42*(1), 160–183.

Featherstone, K. (2011). The Greek sovereign debt crisis and EMU: A failing state in a skewed Regime. *Journal of Common Market Studies, 49*(2), 193–217.

Forbes. (2011, July 19). Frezza, B. *Give Greece what it deserves: Communism* (Op ed. in online ed.). Retrieved from http://www.forbes.com/sites/billfrezza/2011/07/19/give-greece-what-it-deserves-communism/

Frijda, N. H. (2004). Emotion and action. In A. Manstead, N. H. Frijda, & A. Fischer (Eds.), *Feelings and emotions: The Amsterdam symposium* (pp. 158–173). Cambridge: Cambridge University Press.

Frijda, N. H., Kuipers, P., & Ter Schure, E. (1989). Relations among emotion, appraisal, and emotional action readiness. *Journal of Personality and Social Psychology, 57*(2), 212–28.

Graber, D. A. (1990). Seeing is remembering: How visuals contribute to learning from television news. *Journal of Communication, 40*(3), 134–155.

Graber, D. A. (2001). *Processing politics: Learning from television in the Internet age.* Chicago, IL: University of Chicago Press.

Graber, D. A. (2009). *Mass media and American politics* (8th ed.). Washington, DC: CQ Press.

Graber, D.A. (2010). *Media power in politics* (6th ed.). Washington, DC: CQ Press.

Hetherington, M.J. (2004). *Why trust matters.* Princeton, NJ: Princeton University Press.

Karyotis, G. (2014). Protest participation, electoral choices and public attitudes towards austerity in Greece. In G. Karyotis & R. Gerodimos (Eds.), *The politics of extreme austerity: Greece beyond the crisis* (pp. 123–141). Basingstoke: Palgrave Macmillan.

Kelly, B. (2003). *Worth repeating: More than 5,000 classic and contemporary quotes* (p. 263). Grand Rapids, MI: Kreger Publications.

Kinder, D. R., & Sanders, L. M. (1990). Mimicking political debate with survey questions: The case of white opinion on affirmative action for blacks. *Social Cognition, 8*, 73–103.

Lamm, C., & Silani, G. (2014). Insights into collective emotions from the social neuroscience of empathy. In C. von Scheve & M. Salmela (Eds.), *Collective emotions: Perspectives from psychology, philosophy, and sociology* (pp. 63–77). Oxford: Oxford University Press.

Lasorsa, D. L., & Reese, S. D. (1990). News source use in the crash of 1987: A study of four national media. *Journalism Quarterly, 67*, 60–71.

Lazarus, R. S. (1993). From psychological stress to the emotions: A history of changing outlooks. *Annual Review of Psychology, 44*, 1–21.

Le Bon, G. (1896). *The crowd: A study of the popular mind.* London: Ernest Benn.

Lialiouti, Z. (2016). Contesting the anti-totalitarian consensus: The concept of national independence, the memory of the Second World War and the ideological cleavages in post-war Greece. *National Identities, 18*(2), 105–123. doi:10.1080/14608944.2014.987659

Marcus, G. E., Neuman, R., & MacKuen, M. (2000). *Affective intelligence and political judgement.* Chicago, IL: University of Chicago Press.

Marcus, G. E. (2000). Emotions in politics. *Annual Review of Political Science, 3*, 221–250.

McDougall, W. (1920). *The group mind.* New York, NY: Putnam.

McLeod, J. M., Becker, L. B., & Byrnes, J. E. (1974). Another look at the agenda setting function of the press. *Communication Research, 1*, 131–166.

Mitsopoulos, M., & Pelagidis, T. (2011). *Understanding the crisis in Greece: From boom to bust.* Basingstoke: Palgrave Macmillan.

Molokotos-Liederman, L. (2007). The Greek ID card controversy: A case study of religion and national identity in a changing European Union. *Journal of Contemporary Religion, 22*(2), 187–203.

Mouzelis, N., & Pagoulatos, G. (2002). Civil society and citizenship in post-war Greece. *Athens University of Economics and Business Online Papers,* September. Retrieved from http://www.aueb.gr/users/pagoulatos/mouzelis%20civil%20society.pdf

Nimmo, D., & Combs, J. E. (1985). *Nightly horrors: Crisis coverage in television network news.* Knoxville: University of Tennessee Press.

Ottati, V., and Wyer, R. S., Jr. (1993). Affect and political judgment. In S. Iyengar & J. McGuire (Eds.), *Explorations in political psychology* (pp. 296–320). Durham, NC: Duke University Press.

Pappas, T. (2013). Why Greece failed. *Journal of Democracy, 24*(2), 31–45.

Riffe, D., Lacy, S., & Fico, F. (1998). *Analysing media messages: Using quantitative content analysis in research.* Mahwah, NJ: Erlbaum.

Rogers, E. M., & Dearing, J. W. (1988). Agenda-setting research: Where has it been, where is it going? In A. Anderson (Ed.), *Communication Yearbook 11* (pp. 555–594). Newbury Park, CA: Sage.

von Scheve, C., & Salmela, M. (Eds.). (2014). *Collective emotions: Perspectives from psychology, philosophy, and sociology.* Oxford: Oxford University Press.

Sears, D. O. (1993). Symbolic politics: A socio-psychological theory. In S. Iyengar & W. J. McGuire (Eds.), *Explorations in political psychology* (pp. 115–149). Durham, NC: Duke University Press.

Shoemaker, P., & Reese, S. (1996). *Mediating the message: Theories of influences on mass media content.* White Plains, NY: Longman.

SimilarWeb Analytics. (2015). *Traffic rankings and stats for To Vima.* Retrieved August 4, 2015, from http://www.similarweb.com/website/tovima.gr

Singer, E., & Endreny, P. M. (1993). *Reporting on risk: How the mass media portray accidents, diseases, disasters, and other hazards.* New York: Russell Sage Foundation.

Sniderman, P. M., Brody, R. A., & Tetlock, P. E. (1991). *Reasoning and choice: Explorations in political psychology.* New York: Cambridge University Press.

The Economist. (2011, November 26). Charlemagne: "The sinking Euro" (Print ed.). Retrieved from http://www.economist.com/node/21540244

Tzogopoulos, G. (2013). *The Greek crisis in the media: Stereotyping in the international press.* Farnham: Ashgate.

Vasilopoulou, S., & Halikiopoulou, D. (2013). In the shadow of Grexit: The Greek election of 17 June 2012. *South European Society and Politics, 18*(4), 523–542.

Vasilopoulou, S., Halikiopoulou, D., & Exadaktylos, T. (2014). Greece in crisis: austerity, populism and the politics of blame. *Journal of Common Market Studies, 52*(2), 388–402.

Walters, L. M., Wilkins, L., & Walters, T. (1989). *Bad tidings: Communication and catastrophe.* Hillsdale, NJ: Erlbaum.

Weaver, K. (1986). The politics of blame avoidance. *Journal of Public Policy, 6*(4), 371–98.

Wilson, T. D., Dunn, D. S., Kraft, D., & Lisle, D. J. (1989). Introspection, attitude change and attitude-behavior consistency: The disruptive effects of explaining why we feel the way we do. *Advances in Experimental Social Psychology, 22*, 287–341.

Wright, C. R. (1986). *Mass communication: A sociological perspective* (3rd ed.). New York: Random House.

Zaller, J.R. (1992). *The nature and origins of mass opinion.* Cambridge: Cambridge University Press.

5 'The Germans are back'

Euroscepticism and anti-Germanism in crisis-striken Greece[†]

Asimina Michailidou

ABSTRACT

The Eurocrisis has generated a deep and ongoing politicization of the EU within and across national public spheres, fuelling age-old and new political and social conflicts, which in turn shape public perceptions of crisis and the legitimacy of 'crisis government'. Focusing on Greece, an EU member state at the epicentre of the crisis, this paper examines how the European polity was contested in the first five years (2009–2013) of the 'Eurocrisis'. During this period, anti-German stereotypes resurfaced in the Greek public sphere in parallel with increasingly mainstream Euroscepticism. Nevertheless, analysis of news and social media content from this period shows that beneath this new-found scepticism towards the EU and Germany's role in it lie two much broader narratives: that of the power struggle between the people and the political elites; and that of an epic clash between diametrically different political ideologies.

Introduction

The Eurocrisis that broke out in 2009 has given new momentum to the politicization of European integration, turning it into a mobilization force for intellectuals, political actors and citizens' movements (e.g. Statham & Trenz, 2014). From a crisis management and communication perspective, this is hardly a surprising development: crises, as threatening situations that belie expectations of normality and have widespread negative repercussions, inevitably create high levels of uncertainty, focus the attention of the media and increase the public's demand for information and proactive challenging of the decisions taken by political leaders (Seeger, Sellnow, & Ulmer, 2003). The Eurocrisis is the latest in a string of critical situations in the European Union's (EU) history, which have led to the gradual replacement of the 'permissive consensus' characterizing public opinion before the 1990s with a 'constraining dissensus' of heightened public and media contestation (Hooghe & Marks,

---

[†]This is the direct English translation of the tile of a classic 1948 Greek movie ('Οι Γερμανοί ξανάρχονται') with a powerful anti-war message. Shot during a most turbulent time for Greece (the civil-war years that followed the end of the WWII-Nazi occupation of the country), the movie features Theodoros, a quiet, kind man, who one day witnesses a terrifying civil-war conflict while out shopping and upon his return home, he falls asleep and dreams that Hitler is alive and the Nazis are back in Greece with more powerful weapons. The movie – a 'satirical nightmare' as its creators called it – won critical acclaim and is considered one of the best examples of Greek filmography. For the original film poster in English (on which the title is 'The Nazis strike again') and a selection of links with more information on the movie in English, see Βικιπαίδεια (2014).

2009; Statham & Trenz, 2012). This 'EU politicization' sees the simultaneous rise or intensi-fication of insurgent politics (ad-hoc citizens' protests, asymmetric communications), on the one hand, and further depreciation of representative politics, on the other hand (Kriesi, 2012).

In this context, the Eurocrisis is constitutive of a particular kind of public discourse – polarized, emotionally charged, flaming but also frequently evoking democratic norms and European integration core values – that contests the legitimacy of governments, at national and European level (Michailidou, Trenz, & de Wilde, 2014; de Wilde, Michailidou, & Trenz, 2013). The manner in which Eurocrisis contestation unfolds and its content are, therefore, essential factors for the public legitimation and subsequently the success of attempted counter-crisis measures and reforms. Yet, while research has mainly focused on the institutional arrangements of EU 'crisis governance' (Crum & Fossum, 2013; Peters, Pierre, & Randma-Liiv, 2011; Willke, 2010), there is still limited understanding of how public contestation of the Eurocrisis is linked to the struggle of political elites for public legitimacy.[1]

Looking at some of the most sensationalist news coverage across EU countries, one could readily conclude that EU politicization in the context of the Eurocrisis is rapidly degenerating into a 'moral panic' blame-game,[2] whereby certain national and EU political leaders and institutions are invoking the public's wrath on the basis not of their decisions before or during the crisis, but of stereotypical views about their nationality being inher-ently 'evil'. This is what Sierp and Karner (2016) describe as the 'essentialism' of stereotypes in the introductory article of this special issue. Here, I examine this proposition from a crisis management and communication perspective, focusing on the case of the Greek public sphere during the early years of the Eurocrisis (2009–2013). Firstly, I discuss the concept of crisis accountability, as a key phase of crisis management, and identify the conditions under which public accountability of crisis management turns into blame-games. Sub-sequently, the various actors are identified that drive the accountability (or blame-game) process forward and possible outcomes are discussed, drawing on crisis manage-ment and public sphere literature. In the second part of the paper, I combine data from different sources to map how the process of crisis accountability is unfolding in the Greek public sphere. Who contests Eurocrisis measures? Which aspects of Eurocrisis man-agement does public critique focus on? How prominent are stereotypes in the Greek Euro-crisis discourse? The findings are then discussed in the third and final part of the article, where I revisit the concept of 'moral panic' in the context of crisis politics and consider the implications of the Eurocrisis politicization for the public legitimacy – ultimately, pol-itical success – of national and EU leadership in Greece.

Managing crises: from accountability to blame-games

Although approaches to crisis vary in the relevant literature, all categorisations can be neatly captured under Sellnow and Seeger's umbrella-definition that crises 'all generally evoke the notion of some dramatic, unanticipated threat, with widespread and wholly negative impact' (Sellnow & Seeger, 2013, p. 5). Crises violate expectations of what is understood as 'normal' or 'how things should be' and require rapid responses to contain or mitigate the harm (Hermann, 1963; Seeger et al., 2003).[3] Furthermore, crises are disruptive: they interrupt the function of an organization thus posing a threat to the achievement of commonly agreed goals and/or affecting the performance of common problem-solving mechanisms – hence the need for rapid response. The increased levels of public communication due to the heightened media and public attention inevitably enhance the element of conflict in the public and political sphere. Perceptions are crucial, in that they affect the severity of the threat and subsequently the degree of consensus about the measures that need to be taken in order to address it (Coombs, 2010). How public communication and contestation unfold during a crisis can be used as a central indicator for analysing type, dynamics and impact of that crisis on the transformation of political order and legitimacy (Seeger et al., 2003, p. 297).

The basic expectation of any *democratic leadership* is that they will help safeguard society from the adverse consequences of crisis (Boin, 't Hart, Stern, & Sundelius, 2005). This is a complex and delicate process of observation, interpretation, strategic thinking, communication and learning, which is often depicted in literature as neatly linear. In practice, crisis management is a multi-stage process with overlapping components (Allison & Zelikow, 1999; Boin et al., 2005). The main aim of most counter-crisis strategies tends to be the termination of the crisis.[4] It is not only the extent and quality of the introduced counter-crisis reforms that determine the success of a political leadership's attempts to terminate a crisis. Political approval and successful public legitimation of the reforms are also required. These cannot be achieved if the political leadership introducing the counter-crisis reforms is perceived as part or cause of the crisis. Although the outcome of this 'crisis public accountability' process (i.e. accountability attributed through the public debating of the crisis) is determined by several factors – discussed in more detail below – ultimately 'the burden of proof in accountability discussions *lies with leaders* [my emphasis]: they must establish beyond doubt that they cannot be held responsible for the occurrence or escalation of a crisis' (Boin et al., 2005, p. 14). This is not to suggest that political leaders must necessarily be assumed guilty of causing a crisis or its outcomes. It is to stress that political leaders have a responsibility to make themselves and their counter-crisis decisions available to institutional and public scrutiny. Even if they opt for a largely 'silent' crisis management style, their actions will be publicly contested: this is the effect of the democratic public sphere.

The media, political opponents, agencies, legislators, interest groups, investigation committees and citizens all have a say in the evaluation of political leadership in times of crisis and the outcome may be far from fair for political leaders. Yet, by maintaining transparency during the crisis period and facilitating the accountability process, political leaders help safeguard the core functions of democracy and preserve the democratic legitimacy of the system as a whole rather than their personal, short-term political survival. Therein also lays the difference between accountability and blame-games: the former generates valuable feedback that can be used to assess and improve the resilience of people, institutions and political systems (Boin et al., 2005, p. 102). It relies on critical and honest debate of actors acting in good faith (Pidgeon, 1997, p. 9; Seeger et al., 2003). By contrast, blame-games are a race between actors to protect their interests by any means necessary, including defensive rationalization ('we made no mistakes'), covering up or distorting facts, deliberate silences or deflection of blame ('It is not my fault, I was following orders') (Boin et al., 2005, p. 103; Brändström & Kuipers, 2003). Crucially, crises are a test for 'the democratic authenticity of the governance systems' in which they occur (Boin et al., 2005, pp. 111–112). Whether the crisis accountability process aims for 'truth-finding dialogue' or descends into 'inquisition and blame-games' will serve as a proxy indicator for the 'health' of democracy (Boin et al., 2005).

In order to determine which of the two aims are (attempted to be) fulfilled through the crisis accountability process, we must first identify the core arguments that constitute the crisis accountability discourse. How severe is the crisis deemed by the various actors? Where are its causes located? By classifying the answers given to these questions, Brändström and Kuipers (2003) construct an analytical scheme which predicts which actors (individual or collective) will be held responsible for a crisis. Depending on who is held accountable, the Brändström-Kuipers model then proposes four different outcomes of the accountability process, namely:

(1) scapegoating (specific, low-level executive or crisis response agencies or individuals within them are identified as responsible);
(2) organizational mishap (several executive agencies or operational organizations across a range of policies are responsible);
(3) failing policy-makers (specific actors at the strategic political level are identified as responsible) or
(4) policy/system failure (the crisis was caused by a flawed policy, or a flawed system of policy-making and implementation, but senior policy-makers are not necessarily responsible).

The type and extent of reforms (including sanctions) that will follow the crisis accountability process are contingent upon the type of actors found responsible for the crisis. Certain factors may influence the accountability process towards an actor- instead of network-focused discourse. If, for example, the future that the reform promises is not that which the citizens want; or if leaders fail to seize and retain the initiative in the crisis process (thus becoming established in public conscience as part of the crisis rather than the solution to it), then the likelihood of an actor-focused accountability process increases. Similarly, any of the following will quite certainly trigger a strong backlash from society and will likely bias the accountability process towards assigning responsibility and blame to specific actors instead of systems:

• abuse of power (perceived or real) during crisis in order to push through reform;
• failure to effectively communicate and persuade citizens about the need for this reform;
• attempt of superficial rather than substantial reform, that is, appearing to be making changes but not actually incorporating any learning in the attempted reforms (Boin et al., 2005; Seeger et al., 2003).

Existing literature on the chronic malfunctions and weaknesses both of the Greek state apparatus and of the Greek political culture (Lyrintzis, 1987; Pappas, 2013; Vasilopoulou, Halikiopoulou, & Exadaktylos, 2013), leads us to expect that any of the above factors may be have played a role in the way that crisis accountability was publicly attributed during the early Eurocrisis period. Indeed, by the end of 2013, when Greece was entering its fifth year of crisis governance and seventh year of recession, key aspects of the Greek economy, such as government debt, unemployment and economy contraction, remained despairingly high (IMF, 2013a, 2013b). Nevertheless, both Greek and European leaders

appeared optimistic, At the same time, the 'Eurocrisis years' governments had been following a consistently undemocratic path, in terms of both twisting democratic procedures in
order to pass crisis-linked legislation and suppressing dissent among their party ranks and
the public (Michailidou, 2014), more so than in the pre-crisis decades.[5] Certain measures
deemed crucial to improve the state's finances and to redress the social justice imbalances
of previous decades – such as tackling large-scale tax evasion, public sector corruption or
unemployment – remained on paper only. Others, including repeated reductions of salaries, pensions and public welfare spending had further lowered the living standards for
ever wider sections of the population and had in certain cases been deemed unconstitutional by Greek courts.[6] Throughout the studied period, there was thus a strong discrepancy between the reality that the vast majority of Greek people faced daily and the
public claims made by national and EU decision-makers.

Crisis accountability, the media and the public: a public sphere approach

However, the match between counter-crisis reforms and crisis accountability outcomes is
not always guaranteed. In order to determine whether we are dealing with democratic
truth-seeking or self-serving blame-games, we need to look not only at the claims
made publicly by the different actors about who is or should be held responsible, but
also at the ways these claims are publicly presented and justified, as well as the conditions
under which crisis accountability takes place. Is public contestation open to competing
views or do specific actors monopolize the debate? What do crisis evaluations tell us
about the way the crisis is perceived? Is critique focusing on individuals or systems and
policies? In other words, we need to take a close look at the *public sphere*, as the central
locus of political contestation.

My starting point is not the ideal-type, deliberative public sphere, but rather the 'imperfect',
mediatized public sphere, whose democratizing effect rests primarily with its power to 'open
up decision making to public critique' (Statham & Trenz, 2014, p. 7). Conflicts and polarization
are not only expected but also welcome in the case of the EU, in so far as they function as
structuring and integrating elements in an otherwise fragmented public sphere (Michailidou
et al., 2014; de Wilde, Michailidou, & Trenz, 2014). The politicisation of the Eurocrisis and of the
EU's representative system more broadly are understood as a process of mediatization and
mediation through which formalised representative relationships have been conducive to
but also constrained by mass media attention. Mediatization is:

> the interrelation between the operational modes of the mass media and the political system.
> This implies not only media impact on the political process and modes of decision-making, but
> also, in broader terms, impact on the infrastructure of political communication, i.e. on the con-
> tours of the public sphere. (Michailidou & Trenz, 2010, p. 4)

By contrast, 'mediation' reflects the relay function of an actor in the communication
process and as such, it is a broader term that stretches beyond the media's role in the
public sphere.

Such an approach of the crisis accountability mechanism simultaneously emphasizes
the centrality of *mediatized public contestation* in the crisis management process; decou-
ples the *process* of accountability and legitimation through public debate from the
quality of its *outcome* (it may not necessarily lead to the legitimation of political

leadership's choices or to a termination of the crisis); and offers an explanatory framework that allows us to trace the thought process behind different types of crisis contestation arguments and subsequently to hypothesize about the potential outcomes of the accountability process for political leadership. Drawing on this 'mediatized crisis accountability' approach, I take a closer look at the conditions of the mediatized public sphere in Greece during the studied period. The aim is two-fold: firstly, to outline the context and content of anti-German and Eurosceptic public discourse in relation to the Eurocrisis. Secondly, the focus here is on the contestation of German and EU political leadership, but I expand to national politicians and financial institutions in order to put Eurocrisis-related anti-Germanism and Euroscepticism in context.

The Eurocrisis accountability process in Greece: a populist blame-game foretold?

Personifying the causes of the crisis is a strategy commonly favoured by Greek politicians (but certainly not limited to them). As Tzogopoulos (2012, p. 6) observes:

> ... scapegoating has been the persuasion technique of choice for members of both the conservative and the socialist parties for years, helping them to achieve their own priorities at the expense of the Greek population ... Being well-versed in finding scapegoats, it is not surprising that Greek politicians have adopted a similar persuasion strategy since October 2009.

This is frequently directed, but not limited to, the condemnation of Germany for 'the slow death of the Hellenic economy' (Tzogopoulos, 2012). The critique that Greek politicians direct at the German leadership tends to focus primarily on:

(1) Its 'dogmatic' insistence on austerity measures, even though these are strangling the Greek economy. This is the political economy/ideological type of critique, found not only in the public claims of left-wing opposition parties, SYRIZA and the KKE (the leader of SYRIZA and current Prime Minister, *Alexis Tsipras*, frequently referred to *Ms Merkel's* 'economic chauvinism' during the studied period) but also in critique expressed more subtly by members of the government or right-wing, fiscally conservative parties. New Democracy MP, *Dora Bakoyanni*, for example, has often stated both to Greek and German media that the level of austerity imposed on the Greeks is unprecedented in peace times (NewsUp GR, 2012); or

(2) Germany's political arrogance and 'colonial' behaviour towards other EU member states, which is frequently linked to the Nazi occupation during the Second World War. Statements in this category that do not make comparisons of modern German leadership with the Nazis typically unfold like the following:

> ... Our country is experiencing another kind of foreign occupation today, the economic occupation imposed by the lenders and implemented by the government, which executes their orders ... we will not allow anyone to turn our country into a protectorate of Germany, as Merkel and her domestic vassals wish ...

> declared opposition party ANEL leader *Panos Kammenos* on the occasion of Greece's national day, on 25 March 2014 (Enet.gr, 2014). On a similar streak, *Alexis Tsipras* has repeatedly accused *Ms Merkel* and *Mr Schäuble* of 'unashamedly dictating to the Greeks how to vote in the European parliament elections' and of supporting 'Mr Samaras and his extreme-right gang ... This

Europe of division, but also of poverty, of unemployment, of social marginalization, bears no relation to our Europe.' (iefimerida, 2014)

Another set of arguments emphasizes the pride of the Greek people and their moral and democratic superiority vis-à-vis the Germans or other Northern Europeans. A well-publicized example is the strong critique expressed by the Greek President *Karolos Papoulias* in 2012, in response to previous statements by *Wolfgang Schäuble* that Greek politicians may not be that sincere in their intentions to implement the structural reforms required by the 'bail-out' memorandums. Reeling, the Greek President retorted:

I don't accept that my country is vilified by Mr Schäuble. I don't accept it as a Greek person. Who is Mr Schäuble to humiliate Greece? Who are the Dutch? Who are the Finns? We have always been proud to defend not only our freedom, not only our country, but also the freedom of Europe. (TaNea.gr, 2012)

One of the most widely reported in the Greek media cases of 'German resistance' is that of former PASOK member and [subsequently] independent MP *Yannis Dimaras*, who sent an aggressive letter to the chairman of the Legal Committee of the German Parliament, *Siegfried Kauder*, on 30 January 2012. He argued, inter alia, that 'thanks to Greece, Germans have been transformed from cruel and uncivilised Goths into an orderly nation' and assimilated Germany's role in the current crisis to that of Hitler and the Nazis in the Second World War (Ethnos.gr, 2012). The notoriously big-mouthed former Vice President of the government *Theodoros Pangalos* in an interview with the BBC on 25 February 2010, commented:

They [the Nazis] took away the Greek gold that was in the Bank of Greece, they took away Greek money and they never gave it back. He concluded: 'I don't say they have to give back the money necessarily, but they have to say thanks. And they [the German government] shouldn't complain much about stealing and not being very specific about economic dealings.' (Brabant, 2010)

The emotional message thus often sent by Greek political elites is that 'the Hellenic Republic has been imprisoned […] by a country with a catastrophic and unforgivable past' (Tzogopoulos, 2012, p. 7). It is crucial, however, to note that while several politicians conflate modern-day Germany and its political leadership with the Nazis, another group evokes the history of the Second World War and criticizes Germany's Eurocrisis policy without equating it or its people with 'absolute evil'. Perhaps the most recognizable political figure in this camp is 91-year-old *Manolis Glezos*, SYRIZA MP and historic member of the Greek Left, who fought the Nazis and has been a key campaigner for war reparations since then.[7] In an open letter to the German public, published in the Die Welt, Glezos (2013) wrote that:

… you will never hear me speak of REVENGE. We, who lost our loved ones [during WWII Nazi occupation], do not feel hatred for the German people and we do not seek revenge … Every inch of European soil is soaked in blood. We paid dearly for the theories of superior races and nation states. We need a Europe of solidarity, equality and understanding. The recognition by Germany of the war reparations that it owes Greece absolutely serves such a Europe.

Public opinion

Since the outbreak of the Eurocrisis, surveys of Greek public opinion have invariably recorded widespread pessimism regarding both the progression of the crisis and the ability of the national and EU political constellations to handle the crisis. The vast majority of Greeks consistently feel the worst is yet to come both at individual and country level in terms of the economy(for the latest figures, see European Commission, 2015; Public Issue, 2015b). The Eurocrisis is assessed primarily as a symptom of underlying policy failures at national level with external factors such as the global financial crisis and unregulated global stock markets coming second by a great margin. Nevertheless, EU institutions and other EU member state governments are equally little trusted to take Greece and the rest of the union out of the crisis and onto the right path of economic and social recovery (Pew Research Centre, 2013; Eurobarometer 83, 2015). At the same time, support for Greece's membership of the Eurozone has remained high throughout the Eurocrisis period (Metron Analysis, 2015), even though public opinion is deeply divided about the benefits of the common currency. Crucially, from a crisis accountability and legitimation perspective, the feeling of social injustice among the Greek people has been high since the first counter-crisis measures were announced in 2010: with the majority of respondents consistently assessing the economic measures taken in response to the crisis as socially unfair (ΚΑΠΑ Research, 2015; VPRC, 2010).

With regard to Germany in particular, opinion polls in the period 2009–2014 have consistently registered prevalent negative feelings towards this country, most commonly anger, indignation and rage. Such feelings, however, do not necessarily coincide with Nazi stereotypes. In a 2012 public opinion survey, when asked what they associate the word 'Germany' with, approximately one-third of Greek respondents mentioned Hitler, Nazism and/or the Third Reich (32.4%) in general. A much smaller proportion (6%) said that they thought of the Nazi occupation and destruction during the Second World War and the war reparations issue (VPRC, 2012). More than twice as many, though, perceive Germany as hostile towards Greece, insofar as German political leadership is concerned (Pew Research Centre, 2013). Not surprising, then, that Greek public opinion is not well disposed towards Chancellor Angela Merkel, with approximately 7 out of 10 Greeks consistently having a negative opinion about her (for the latest poll, see Public Issue, 2015a). On the day of Angela Merkel's second visit to Athens, on 10 April 2014, the well-established liberal tabloid newspaper *To Pontiki* published a survey that not only highlighted the unpopularity of the German chancellor, but also that half of the Greek population support the SYRIZA view that Merkel's policies are tearing the EU apart (Pulse RC, 2014). Four out of five respondents also agreed that the then Greek Prime Minister, Antonis Samaras, ought to put the issue of the Second World War reparations on the agenda during his meeting with the German chancellor.

From the above, it becomes clear that anti-German public opinion in Greece is specifically directed not at the German people as a whole, but the German political leadership in particular. Given Germany's role in the Eurocrisis, this is entirely predictable from a crisis management perspective. That a substantial proportion of the population conflates today's German leadership with the Nazis confirms the presence of the discursive 'seeds' that could lead to an actor-focused blame-game 'witch hunt', whereby senior political leaders are held responsible for the crisis and their legitimacy is questioned on the grounds of them being inherently 'evil'; with that attribution of 'evil' then extrapolated to the entire peoples these leaders represent.

Nevertheless, a closer reading of opinion poll statistics conducted before and during the crisis, points to a deeper-running 'anti' attitude among the Greek people and a potentially more damaging one for the EU polity: one of general scepticism towards national political institutions and the leaders of the biggest (and traditionally also perceived as the most powerful and influential) EU member states. Greek political parties have always enjoyed poor or abysmally poor trust rates, which a look at all *Standard Eurobarometer* surveys can quickly confirm. However, the parliament as an institution has in pre-crisis years always enjoyed the Greek public's trust and so have the EU institutions. The Eurocrisis appears to have dealt this trust a near-fatal blow. Crucially, a cross-referencing of polls from different sources shows that the perception of a power imbalance within the EU runs back a decade (at least in terms of opinion poll data) and is widespread across EU member states (European Commission, 2004; Pew Research Centre, 2013; Scharioth, 2012).[8] The Eurocrisis has strengthened the view that the EU system is built on inequality of power and now also of access to resources. The conditions are therefore favourable for a more generalized system-focused accountability result, whereby the EU's legitimacy to represent the people of Greece and to handle the current crisis is questioned and possibly revoked.

Crisis, mediatization and the Greek public sphere

Greek news media sphere in transition. The Eurocrisis has had a profound impact on the Greek media sphere. The decline in media economic performance and journalism standards during the Eurocrisis has been such, that Greek journalists have been reported to 'operate in disastrous social and professional atmosphere' (Reporters without Borders, 2013b), where freedom of information is 'repeatedly and blatantly flouted [...] a dizzying fall for the world's oldest democracy' (Reporters without Borders, 2013a). The sudden and unconstitutional closure of the public broadcaster, ERT, in 2013 by the then ND-PASOK-DIMAR coalition government contributed to the negative evaluations of the Greek media sphere.[9] Mainstream media, especially the highly influential private TV channels, have been shown to have consistently broadcast one-sided, heavily austerity-biased coverage of the Eurocrisis (Grey & Kyriakidou, 2012). This is hardly surprising, in a country that epitomises the 'polarized pluralist' media system model (Hallin & Mancini, 2004) of close media links with the PASOK-ND bi-partisan political establishment of the post-junta (*Metapolitefsi*) era;[10] extensive state intervention and/or control; and the domination of media ownership by industrialists (Kontochristou & Terzis, 2007; Papathanassopoulos, 2001). From a democratic media perspective, the Greek media sphere has, therefore, never been a particularly healthy environment. This hampers its ability to meet the conditions of *publicness* that is, to make political authority visible and expose them to the public's scrutiny. Weak or unhealthy media systems such as these entail diminished autonomy and accountability functions for the media professionals as well as reduced quality of the news services provided. Greece is not alone in this respect: Europe-wide and beyond, scholars point to the mainstream media being directly responsible for systematic misinformation, abusing power, restricting the diversity of political views and manipulating public opinion in the case of the Eurocrisis (Tracy, 2012; Tzogopoulos, 2013). Some journalists are fighting back by challenging the editorial lines of the crisis reporting.[11]

At the same time, the Greek online public sphere offers a reporting 'escape route' to journalists who lost their jobs in established news media outlets either because of the financial crisis, or because they diverged too much from the editorial/ownership line, or both. From this perspective, the Greek news media landscape has been dramatically trans-formed with the rise of news blogs and online news media platforms, several of which are owned and run by prominent journalists without any links (visibly at least) to powerful media conglomerates or other business interests. Such news sources now match estab-lished newspapers and even TV political talk shows in popularity and offer an alternative to the mainstream line of reporting (the quality of this alternative reporting is not necess-arily better than what established TV channels broadcast, but what is crucial here is the very existence of riposte) (Michailidou et al., 2014).

News frames: 'Repent ... Merkel is coming ... '[12]

There is no doubt that for the studied period 2009–2013, the Eurocrisis is a near-perma-nent fixture in the Greek news sphere. Findings reported here were collected in the context of the 'Eurocrisis in the media' study, part of the ARENA EuroDiv project. Pertaining to the case of Greece, in particular, the following data sets are quoted in this paper:

- Political cartoons: quantitative and qualitative analysis of the work of six prominent pol-itical cartoonists (Stathis, Kostas Mitropoulos, Dimitris Hantzopoulos, Giannis Kalaitzis, Ilias Makris and Andreas Petroulakis) over a period of four constructed weeks (dates ran-domly selected) in 2009–2011. In total, 172 cartoons were collected, of which 120 were about the Eurocrisis. Only 18 portrayed Germany or a German official in a negative light and only four had a Nazi theme.
- RSS feeds: 183,128 news feeds collected from the politics and economy sections of the top five news websites in Greece (according to Alexa.com rankings): in.gr, protothema. gr, newsit.gr, newsbeast.gr, zougla.gr, over the period January–August 2012. Of these, 104,382 were relevant to the Eurocrisis and were further quantitatively coded. Angela Merkel was mentioned in 1445 news feeds, while the Troika (IMF, European Commis-sion, European Central Bank all together or separately) in 2978 news feeds.
- Newspaper front pages: the front pages of all 31 newspapers of national circulation at the time of Angela Merkel's two visits in Athens (9 October 2012 and 11 April 2014) were coded to determine the visibility of the German chancellor's visit in print media and the framing of the events (positive/negative; mention of war reparations). Our sampling stretched over a two-day period for each visit (date of visit and following day) which yielded 89 newspaper front pages in total. 77 of these mentioned the chancellor's visit and in 43, the visit was the main front-page news. The issue of the Second World War reparations appeared in only two front pages in 2012 and in eight in 2014.
- 364 online news articles and accompanying reader comments from two of the most popular online news media (according to Alexa.com rankings) during the period 2010–2012, namely protothema.gr and zougla.gr. Articles were collected in relation to three specific Eurocrisis events: the agreement on Greece's first loan ('bail-out') and establishment of the EFSF in May 2010; the 2011 announcement by then-Prime Minister of Greece, George Papandreou, of a referendum on whether Greece would accept a second loan agreement (the actual question of the referendum was never clari-fied, but when announced, the other EU leaders made it clear that any referendum would ultimately affect Greece's Eurozone membership regardless of how the question

would be formulated); and the ratification by the German parliament of the second loan agreement for Greece in December 2012.

Longitudinal and event-based analysis of the above data[13] shows that, overall, technocratic and political elite actors (i.e. political actors in decision-making positions) dominate media coverage of the Eurocrisis in professional news platforms and their public statements virtually never contain any critique or hint of doubt of their own actions. Greek journalists largely opt for seemingly 'neutral' crisis reporting that simply presents the actions of various decision-makers as facts rather than provide commentary or analysis of those. The technocratic hegemony discourse thus remains virtually unchallenged. There is, however, a distinct divide among professional journalism sources, which runs in two dimensions. Firstly, there is a divide between pro- and anti-'bail-out' agreement news outlets,[14] with very few news sources offering pluralistic coverage that allows both sides to be heard. Those that support the 'bail-out' reforms are also pro-government and supportive of the actions and demands of the European Commission, the European Central Bank and the International Monetary Fund (the three institutions that form Greece's international lenders and are most commonly referred to as 'the Troika'). Secondly, there is a divide between internet-only news sources and news media with a dual online–offline presence (print media, TV), with the former largely falling under the anti-'bail-out' block. Since the media provide the structure for the public sphere, it follows that the Greek public sphere is a divided space; the extent to which a member of the public will be exposed to technocratic hegemony discourse, or competing views about the Eurocrisis depends not only on their preference for online or offline news but also on the political views they and their preferred newspaper supports.

Sensationalist framing with strong anti-German, Nazi connotations is actually not that prominent. In fact, the vast majority of news feeds and complete articles referring to the Eurocrisis (80% of all complete articles coded and 70% of the RSS feeds) have a national perspective. We can broadly classify articles with a national perspective under two categories: those that highlight a 'national interest' angle of specific EU politics events or developments, such as news items in Greek online media covering the establishment of the EFSF mechanism and discussing the implications of this for Greece's economy and fiscal policy; and those that turn specific EU events or developments into a backdrop story for national politics, particularly inter and intra-party conflicts. Critique on German or EU leadership may be present in such articles, but then it tends to focus on the specific decisions or statements rather than portray the German chancellor or any other EU leader as a Nazi. During the studied period 2010–2013, he news sources that can be classified as anti-German 'moral panic' instigators fall mostly, though by no means exclusively, under either the nationalist/extreme-right side of the political ideology spectrum or the sensationalist tabloid type of journalism. The former tend to be low-circulation newspapers offering a curious mixture of religious, apocalyptic analysis of current events, conspiracy theories about extra-terrestrials, strong anti-Semitism and of course strong anti-government and anti-German rhetoric based on the Second World War experience. The latter pose a bigger challenge, in that they are popular with the public, have a 'mainstream news' reporting style and their anti-Germanism is more sophisticated, thus more credible.

Readers' frames. The image that jumps out of readers' comments is of a nation in turmoil that is struggling to find a way out of a precarious situation in a united manner. The Greek political system is rejected as shamelessly corrupt and self-serving; particularly the Socialist party PASOK and conservative New Democracy that until January 2015 had been either alternating in government or governing in coalition. The majority of the analysed comments reject the Greek political system because they equate it with whichever of the two parties they oppose. The ills of the Greek political system are thus acknowledged but arguments are so tied up to specific political parties or even individual political actors, that all debates inevitably degenerate to emotive, 'enraged fan' behaviour (personal attacks, outright dismissal of different points of view, slogan-style comments and denial of facts). Debates are introvert in that 'others' (EU partners, EU peoples, EU institutions or countries beyond the EU) are sparsely mentioned and then largely to appoint blame (it is the EU/Troika/Germany/global markets' fault). There is hardly any mention of other EU countries in crisis (Ireland, Spain, Portugal and Italy) and in the few instances that these countries do appear in the conversation, it is either to remind us that Greece is in a worse position (i.e. the others countries got a better 'deal' because they 'played the game more smartly') or to warn us and the people of other EU countries that we are all on the same boat and will soon be sharing the same 'austerity fate'.

Us versus them. Comments that make explicit or implicit references to two of the darkest periods in Greece's recent history, the Second World War Nazi occupation of 1941–1944 and the civil war of 1946–1949, are encountered often. The role of Germany in the Greek crisis has re-awoken bitter memories of military occupation, torture, humiliation and heroic resistance and has brought to the fore the unresolved issue of war reparations. There is at least one mention of Germany, the German government or chancellor Merkel in such context in all articles of the Greek data set, including the top commented and shared ones. Articles or readers supporting the Memorandum agreements and austerity measures that come with these or comments that convey any support or alignment with 'hard-working Germans' are instantly labelled 'traitors', 'collaborators of the German occupation forces' or 'spivs' (in direct reference to those who profiteered during the Nazi occupation at the expense of the Greek people). Similarly, references to specific gruesome events of the civil war period – atrocities committed both by the right-wing government forces and the Communists – are used to threaten or warn other readers that such a fate awaits Greeks in general or the collaborators of the new 'occupying forces' (The EU, the IMF and Germany or Germany and France).[15] The brutalities committed against Communists or their suspected collaborators by the right-wing government forces during the civil war are also used by those who support the austerity measures and the role of Germany and of the EU in the Greek crisis, to warn anti-austerity protesters in general or specific commentators with anti-austerity/anti-German/anti-EU views, of the gruesome end 'communists' will have if they try to impose 'red fascism' on the Greek people once more. Foreign news media are often perceived as serving strategic interests of foreign or global powers, invariably 'the Americans', 'the markets', 'the British' or 'crook investors'.

Conclusion

Combining insights from crisis communication and public sphere theories, I have analysed the politicization of the Eurocrisis in Greek public discourse with two aims: Firstly, to create a general map with the actors and types of claims made publicly about the causes and effects of the Eurocrisis, and secondly, to more specifically determine the prominence of Eurosceptic and anti-German discourse.

The Greek public sphere of the Eurocrisis years emerges from the analysis as deeply divided along the pro- and anti-crisis management strategy followed by the Greek governments at the behest of EU institutions and other member-state governments. The Greek media sphere offers crisis coverage that is deeply flawed, from a journalist credibility perspective. Most events or developments regarding the Eurocrisis are presented in a seemingly neutral manner, without journalistic analysis or commentary. There is a strong focus on the national politics, with the social and EU/transnational dimensions of the crisis rather overlooked. Sensationalist anti-German frames are not frequently encountered but the fact that they appear in high-popularity media and coincide with the general public's feelings towards Germany makes such frames more powerful. Sensationalist anti-German frames are also used occasionally by politicians of various ideological and party backgrounds, though the vast majority of anti-German or anti-EU critique coming from politicians' lips is mostly focused on a vision of an alternative Europe and the shortcomings of the crisis management strategy currently being followed. Crucially, the Greek public identifies the national, German and EU leaderships as directly responsible for the crisis and the subsequent suffering of the Greek people.

On the basis of the presented evidence, we can speculate that the most likely outcome of the current crisis accountability process would be an actor-focused one, whereby responsibility is attributed to senior policy-makers or political leaders and sanctions follow (or at least are proposed). The ingredients for a generalised 'moral panic' whereby all Germans will be collectively held responsible for the ills of Greece due to the former's inherent 'evil', are present but not in sufficient doses to make such a moral panic likely. Nevertheless, a focus on individual actors – be that Ms Merkel, Mr Samaras or Mr Barroso – prevents the system from learning and taking deep reformative action to restore the people's trust and to substantially reduce the risk of similar crisis in the future.

Notes

1. Statham and Trenz (2014) identify this gap in research and propose an EU politicization research agenda that is based on contestation mechanisms in the public sphere.
2. I use the term 'moral panic' here as a blanket concept that defines '[a] condition, episode, person or group of persons [which] emerges to become defined as a threat to societal values and interests' (Cohen, 1973, p. 9) and which is characterized by disproportionality (i.e. the perceived threat is disproportional to the real threat), whereby the perceived threat takes the shape of 'folk devils' (Thompson, 2006).
3. That a crisis is almost always unanticipated does not mean that there are no warning signs before its outbreak. It is more the case that key stakeholders fail to notice or act upon those signs, as has been the case with the Eurocrisis.
4. Learning from a crisis is also a key aim of crisis-management but usually comes secondary. This is despite the fact that it pays off in the long term for an organization or system as a whole to give this at aspect as much attention, because it constitutes a solid way to safeguard a system from future similar crises (Boin et al., 2005).
5. The quality of Greek democracy has been critically assessed and found lacking by several scholars. See, indicatively, Diamandouros and Gunther (2001).

6. One in five Greeks are at risk of poverty according to the recent data released by Eurostat, but a careful reading of the report reveals that 'at risk of poverty' is a person in a household whose disposable income is already *below* the 'at risk of poverty' line (Eurostat, 2013).

7. Campaigning for the Greek War Reparations case has been ongoing for decades, but the Eurocrisis has focused the media's attention on it and made it part of parties' political agenda. For an overview of the Greek reparations case, including the confidential report produced for the Greek government see Lowen (2013). For an insight into some of the legal arguments produced by the German side in the case of the Distomo Nazi massacre in particular see Rau (2005).

8. The issue of trust/distrust of citizens towards EU institutions and how this links to Euroscepticism, has been the subject of extensive scholarly research. Indicatively, see Hooghe and Marks (2007), Hudson (2006), Harteveld, van der Meer, and de Vries (2013).

9. The ERT was closed down in an attempt to meet the target of dismissing 4000 public sector employees by the end of 2013, as part of the conditions of the Second Economic Adjustment Programme (bailout). The ERT was eventually reinstated in early 2015, by the SYRIZA-ANEL government, which has vouched to safeguard the independence of the public broadcaster. Thus far, news production has maintained the co-operative, interactive, employee-led style of news making that the ERT journalist teams established successfully in the 'closure period' of the public broadcaster. Citizens will also have a direct say in the evaluation of the ERT, through the recently announced Social Control Councils (SCCs). Any citizen or civil society organization can apply to become a member of their regional SCC, whose role is to communicate to the Board of Directors their views on the content of the ERT's programme, to make recommendations for the proper functioning of the ERT and to monitor the compliance of the ERT's operations with the obligations envisaged in its founding manifesto.

10. Metapolitefsi is the period that started with the restoration of democracy in 1974 and ended with the collapse of the PASOK-ND bi-partisan political establishment during the Eurocrisis years. Although this collapse has been gradual since 2009, the definitive moment that sealed the end of the Metapolitefsi was 25th January 2015, when SYRIZA won the national elections and formed the first-ever left wing government in Greece (albeit in coalition with the smaller, right-wing populist party Independent Greeks-ANEL).

11. One example is the case of Greek journalist Kostas Vaxevanis, who published the infamous 'Lagarde list' of potential Greek tax evaders against the intentions of the Greek government, who were apparently trying to 'bury' the case and prevent investigations. Such has been the notoriety and impact of the Lagarde list scandal on international public discourse that the Financial Times now include it in their influential Lexicon of 'economic, financial and business terms' (Financial Times Lexicon, 2014).

12. Political cartoon by Dimitris Hantzopoulos (2012) depicting former Prime Minister of Greece *Antonis Samaras* on the roof of the Greek Parliament in a Messiah pose.

13. All quantitative coding was carried out with DiscoverText, while for the qualitative analysis we followed a combined discourse and concept mapping approach. The concept-mapping component was carried out using Leximancer. For more details on the sampling strategy, quantitative and qualitative coding, as well as validity and reliability scores, see Michailidou et al. (2014).

14. The more common terms used to define the two opposing opinion camps are pro- and anti-Memorandum, after the Memoranda of Understanding that accompany the loan agreements by the EU, the IMF and the European Central Bank that the Greek government has signed.

15. For a concise history of Greece's civil war years and the atrocities committed by both warring sides see (Close, 2013; Hamilakis, 2002; Mazower, 2000; Voglis, 2002).

Acknowledgements

The research presented in this article was completed as part of the EUROTRANS and EURODIV projects, which are run by the ARENA *Centre for European Studies* in Oslo and funded by the *Research Council of Norway*. I wish to thank the special issue editors, Aline Sierp and Christian Karner, for their constructive feedback and support during the publication process. I also thankful to the three anonymous reviewers who provided detailed and constructive reviews of my article, as well as to my colleagues at ARENA, *Prof. Helene Sjursen* and *Dr Mai'a Davis Cross* for their inspirational comments that helped focus my analysis. Many thanks also go to *Elina Roinioti*, PhD candidate at the *Panteion University* of Social and Political Sciences in Athens, for her thorough coding of the Greek news data set.

Disclosure statement

No potential conflict of interest was reported by the author.

References

Allison, G. T., & Zelikow, P. (1999). *Essence of decision* (2nd ed.). New York, NY: Longman.
Βικιπαίδεια. (2014). Οι Γερμανοί ξανάρχονται. Retrieved from April 3, 2014. Available on the Greek Wikipedia website, http://tinyurl.com/ybkm6ff
Boin, A., 't Hart, P., Stern, E., & Sundelius, B. (2005). *The politics of crisis management: Public leadership under pressure*. Cambridge: Cambridge University.
Brabant, M. (2010). Greece angers Germany in gold row. *BBC News*, February 25, 2010. Retrieved from April 4, 2014. the BBC website at http://news.bbc.co.uk/2/hi/8536862.stm
Brändström, A., & Kuipers, S. (2003). From "normal incidents" to political crises: Understanding the selective politicization of policy failures. *Government and Opposition*, *38*(3), 279–305.
Close, D. H. (2013). *The origins of the Greek civil war*. Oxon: Routledge.
Cohen, S. (1973). *Folk devils and moral panics*. St Albans: Paladin.
Coombs, W. T. (2010). Parameters for crisis communication. In W. T. Coombs, & S. J. Holladay (Eds.), *The handbook of crisis communication* (pp. 17–53). Oxford: Wiley-Blackwell.
Crum, B., & Fossum, J. E. (Eds.). (2013). *Practices of inter-parliamentary coordination in international politics*. Colchester: ECPR Press.
Diamandouros, P. N., & Gunther, R. (Eds.). (2001). *Parties, politics, and democracy in the New Southern Europe*. Baltimore, MD: The Johns Hopkins University Press.
Enet.gr. (2014). Π. Καμμένος: Δεν θα γίνει η χώρα προτεκτοράτο της Γερμανίας. Retrieved from April 5, 2014. http://enet.gr/?i=news.el.article&id=422373
Ethnos.gr. (2012). ΕΠΙΣΤΟΛΗ ΔΗΜΑΡΑ ΣΤΟΝ KAUDER: «Άγριοι και απολίτιστοι Γότθοι». Retrieved from April 8, 2014. http://ethnos.gr/article.asp?catid=22767&subid=2&pubid=63609446
European Commission. (2004). Standard Eurobarometer 62.
European Commission. (2015). Factsheet on Greece, Standard Eurobarometer 83.
Eurostat. (2013). European social statistics pocketbook: All social statistics on the EU in one publication. Eurostat Press Office release, July 17 2013. Retrieved from March 22, 2014. http://europa.eu/rapid/press-release_STAT-13-112_en.htm?locale=en
Financial Times Lexicon. (2014). Definition of Lagarde list. The Ltd 2014. Retrieved from March 18, 2014. http://lexicon.ft.com/Term?term=Lagarde-list
Glezos, M. (2013). Was Deutschland meinem Land heute noch schuldet. Retrieved from April 4, 2014. Die Welt website at http://www.welt.de/politik/ausland/article115831049/Was-Deutschland-meinem-Land-heute-noch-schuldet.html

Grey, S., & Kyriakidou, d. (2012). Special Report: Greece's triangle of power. December 17 2012. Retrieved from March 18, 2014. Reuters website at: reuters.com/article/2012/12/17/us-greece-media-idUSBRE8BG0CF20121217

Hallin, D. C., & Mancini, P. (2004). *Comparing media systems: Three models of media and politics.* Cambridge: Cambridge University Press.

Hamilakis, Y. (2002). The other "parthenon": Antiquity and national memory at Makronisos. *Journal of Modern Greek Studies, 20*(2), 307–338.

Hantzopoulos, D. (2012). Antonis Samaras cartoon, 6 October 2012, first published in newspaper Ta Nea, Retrieved from April 3, 2014. hantzopoulos.gr/photos/caricatures/caricatures_1349508095/121005b.png

Harteveld, E., van der Meer, T., & de Vries, C. E. (2013). In Europe we trust? Exploring three logics of trust in the European Union. *European Union Politics, 14*(4), 542–565.

Hermann, C. F. (1963). Some consequences of crisis which limit the viability of organizations. *Administrative Science Quarterly, 8*(1), 61–82.

Hooghe, L., & Marks, G. (2007). Sources of Euroscepticism. *Acta Politica, 42*, 119–127.

Hooghe, L., & Marks, G. (2009). A postfunctionalist theory of European integration: From permissive consensus to constraining dissensus. *British Journal of Political Science, 39*(1), 1–23.

Hudson, J. (2006). Institutional trust and subjective well-being across the EU. *Kyklos International Review for Social Sciences, 59*(1), 43–62.

Iefimerida.gr. (2014). Ολοι οι υποψήφιοι του ΣΥΡΙΖΑ για το ευρωψηφοδέλτιο [λίστα]. Retrieved from April 29, 2014. http://iefimerida.gr/node/152889#ixzz30MlZRJpB

IMF. (2013a). Country Report No. 13/154, GREECE ARTICLE IV CONSULTATION, 2013.

IMF. (2013b). Country Report No. 13/241, Greece: Fourth Review under the Extended Arrangement Under the Extended Fund Facility, and Request for Waivers of Applicability and Modification of Performance Criterion.

ΚΑΠΑ Research. (2015). Έκτακτη Πανελλαδική Έρευνα για τη νέα συμφωνία, opinion poll conducted on behalf of newspaper To Vima, 17/07/2015. Retrieved from August 19, 2015. To Vima website at: http://www.tovima.gr/files/1/2015/07/14/Kapar.pdf

Kontochristou, M., & Terzis, G. (2007). The media landscape in Greece. In G. Terzis (Ed.), *European media governance: National and regional dimensions* (pp. 225–237). Bristol, CT: Intellect Books.

Kriesi, H. (2012). The political consequences of the financial and economic crisis in Europe: Electoral punishment and popular protest. *Swiss Political Science Review, 18*(4), 518–522.

Lowen, M. (2013). The war claims dividing Greece and Germany. Retrieved from April 5, 2014. *The BBC News* website at http://bbc.com/news/world-europe-22470295

Lyrintzis, C. (1987). The power of populism: The Greek case. *European Journal of Political Research, 15* (6), 667–686.

Mazower, Mark. (2000). The cold war and the appropriation of memory: Greece after liberation. In Istvan Deák, Jan T. Gross, & Tony Judt (Eds.), *The politics of retribution in Europe: World war II and its aftermath* (pp. 212–232). Princeton: Princeton University Press.

Metron Analysis. (2015). Πανελλαδική Έρευνα Κοινής Γνώμης, Ιούλιος 2015, public opinion poll conducted in July 2015 on behalf of online news platform Parapolitika.gr. Retrieved from August 19, 2015. the Metron Analysis website at: http://www.metronanalysis.gr/category/2015/

Michailidou, A. (2014). Crisis and change in Greece: What price democracy? In J. E. Fossum, & A. J. Menendez (Eds.), *The European Union in crises or the European Union as crises?* (pp. 245–276). Oslo: ARENA Report Series.

Michailidou, A. & Trenz, H. J. (2010). Mediati(zi)ng EU Politics: Online news coverage of the 2009 European parliamentary elections. *European Journal of Communication Research, 35*(3), 327–346.

Michailidou, A., Trenz, H. J., & de Wilde, p. (2014). *The internet and European integration.* Berlin: Barbara Budrich.

NewsUp Gr. (2012). 'Ntora Bakoyanni ZDF' video clip of Dora Bakoyanni speaking at the German Banks Union event 'The euro and the European economic crisis'. Retrieved from April 4, 2014. YouTube at http://youtube.com/watch?v=gbi5NLaNzr0

Papathanassopoulos, S. (2001). Media commercialization and journalism in Greece. *European Journal of Communication, 16*(4), 505–521.

Pappas, T. S. (2013). Why Greece failed. *Journal of Democracy, 24*(2), 31–45.

Pidgeon, N. (1997). The limits to safety? Culture, politics, learning and man-made disasters. *Journal of Contingencies and Crisis Management, 5*(1), 1–14.

Peters, B., Pierre, J., & Randma-Liiv, T. (2011). Global financial crisis, public administration and governance: Do new problems require new solutions? *Public Organization Review, 11*(1), 13–27.

Pew Research Centre. (2013). The New Sick Man of Europe: the European Union. Pew Research Global Attitudes Project, May 13, 2013. Retrieved from April 2, 2014. the Pew Research Centre website at http://www.pewglobal.org/2013/05/13/the-new-sick-man-of-europe-the-european-union/

Public Issue. (2015a). Political Barometer 141/2–2015 Special Issue 2: Attitudes towards Germany and the Greek-German relations. Retrieved from August 19, 2015. The Public Issue website at: http://www.publicissue.gr/en/2024/pol-bar-141-special-issue-2/

Public Issue. (2015b). Πολιτικό Βαρόμετρο 145, Ιούνιος 2015, Retrieved from August 19, 2015. Public opinion poll available on the Public Issue website at: http://www.publicissue.gr/11580/varometro-june-2015/

Pulse RC. (2014). Δημοσκόπηση: Επιφυλακτική έως εχθρική, opinion poll conducted on behalf of the newspaper To Pontiki, Issue 1807. Retrieved from April 13, 2014. To Pontiki website at http://topontiki.gr/archive-new.php?acat=2&aid=2331, 12–13 (12–13)

Rau, M. (2005). State liability for violations of international humanitarian law – The distomo case before the German federal constitutional court. *German Law Journal, 7*(7), 701–720.

Reporters without Borders. (2013a). European Union and Balkans: European Union – Rights guaranteed but under threat. Retrieved from April 2, 2014. The Reporters Without Borders, World Press Freedom Index 2014 at: https://rsf.org/index2014/en-eu.php

Reporters without Borders. (2013b). World Press Freedom Index 2013. Retrieved from March 18, 2014. The Reporters without Borders website at: http://fr.rsf.org/IMG/pdf/classement_2013_gb-bd.pdf

Scharioth, N. (2012). Changes in the image of Germany – 2006 to 2011: Evidence from the gallup world poll. In M. Almut, & R. Parkes (Eds.), *Germany as viewed by other EU member states* (pp. 1–5). EPIN Paper no. 33 / June 2012.

Seeger, M. W., Sellnow, T. L., & Ulmer, R. R. (2003). *Communication and organizational crisis.* Westport, CT: Praeger.

Sellnow, T. L., & Seeger, M. W. (2013). *Theorizing crisis communication.* West Sussex: Wiley-Blackwell.

Sierp, A., & Karner, C. (2016). National stereotypes in the context of the European crisis. National Identities 18.

Statham, P., & Trenz, H. J. (2012). *The politicization of Europe: Contesting the constitution in the mass media.* London: Routledge.

Statham, P., & Trenz, H. J. (2014). Understanding the mechanisms of EU politicization: Lessons from the Eurozone crisis. *Comparative European Politics Advance Online Publication,* March 3 2014, 1–20.

TaNea.gr. (2012). Παπούλιας: «Ποιος είναι ο κύριος Σόιμπλε που λοιδορεί την πατρίδα μου;». Retrieved from April 8, 2014. Ta Nea website at http://www.tanea.gr/ellada/article/?aid=4694861

Thompson. (2006). The history and meaning of the concept. In C. Critcher (Ed.), *Critical readings: Moral panics and the media* (pp. 60–66). Berkshire: Open University Press.

Tracy, J. F. (2012). Covering "financial terrorism". *Journalism Practice, 6*(4), 513–529.

Tzogopoulos, G. N. (2012). It's Germany Stupid! The Greek-German Misunderstanding. In A. Möller, & R. Parkes (Eds.), Germany as Viewed by Other EU Member States (pp. 6–9). EPIN Paper no. 33/June 2012. Retrieved from April 3, 2014. The CEPS website at http://www.ceps.eu/book/germany-viewed-other-eu-member-states

Tzogopoulos, G. N. (2013). *The Greek crisis in the media: Stereotyping in the international press.* Farnham: Ashgate.

Vasilopoulou, S., Halikiopoulou, D., & Exadaktylos, T. (2013). Greece in crisis: Austerity, populism and the politics of blame. *Journal of Common Market Studies, 52*(2), 388–402.

Voglis, P. (2002). *Becoming a subject: Political prisoners during the Greek civil war.* New York: Berghahn Books.

VPRC. (2010). Greek society's attitudes towards the economic crisis. Retrieved from April 3, 2014. The VPRC website, at http://www.vprc.gr/article.php?id=934

VPRC. (2012). Η Εικόνα της Γερμανίας και της γερμανικής πολιτικής στην ελληνική κοινή γνώμη, opinion poll conducted on behalf of weekly magazine Epikaira, 2012. Retrieved from April 3, 2014. The VPRC website at: http://www.vprc.gr/article.php?id=1144

de Wilde, P., Michailidou, A., & Trenz, H. J. (2013). *Contesting Europe*. Essex: ECPR Press.

de Wilde, P., Michailidou, A., & Trenz, H. J. (2014). Converging on Euroscepticism: Online polity contestation during European Parliament elections. *European Journal of Political Research*, Early View (online), 1–18.

Willke, H. (2010). Transparency after the financial crisis. Democracy, transparency, and the veil of ignorance. In S. A. Jansen, E. Schröter, & N. Stehr (Eds.), *Transparenz* (pp. 56–81). Wiesbaden: VS Verlag für Sozialwissenschaften.

6 Pictorial stereotypes and images in the Euro debt crisis

Horst-Alfred Heinrich and Bernhard Stahl

ABSTRACT

In the Euro debt crisis, it is hardly surprising that reciprocal stereotyping is carrying the day in the national media reviving old images of the respective 'other'. The study asks how covers of German news magazines are shaped by the use of national stereotypes and images when reporting about this crisis. The paper seeks to build a bridge between the seemingly distanced disciplines arts and political science by offering a lean framework for analysis. It uses some cover images taken from two German weeklies and modifies Panofsky's semiotic model revealing traditional stereotypes and images of Greece.

Introduction

Germany is currently considered to be the most powerful economy in Europe, with a political élite pushing for an austerity policy in other European countries. Against this background, it is hardly surprising that Germans and in particular German political leadership are caricatured in the European media. In one of the most striking examples, Chancellor Angela Merkel is depicted wearing a uniform while commanding a helicopter attack against the Acropolis.[1] The suggestion behind the picture refers to a long-lasting stereotype well-known in several European countries: Germany's claim for power over Europe (Wippermann, 1981).

As we are dealing with a distorting articulation of reality, insulting reactions by German media to these and similar images may not be surprising either. However, this should not distract from the fact that German news coverage has also employed similarly prejudiced statements about its neighbours (Hahn & Hahn, 2002). In general, one can assume that all media outlets working with these kinds of stylistic devices expect greater news value and greater attention among their audience. At the same time they can surely count on recognition effects.

The literature on stereotypes has become very comprehensive (Dovidio, 2010; Fiske, 1998; Hinton, 2000) and, therefore, this paper will not cover the causes that lead to the use of stereotypes. It shall suffice to locate the construct *stereotype* on a theoretical level. Instead, we raise the question to what extent stereotypes are linked to symbols which in turn enhance or add a specific meaning to a pictorial stereotype. Based on an exploratory analysis of cover images taken from two German weekly political magazines, we investigate this aspect here. Evidently, stereotypes associated with a foreign group (here: the Greeks) are not meant to adequately represent a complex issue such as the Euro crisis. Rather, recipients of the weeklies are presented with simplistic messages regarding the alleged causes of the crisis. Messages referring to stereotypes are bound to convince recipients if they match their national identity.

Theoretical and methodical considerations

On a theoretical level, our research draws on various approaches of stereotypes, social categorisation theory (SCT), as well as the image approach. Our research interest touches upon the question how pictorial articulations of other nations can be investigated. Moreover, the extent to which pictorial images fulfils the function of simplification and which stylistic devices are of particular importance become relevant.

Theoretical assumptions on stereotypes

Despite the fact that *nation* and *membership to a nation* represent contested analytical terms,[2] the terms' underpinning structural principle seems useful due to its multidimensionality, functionality, and adaptability. The term *nation* refers to civic rights and territory, as well as to an ethnic and genealogical dimension without clear differentiation (Smith, 1991, p. 15). At the political level, this vagueness allows for pursuing a national interest, 'which is presumed to reflect the national will and national identity of the inclusive population' (Smith, 1991, p. 16). To the extent that we are dealing with an imagined community (Anderson, 1983), the question is raised how in-groups and out-groups (e.g. migrants within a nation or members of other European nations) are seen. On the one hand, the unknown other may be fascinating; on the other hand, it may induce fear. Hence, in order to create acceptance for common European solutions, a European policy must not only forge a compromise between national interests at the macro level but reduce and balance animosities at the micro level too.

In this context, stereotypes play an important role. In everyday language the term *stereotype* is used synonymously with prejudice. In the academic literature, however, the term is understood in various ways.[3] Within the framework of attitudes (Eagly & Chaiken, 1998) Susan Fiske (1998, p. 357) defines a stereotype as a cognitive element of categorisations while prejudices constitute the emotional dimension of the construct. Discrimination is, then, seen as the behavioural component. We do not follow this conception since the analytic differentiation between the facets of attitudes focuses on mental activities. Therefore, Fiske's conception does not allow for the analysis of arguments in textual or visual material which can be used as stereotypes with the aim of devaluation of out-groups.

Instead, we draw on a definition proposed by Pierre van den Berghe (1997) and differentiate between a categorical and statistical classification tendency (Kindervater, 2007, pp. 47–48). The categorical variant refers to the negative prejudice as a classification of persons defined as out-group members who are depreciated and devalued because of their otherness. This type fulfils the function of legitimating discriminatory attitudes and actions. That is why a prejudice will not be adjusted even if confronted with its empirical counter-evidence. Assuming a lack of information, statistical classification aims at characterising individuals or groups. A stereotype of this kind enables orientation in order to take quick decisions in time as well as in resource-constrained situations (Kindervater, 2007, p. 48). This conception may undergo change, if empirical counter-proof is provided.[4]

Van den Berghes concept is helpful for the analysis of pictures because visual categorisations might be based on generalisations (Schneider, 2004, p. 12). Yet, they are not necessarily linked to prejudices which in turn aim at devaluing out-groups. Consequently, the analysis of a picture has to answer the question in how far the visual content refers to stereotypes known for their use as categorical classification.

Insofar as stereotypes provide individuals with a frame of reference, the concept can be connected with the SCT. According to this approach human action in social situations is based on the ability to classify the self and other individuals or groups and thus to reduce the need for information which in turn saves cognitive resources (Turner & Reynolds, 2012, pp. 404–405). Given contextual principles like accessibility of categories as well as normative and comparative fit, de-personalising individuals serves the goal of comprised information. It can be assumed that the conditions for categorisation are usually given in the case of media reports about topics like foreign politics or economic issues.

Under the above-mentioned conditions such articles portray life conditions or experiences of particular people. But they only function as prototypical examples demonstrating the specific situation of groups (the government, 'the' working class, 'the' Greeks, etc.). Hence, they merely appear as interchangeable entities of a collective to which they are attributed. Their personal characteristics are no longer recognised (Ellemers & Haslam, 2012, p. 388). Referring to this theoretical assumption, within this paper it is explored in how far political magazines use stereotypes which might heighten the salience of the social categories presented to the readership.

Levelling down differences between members of the same group enhances the affiliation with the in-group while inter-group differences become more pronounced. Such simplified observations allow for a quick evaluation of social situations due to the substantial reduction of information. This is also an important aim of media reporting. The reader should get a straightforward insight into complex issues. Nevertheless, making life easier bears a disadvantage: According to social identity theory (Tajfel & Turner, 1986) preferring in-group members occurs at the expense of out-groups.

Stereotypes unquestionably correspond to social categories. But they are specific as they only apply to certain types of human groups. Following social dominance theory (Sidanius & Pratto, 1999) modern societal order corresponds to a categorical status system. It determines dominant as well as subordinate status positions which result from group membership such as gender, ethnic, or religious affiliation (Küpper & Zick, 2005, p. 33). In contrast to other social categories, stereotypes always entail a dominant group as a reference point, a principle on which the media usually count on. A dominant group sets the standards of everyday-type communication, that is, speaking of US citizens implicitly refers to white heterosexual men (Fiske, 1998, p. 366). When people communicate, this categorisation is taken for granted and thus immediately understood by the recipient. Attributing *black woman* to a person in a leading management position is usually mentioned explicitly because the person does not conform to the stereotype. The latter ascribes other roles to black women which renders it necessary to complement the stereotype.

The implicit use of stereotypes describing a dominant or a subordinate group refers to the concept of statistical classification tendency. People know about the different stereotypes which are attributed to the several groups and they employ them as a proper instrument for fast communication on the basis of limited information. As the example of the black manager shows stereotypic categories allow for deviations. They are not necessarily categorical classifications. This is also true for the stereotypes presented by the media. Whether they are interpreted as a devaluation of out-groups or not depends not only on the current public discourse as broader context but also *inter alia* on the recipients' degree of social dominance orientation.

Assuming that there are diverging national interests in the Euro debt crisis, we apply the theoretical considerations outlined above to the European Union. In this case, national sensitivities are affected and public communication reproduces national stereotypes which, in turn, reflect power relations between the particular societies. The media, in particular, tends to categorise other nations enabling quick and simple recognition. Furthermore, this kind of articulation creates attention. To what extent such stereotyping also serves furnishing prejudices, and whether they devalue the respective out-group are questions we turn to in the empirical section. In addition, we will explore how symbols are used thereby potentially leading to negative effects.

Conceptualisation of visual stereotypes

As pointed out above, the literature on stereotypes has become very extensive. It is noticeable, however, that there are different approaches to analysing pictorial stereotypes in the social sciences and humanities respectively, which are rarely combined or even related to each other. Cognitive approaches clearly dominate in political sociology and social psychology. Various studies deal with the function of prejudices and their causes, as well as their effects on devalued groups. Visualisations only play a limited role in this research field.[5] However, it can be assumed that pictorial images have a stronger impact on recipients than the mere verbalisation of stereotypical categories (Beckett & Park, 1995).[6]

Historiography, history of art and linguistics are the humanities' disciplines with primary interests in pictures' different layers of meaning. They investigate, in a contextualised approach, the meaning associated with visual articulations. These approaches assume a recipient who either is a 'normal' observer (Eco, 1991) or the 'knowledgeable' art historian (Panofsky, 1932). They offer insights into encoded interpretations which are reproduced and circulated to the readership of print media. Well in line with Stuart Hall's studies on television, encoding does not determine how the respective meanings of stereotypical articulations are actually adopted, that is, decoded (Hall, 1999). It is conceivable that the recipient may recognise a particular detail as the central feature of a stereotype and, subsequently, communicate the content of the image without any further reflection.

Image theory

Regardless of the disciplinary approach chosen, most publications fall short of theoretically linking the concept of stereotypes to visual representation. This research gap can be closed by drawing on Kenneth Boulding's image concept (Boulding, 1956). It assumes that images constitute subjective knowledge, including cognitive, emotional, and evaluative components. They are stored as experiences on which we rely whenever needed (Boulding, 1956, pp. 8–10). When this subjective knowledge is activated our behaviour will be guided by these images (Boulding, 1956, p. 10). Although Boulding makes no distinction with regard to the different terms of perception (Goldstein, 2001),[7] it is quite clear that images – as condensed signification concepts of the world around us – still point beyond action schemes which refer to automated processes.[8] On the contrary, they are quite similar to statistical stereotypes, since both – images and statistical stereotypes – aim at simplifying complex issues by emphasising a few central categories.

Boulding stresses the role of national stereotypes (Boulding, 1961, p. 393) when arguing that national images derive from shortened and distorted narratives of national history. By communicatively re-iterating selected events of the past, members of a nation produce an image of the collective 'self' with corresponding characteristics. The latter result from the assumption that a nation defines itself by shared experiences and has been shaped accordingly. Certain properties are derived from these community-building experiences which are, on the one hand, attributed to the national in-group, and on the other hand, to nations defined as foreign out-groups (Alexander, Brewer, & Hermann, 1999, pp. 79–80). These characteristics, in turn, correspond to stereotypes.

Although Boulding's (1961, p. 392) concept is generally located at the macro level in order to explain state interactions, it also allows for feedbacks on the micro (i.e. domestic) level. Outcomes of political systems, here: nations, may be a resultant of interacting political élites and public. They may not share the same images but usually a significant overlap can be expected. Images or stereotypes have a long-term effect because they are recalled and reproduced through various socialisation institutions and the media (Boulding, 1961, p. 393) – the latter serving as a mediator between macro and micro levels. Within these processes symbols are of particular relevance since they allow for a broad range of interpretation.

Another asset of the image concept is Boulding's (1961) recognition of the images' visual dimension. Messages will affect an image, if they refer to a symbol. In our view, a symbol can be understood as a sign denoting a representation which cannot be perceived directly (Voss, 2006).[9] Symbols might be connected to the image concept since symbols can be conceived of as pictorial signs. They address cognitive constructs which are not explicitly presented in the picture.[10]

Even though Boulding (1956) primarily relates his idea to spoken communication, the concept might 'travel' to visual representations. The latter create an image of the empirical reality and – in turn – may change our beliefs. On the one hand, the combination of visual images and pictorial symbols should entail the potential for new insights on behalf of the recipients. On the other hand, it may also reinforce existing stereotypical views by applying them to new contexts. Where symbols point to a cognitive construct which cannot be immediately taken from the image, the empirical observation does not directly correspond to the picture. Due to this interpretative room of manoeuvre the combination of visual image and pictorial symbolism allows for two consequences:

- the creation of new ways of consideration by developing novel meanings triggered by the pictorial content;
- a strengthening of well-known stereotypic articulations which are adapted to new visual habits.

Exactly these options are explored in the ensuing analysis.

A model for pictorial analysis

Our pictorial analysis is embedded in a wider understanding of discourse analysis. In a narrow sense, the discourse analysis has been conceived of as interpretation of a text corpus.[11] In a wider sense, though, discourses can be comprehended as a formation of signs. Such a semiotic perspective would include audio-visual media, that is, photos, films, and pictures. For analysing pictures, we base our approach on theoretical insights provided by Panofsky (1978) which have been developed further by Marotzki and Stoetzer (2006). They have advanced Panofsky's iconological method by integrating findings from film studies; hence, their model seems particularly well suited to deal with pictorial analyses of social situations. We have slightly modified their approach and suggest transferring it to the field of political science in general and international relations in particular. The approach suggests four steps:

1. Denotation
First, the most evident objects on the picture are identified (Marotzki & Stoetzer, 2006, p. 17). This requires a simple description of what can be seen on the picture without reflecting on any deeper context knowledge.[12]

2. Connotation
In the second step, the cultural-specific meaning is crucial. Existing or dominant cultural interpretations of the objects depicted shall be interpreted. For instance, if the picture shows a man in a black suit, the denotation in step 1 will describe just that. Our cultural knowledge tells us that the man may be involved in a serious business or social event which would require this dressing. In the Christian culture, one might add, a black suit is often linked to religious celebrations such as weddings or funerals. Going beyond the mere visual content, in the analysis of weekly covers the added title, headers, and subtitles play an important role since they provide further information concerning different versions of how the picture can be understood.

3. Mise-en-scène
After having analysed *what* can be seen on the picture, step three is devoted to *how* the objects are placed. This endeavour is based on the semiotic insight that the way an object is presented largely impacts on its meaning (Krah, 2011, p. 40). Drawing from film studies one might distinguish between colour, line, and form which focuses on arrangements of space (foreground – vs. background), frames, and (a-)symmetries, and sharpness as well as light effects.

4. Synthesis
Finally, the societal context has to be linked to the picture. This 'iconological interpretation' (Panofsky, 1978, p. 50) refers to the *Zeitgeist*, to the historical trends of the time, to societal conditions. This background knowledge has to be combined with the results of the visual investigation and refers to survey and other research. For practical reasons, this

methodological step will be undertaken after having examined the two magazine covers chosen for analysis here.

Empirical analysis

The context of the Euro debt crisis

By exemplifying the Euro debt crisis we examine pictorial symbols in connection with stereotypes. This idea looks rewarding taking into account that the crisis has led to huge interest conflicts between European nations. Considering the media's limited capacity to comprehend complex economic situations as well as national politics, we expect rather stereotypic simplifications.

The Euro debt crisis did not happen overnight and due to the various factors which played into its evolvement, there is no consensus as to when exactly it began. There are those who see a seamless transition from the Global financial crisis which started in 2007 to the Euro debt crisis (Chronology, 2013), whereas some would mark the revelation of Greece's true budget deficit in the autumn of 2009 as the beginning of the crisis (Euro-zone Crisis, 2013). Yet, arguably the budget deficit did not suddenly appear, for Greece already had a heightened debt load when it joined the Euro in 2001. Without a doubt, a closer look at the whole political process goes beyond the scope of this paper. Therefore, this section only concentrates on a rough sketch of what happened in years 2009–2013. The brief description provides the context within which the magazine covers were published.[13]

In autumn 2009, the Greek budget deficit was no longer manageable by the state institutions. As a consequence, in March 2010, Greece presented its austerity package. This in turn led to a downgrading by the ratings agency Fitch. EU ministers reacted by setting up a €500 billion fund which was enabled through the newly established rescue mechanisms. This was the beginning of an ongoing economic as well as political process with the superficial aim of stabilising both the Greek budget and economy with the help of the International Monetary Fund (IMF) and the European institutions. But it was also a fundamental struggle over the validity of political–economic paradigms, the scope of the European integration, and the willingness to solidarity between the EU member states.

The public sphere does not seem the appropriate forum to come to terms with a comprehensive understanding of the diverse and contrary interests in a specific issue area. Hence, it seems reasonable to assume that both the political actors and the media tend to reduce complexity by reverting to available images which are connected with stereotypes. To what extent the members in the target groups of the political messages interpret them as statistical or categorical classifications must remain open for it depends on individual properties. Yet, concerning the media it is claimed here that the economic reverberations of the debt crisis not only triggered serious consequences in the political realm but also opened Pandora's box of historical stereotypes.

German stereotypes on Greece and the Greek

Some negative German stereotypes of Greece are old and persistent. Evidently, we cannot provide an extensive historical analysis of the Greeks' image in German literature and media here. Yet some historical aspects which led to Germans' contemporary articulations concerning Greece and the Greeks deserve attention.[14]

One of the oldest roots of negative considerations in entire Europe goes back to year 1054 (during the Byzantine era), when the division of Christianity into Catholic and Orthodox faith was taking place. This schism brought about mutual mistrust between Catholic Europe and the Orthodox world (in this case Greece).[15] Subsequently, this enforced another, more current stereotype which assigns Greece to the Balkans – a region ascribed to as instable, uncivilised, and backward (Todorova, 1997). One of the oldest examples of such historical descriptions is the *Völkertafel* of 1730 (Stanzel, 1998, p. 14). It is an illustrated cross-table which lists several European nations, populations, and ethnic groups. It ascribes specific stereotypical characteristics and behaviour to each of them. If one checks this peoples' table one can find under the rubric *Greek* the attributes 'lying devil' ('Lung Teüfel', i.e. lügender Teufel), 'even more treacherous than Russians' ('noch verräterischer'), 'lazy' ('gar faul'), and 'slightly ill' ('kränkeln als Zeitvertreib'). Following the peoples' table a Greek would even pass away 'in treachery' ('Ihr Leben Ende: In betrug') (Stanzel, 1998, p. 14). This reference shows that negative stereotypes ascribing members of an ethnic group a specific 'national character' tend to be old. Furthermore, the prejudice of the workshy, cheating Greek is long lasting as the analysis of several encyclopaedia articles shows.

Another aspect is the continuous articulation of Greece's budget problems which can be observed over more than the past 100 years (Busch, 2005, pp. 50–65). Independent of the question whether these statements were connected to a stereotype or were claimed as a matter of fact, these descriptions outlined the image of a country with a disastrous economy.

Yet the Greek image has not always been a negative one. The Philhellenes – a movement that commanded admiration for ancient Greece – was praised in Germany in the eighteenth and nineteenth centuries. Some of this admiration accompanied the Greek rebellions in the early nineteenth century against the Ottoman domination. German and west-European sympathy and compassion went with those who fought for their freedom. But this admiration turned into disappointment when confronted with the Greek reality documented in diaries published by travellers. One of them, Urquhart (2008), pronounced Greece as the cradle of democracy but experienced an undeveloped Balkan country instead. Such travel reports were widely spread at the time and probably enhanced already existing negative stereotypes.

Interestingly, the political élite of the 'Third Reich' propagated a rather positive image of Greece and provided an example of contradictory articulations concerning this country. Hitler was greatly attracted to ancient Greece. He admired the antiquity, and the Nazi ideology saw itself as being a descendant of the old Hellenes. However, this positive perspective came to an end after German troops invaded the country in 1941 due to strategic reasons. When Greeks started to fight the occupation (1941–1944), the favourable attitude vanished and the German state launched a negative propaganda campaign against the Greeks naming them a 'nation of swines' ('Sauvolk') (Fleischer, 1998) or defining them as criminal, lazy, and corrupt. This aversion should be understood against the background of the war crimes committed by the Wehrmacht (Coulmas, 2012, pp. 39–40; Rondholz, 2012, p. 53) for which Greece claims compensation until today.

After the Second World War the negative discourse about Greece underwent a transformation. In the 1960s and 1970s, the country became a popular destination for German tourists, and Greek *Gastarbeiter* effectively contributed to the German *Wirtschaftswunder*. Positive views found their way into German society with popular Greek film figures such as Alexis Sorbas and singers such as Nana Mouskouri who was very successful with her hit 'White Rose of Athens' describing Greece as both *Heimat* and a land of people's dreams (Mouskouri, 1961).[16] This story was similar to those of the German bourgeoisie expressed in travel books written by several well-known novelists (Meid, 2012). They described a Greek countryside which appeared as contrast to the modern industrial society by searching for the ancient Greece or for a supposedly virgin nature.

Within this broad context one should assess the reactions of many German journalists on Greek application for EC membership which they welcomed describing it as the return to the cradle of humanity (Höhler, 2011) – despite the fact that the European Commission had spoken against early membership.

This overview shows that not only negative stereotypes on Greeks carried the day but a broad repertoire of diverse images can be found in history. It is important to note that the categorisations do not always ascribe specific attitudes to the Greek as stereotypes do. Several categorisations draw up images about Greece in Boulding's sense. These articulations range from the negatively evaluated economic situation to the portrayals of a pleasant natural scenery or of fine works of art expressing a reserve against today's problems. All these categorisations form a corpus of concepts which may be used by the media and political actors, as well as individuals. The stereotypes and images are invoked in different political situations and users can be sure that their audience will probably have the knowledge to recognise them.

Stereotypes in news magazines

As the theoretical considerations have already demonstrated, stereotypes are more than verbal concepts. They often refer to visual images of the 'other' to whom they are ascribed (Schweinitz, 2006, p. 49). Such visual stereotypes can be understood as pictorial schemes with few distinctive attributes which are part of common knowledge (Schweinitz, 2006, p. 49). Therefore, we can assume that the media operates with these visual images because they provide plausible analogies which allow an easy understanding of complex issues. Nevertheless, one has to bear in mind that visualisations always appear as polysemous. The individual has at least some degree of freedom when interpreting visualised stereotypes.

Following from this, we analyse two weeklies' covers as illustrative examples. It shall be demonstrated how visualisations of the Euro crisis can be used to link economic issues with implicit 'explanations' referring to national stereotypes or images. As our objects of analysis we decided on covers presented by two weeklies located in different sections on the German political spectrum. *Focus* aims at a more conservative clientele and was founded to challenge the supremacy of the more liberal-left *Der Spiegel*, which is known for its critical and insisting news style (Schrag, 2007). For the *Focus* we chose the February 2010 cover. The *Spiegel* cover was published in May 2012.[17]

Figure 1. Focus cover from February 22, 2010 (no. 8).

Ad Focus cover (Figure 1)

Denotation

Depicted, here, on the cover page of the February 2010 *Focus* magazine, is a marble statue of a woman who is missing her left arm and who is showing the middle finger of her right hand. The background resembles a blue, partly cloudy sky. The statue fills the right side of the cover page and faces the viewer. Her body below the waist is covered by a cloth with blue and white stripes. She is nude from the hips upwards. Half of the statue's face is covered by a shadow and she is looking away from the viewer. On the left there is a title in large white letters; underneath, at the same level as the statue's hips, a question is written in smaller black letters.

Connotation

The statue shown is unmistakably an altered version of the Venus of Milo – the famous Greek statue which is missing two arms and is believed to portray the Greek goddess Aphrodite. Aphrodite – in most sagas – not only stands for beauty but also bears traits of egocentrism and infidelity. Two alterations were made, here: an arm was added and the cloth she is wearing has blue and white lines; so far, two hardly offensive additions. The arm which was added, however, shows the middle finger, a gesture which is known as indecent in Western countries. The blue and white cloth immediately recalls images of the Greek flag – a blue and white cross and lines. This epitome of Greek culture – world famous ancient art and the national flag therefore – is showing others the middle finger. Who are the others? The title (translated) *Swindlers in the Euro family* implies that the Greeks are signalling the other Europeans that they could not care less. The question underneath reads, 'Is Greece cheating us out of our money – and what about Spain, Portugal, Italy?'

Mise-en-scène

The statue is placed in a deep blue background which leads the observer to think of a Mediterranean sky which German tourists used to adore. The Venus seems to be illuminated from the left-hand side, her right half is partly dark. The Venus is thus spotted half-light-half-shade which may look dodgy as well as shady and alludes to twilight, lack of transparency, and secrecy.

Ad Spiegel cover (Figure 2)

Denotation

The cover page of the *Spiegel* magazine from May 2012 focuses on the remains of a broken pillar with a small fragment of a coin fixed at the top of the capital. The rest of the coin leans against the column. The objects are located on a field covered with smashed stones. Only three pillars are still standing upright in the middle ground. In the background the view is limited by the black shadow line of a hilly landscape with few treetops stretching to the dark blue, cloudless night sky. At the top of the photomontage a headline in

Figure 2. Spiegel cover from May 14, 2012 (no. 20).

light blue and white letters is placed. Below on the right margin the subtitle follows with small white letters.

Connotation

Overall the picture conveys the impression of devastation. The column with its Ionic capital and the Mediterranean night scenery can be interpreted as visual symbols standing for Greece. The headline reading 'Acropolis adieu' explicitly points to Greece's worldwide known ancient monument. The colours of the headline's letters (light blue and white) refer to the Greek flag as the other national symbol. Following the visual message the cultural heritage of Greece which stands for the birth of democracy appears to be ruined. Consequently, the European currency is broken off from Greece (the pillar) with relevant damages. The text message supports the visual interpretation. It takes up a well-known chanson title sung by Mireille Mathieu in 1971. Whereas the song describes the nostalgic farewell from Athens as an unrealistic dream location (Mathieu, 1978), the subtitle ('Why Greece has to leave the Euro, now') confronts the reader with the supposed necessity of Greece's exclusion from the Eurozone.

Mise-en-scène

The impression mentioned above is supported by the arrangement of the objects. In the foreground the pillar as well as the broken Euro appears in glaring light from both the left and the right sides which leaves sharp shadow lines on the objects. One cannot ignore the disaster. In contrast, middle and background interact with the message of the headline. The artist created an atmosphere which appeals to a romantic conception of vacation and mild summer nights in the Mediterranean region.

Synthesis of both covers

The two covers were launched when the debt crisis had reached different moments of culmination between 2010 and 2012. These years were the time when the international and EU institutions and the member states were desperately trying to build new institutions in order to cope with the looming Greek (and Spanish and Irish) bankruptcy. Yet, and this is a first insight, the covers do not deal with institutional design. Nor do they allude to the EU or global issues. In both cases, the crisis is portrayed as a nation-state affair only. One might object that it is not entirely clear what the 'we' on the *Focus* cover stands for. But the mention of other states (Spain, Italy, and Portugal) does not support the thesis that 'we' alludes to the EU or the net-payer countries. One year later, the *Spiegel* explicitly refers to Greece by the statement that this nation would have to leave the Eurozone. In this regard, the pictorial nation-state centrism falls well in line with the 'net-payer debate' ('Nettozahlerdebatte') which has been haunting the German discourse on European affairs since the mid-1990s. After having decided to introduce the Euro and to compensate the southern member states for the necessary economic adjustments (summits of Maastricht 1991 and Edinburgh 1992) the prospect of Eastern enlargement triggered an animated debate on the German fiscal contributions to the EU budget. Due to the relative strength of the German economy and the small size of its agrarian sector, Germany's net contributions tended to rise until 1994 (Jeřábek, 2011, p. 174). From that time onwards, the debates have been popping up in the German public: the issue of Germany's financial contributions to the European Stability Mechanism (ESM) – in the eyes of many

Euro-sceptics – only varied the theme. In short – the EU does not play any role in the magazines' visual articulations. However, *Focus* speaks of the 'Euro family' which adds a community flavour to the crude picture. But this is the only remnant of a community value. On the whole, the two covers serve national stereotyping.

Now, how are 'the' Greeks depicted and what might this view tell us about subliminal messages which we are willing to follow? Again, the topic is one that should be dealt with as an institutional as well as transnational problem.

Regarding the *Focus*, the Greek nation (flag) is tied to the Greek culture (Venus of Milo) but in this case both stand for cheats ('Betrüger'). This demeaning attitude is complemented by a purported disrespect of the other 'family members' as the middle finger gesture reminds us of. At best, in the context of the 'Euro family', Greece is presented as a naughty, ill-mannered, and treacherous child. Considering the *Völkertafel* quoted above, this image of Greece follows up on old ones. In their endeavour to get their message across, the media tends to link its images to established stereotypes, which the potential reader can be assumed to recognise.

In the *Focus* case, the Germans stand outside the picture – as observers, while the disrespectful gesture and text suggest that Greeks are free to waste their money. It even seems that Aphrodite (Greece) is on stage while the German audience is doomed to silently acknowledge the drama. But the observers will have to pay for the performance. This image of a German 'paymaster' who cannot control events is implicitly referred to in the picture.

Where *Focus* pinpoints the Germans as passive paymasters who are encouraged to mistrust Greece with its incredible behaviour (the middle finger), the *Spiegel* suggests the 'Grexit' – a word unknown in 2012 – as a matter of fact. As the Greek culture (the ancient heritage) appears to be completely destroyed, it threatens 'our' currency which will be demolished. Referring to the old stereotype mentioned above, the cover presents Greece as the sick patient beyond all hope. Similar to the disappointment of German travellers in former centuries who could not confirm their dreams of modern Europe's birthplace when visiting nineteenth-century Greece, here, the *Spiegel* reader is indirectly asked to say goodbye to her/his dreams about a non-existent easygoing life somewhere in the south. Concerning this interpretation one has to bear in mind that Mathieu refers to Mouskouri's *White Rose of Athens*. This flower symbol reminded Greeks as well as Germans that they had lost something when leaving their home and that they will only return in the distant future (Mouskouri, 1961). Ten years later, Mathieu (1978) told us that the *White Rose* is wilted. The message is similar to the picture as well as to headline and subtitle in the *Spiegel* cover: Greece appears to be shattered; we have to leave it forever because the dream is over.

Further examples of cover images

As the interpretation of two magazine covers might limit the scope of the exploratory analysis, this chapter concentrates on the synthesis of two other covers depicted in Figure 3. They demonstrate that the articulation of national stereotypes in cover pictures is not a unique case.[18]

Again, Greece is symbolised by the Acropolis and the head of Aphrodite – the two most important attractions of Greek culture. But in these cases the ancient relics are in danger of

(a)   (b)

Focus no. 38, September 19, 2011   Spiegel no. 18, May 3, 2010

Figure 3. More cover pictures presented in Focus and Spiegel in 2010 and 2011.

being flooded (3a) or of being burnt (3b). Similar to the covers analysed in detail above, the Euro crisis is not articulated as an institutional affair and a clash of societal and political interests. Instead, the message is a simple one: The *Focus* headline in Figure 3a insinuates that Greece threatens 'our' money. The old culture with its ancient monuments seems to be lost. But as they are part of the Eurozone 'they' will get 'us' into troubles, too. The European flag is going up in flames right now (Figure 3b).

The covers do not reveal anything about the catastrophe's causes. On the contrary, the photomontages suggest that stereotypical behaviour led to the decline. Greece is portrayed as ill and lazy (the crumbling monuments – and nothing happens). The pictures repeat the image of the severely ill European patient (the Greek economy) who is irretrievably lost. At the same time the monuments, the sea, and the sky remind the reader of Greece as something which never really existed. It is this combination of a desired outgroup image located in a dreamland with a threat of the in-group in the present which takes up old stereotypes of 'the' Greeks.

Conclusion

This paper has enquired into the meaning of visualisations in the case of media reports on complex political–economic issues. By conducting an exploratory analysis of the covers presented by two German weeklies we can show to what extent the media refers to national stereotypes and images simplifying complex political matters.

The ancient world symbolised in classical remnants like statues or temple columns proved to be the pre-dominant image of Greece on several pictures. The *Focus* cover provided us with a vulgar gesture, which alludes to an alleged evil-minded attitude of the Greeks uttering disrespect for the other 'family members' of the 'Euro family'. This symbol enhances the standard representation of the conflict, namely that the Euro debt crisis is a conflict between nation-states and perhaps even more profoundly – considering the cultural impact of the Venus of Milo – a conflict of civilisations. These images serve the German stereotype of the 'Greek cheater' well. The *Spiegel* cover reminds us of assumed German reveries about Greece as an inaccessible aim of a better life. This view is contrasted with the assertion of Greece as the incurable society and economy.

Referring to Boulding's (1956) image concept our exploratory semiotic analysis offers some insights for understanding German policy in the Euro debt crisis. Responsibility for the crisis is attributed to Greece alone – its reckless and excessive accumulation of debts. Hence, the political solution of the problem offered can only mean a 'Spardiktat' which led to the fiscal compact and severe conditioning of financial assistance: Greece has to be forced to substantially reduce its debt. Probably, so the suggestion goes, Greek bankruptcy and a credit crunch are inevitable (the destruction seems to be immense). Thus, in the view of the anticipated *Spiegel* and *Focus* readers the German government should minimize possible reverberations on the German budget and its economy by calling for safeguards and limits to the German commitment. This means including other lenders (such as the IMF), to condition German contributions to the ESM, and to hinder EU institutions (European Central Bank) and member states to draw German money 'through the loophole' (i.e. Euro bonds).

Taken together, this paper offers a lean framework for visual analysis in political science. Pictures provide us with information which nurtures our (stereotypical) images – images of the world, our society, and on politics. Particularly, symbols are well suited to transport such images. Surrounded by an information over-flow and facing the complexities of social relations, human beings tend to build social categorisations, of which stereotypes are one. Groups of people are thereby defined and characterised by attribute classifications which make them different from one's own group. Such stereotypes – and this is our epistemological assumption – enable political action in two ways. First, they make it easier for political élites to justify and legitimate political decisions vis-à-vis the public. The media serves as a transmitter, dressing stereotypes in pictures – on covers of magazines as we have seen, here. Second, stereotypes pre-frame political decisions by limiting the space of political options. For instance, when Greeks are characterised as cheaters in the public sphere and when Greece is articulated as an ailing culture it is harder and less likely that decision-makers take solidarity measures. Admittedly, our semiotic analysis bears methodological caveats. A hermeneutical approach may overstate the pictorial impact and, consequently, the meaning of the covers may be different 'in the eyes of the public'. To further develop this line of research, we anticipate future studies confronting test groups with the pictures in order to find out whether our preliminary findings garnered by the exploratory semiotic analysis are reliable.

Some methodological limitations of this exploratory analysis notwithstanding, the findings illustrate the benefits of integrating the visual into the method spectrum of political science in general and of research on stereotypes in particular. In our view, the media's use of visual symbols induces stereotyping. Admittedly, recipients may not believe in them and may not be touched by such endeavours. Yet, the use of symbols facilitates the comprehension of issues which otherwise would be difficult to grasp and paves the way for what is politically possible. Further research has to clarify what impact such simplistic images regarding economic politics have not only on the public but also on political élites.

Notes

1. Acropolis now (2010, May 1). *The Economist*.
2. Some scholars define nation membership by using essentialist criteria while others prefer attributed ones. Furthermore, it is contested whether nation building is rather a primordial or a modernist phenomenon (Ichijo & Uzelac, 2005).
3. See for example Petersen and Schwender (2009). Here, stereotypes are partly associated with categorisations, and partly with negatively loaded prejudices. For a comprehensive literature review see Fiske (1998) and Quinn, Macrae, and Bodenhausen (2010).
4. Change of this sort may not fully transform the stereotype at once. It can also occur, if some exceptions from the rule constituted by the simplified perception are accepted (Hahn & Hahn, 2002, p. 22).
5. For an overview see Schweinitz (2006).
6. For further studies see Fiske (1998, p. 375).
7. Goldstein explains in his chapter how we perceive art and how a work of art may exploit the given circumstances in order to deceive the observer. Our perceptions are vulnerable and can easily be led astray. Perceptions, therefore, are highly susceptible.
8. The scheme concept is explained by Smith and Queller (2001).
9. We are mindful of the fact that scholars do not share a common definition of the term symbol (see Berndt & Drügh, 2009; Warnke, 2005; Zerbst & Waldmann, 2006). Yet, our definition enables to draw a relationship between Boulding's image concept and the world of pictures – regardless of the fact that Boulding constrains his idea to conversation – the spoken word.
10. According to Boulding (1956), symbols are similar to stories about issues or (hi-)stories.
11. For a broad overview concerning the different approaches of discourse analysis see Keller (2007).
12. Panofsky speaks of 'pre-iconographic description' (1978, p. 50).
13. For an overview see Panagiotarea (2013).
14. This summery is based on the review of a context analysis of newspapers published between 1997 and 2004 and encyclopaedias edited in the last 150 years (Busch, 2005), of the hermeneutic analysis of German twentieth-century travel stories (Meid, 2012), of the description of journal articles printed between 1918 and 1944 (Thanopulos, 1987), and of the analysis of survey data collected under German tourists in 1992 (Papadimitriou, 1995).
15. This conflict (clash among fault line) has also been made popular by Huntington (1993, pp. 30–32).
16. The white roses as symbol are important insofar as they play a role in the pictorial analysis.
17. In our denotative descriptions we do not mention the magazine logo, number and date of edition, price quotation, or small info boxes with textual hints concerning other topics within the magazine. Rather, we are only interested in the visual articulation of the Greek case.
18. In *Focus* and *Spiegel*, four further covers were published between 2009 and 2012 referring to Greece and the debt crisis. One is very similar to that in Figure 1 (Focus no. 38, September 19, 2011) showing Aphrodite as beggar. The *Spiegel* (no. 25, June 20, 2011) presented an obituary at the Euro showing Greece as a coffin shaped with the national flag. In these examples, too, the Euro crisis is depicted as a simple nation-state affair using explicit (beggar) or implicit (cannot economise) national stereotypes. In two other Spiegel covers (no. 10, March 8, 2010; no. 49, December 6, 2010) the Euro coin is depicted showing the front side with the map of all Euro countries. In both cases, Greece disappeared from the map.

Disclosure statement

No potential conflict of interest was reported by the authors.

References

Acropolis now. (2010, May 1). *The Economist*. Retrieved from http://www.economist.com/printedition/2010-05-01

Alexander, M. G., Brewer, M., & Hermann, R. K. (1999). Images and effect: A functional analysis of out-group stereotypes. *Journal of Personality and Social Psychology, 77*, 78–93. doi:10.1037/0022-3514.77.1.78

Anderson, B. (1983). *Imagined communities: Reflections on the origin and spread of nationalism.* London: Verso.

Beckett, N. E., & Park, B. (1995). Use of category versus individuating information making base rates salient. *Personality and Social Psychology Bulletin, 21*, 21–31. doi:10.1177/0146167295211004

van den Berghe, P. L. (1997). Rehabilitating stereotypes. *Ethnic and Racial Studies, 20*, 1–16. doi:10.1080/01419870.1997.9993945

Berndt, F., & Drügh, H. J. (Eds.). (2009). *Symbol. Grundlagentexte aus Ästhetik, Poetik und Kulturwissenschaft* [Symbol. Basic Texts from Aesthetics, Poetics, and Cultural Studies]. Frankfurt am Main: Suhrkamp.

Boulding, K. (1956). *The image*. Ann Arbor: University of Michigan Press.

Boulding, K. (1961). National images and international systems. In J. N. Rosenau (Ed.), *International politics and foreign policy: A reader in research and theory* (pp. 391–398). New York: The Free Press.

Busch, D. (2005). *Das Bild Griechenlands zwischen Fremd- und Selbstwahrnehmung*. [The Image of Greece between others and self-perception]. Berlin: Frank & Timme.

Chronology (2013). Die Chronologie der Krise [The chronology of the crisis]. (2013). *Tagesschau.de*. Retrieved from http://www.tagesschau.de/wirtschaft/chronologiefinanzmarktkrise100.html

Coulmas, D. (2012). Von der Ungleichzeitigkeit der Kulturen oder: Das „schwierige Geschäft, Grieche zu sein" [On the asynchrony of cultures or: The difficult business of being a Greek]. *Zeitschrift für Außen- und Sicherheitspolitik, 35–37*, 36–42. Retrieved from http://www.bpb.de/apuz/142835/von-der-ungleichzeitigkeit-der-kultur?p=all

Dovidio, J. F. (Ed.). (2010). *The SAGE handbook of prejudice, stereotyping, and discrimination.* Los Angeles: Sage.

Eagly, A. H., & Chaiken, S. (1998). Attitude structure and function. In D. T. Gilbert, S. T. Fiske, & G. Lindzey (Eds.), *The handbook of social psychology* (4th ed., pp. 269–322). Boston: McGraw-Hill.

Eco, U. (1991). *Einführung in die Semiotik* [Introduction to semiotics]. München: Fink.

Ellemers, N., & Haslam, S. A. (2012). Social identity theory. In P. M. V. Lange, A. W. Kruglanski, & E. T. Higgings (Eds.), *Handbook of theories of social psychology* (Vol. 2, pp. 379–398). London: Sage.

Eurozone Crisis. (2013). *Eurozone Crisis: Three-and-a-half years of pain* (March 28, 2013). *The Guardian*. Retrieved from http://wallstreetexaminer.com/2013/03/eurozone-crisis-three-and-a-half-years-of-pain-the-guardian/

Fiske, S. T. (1998). Stereotyping, prejudice, and discrimination. In D. T. Gilbert, S. T. Fiske, & G. Lindzey (Eds.), *The handbook of social psychology* (Vol. 1, 4th ed., pp. 357–411). Boston: McGraw-Hill.

Fleischer, H. (1998). Die 'Viehmenschen' und das 'Sauvolk'. Feindbilder einer dreifachen Okkupation: Der Fall Griechenland ['Beastmen' and 'Swinefolk'. Enemy images during a threefold occupation: The case of Greece]. In W. Benz, G. Otto, & A. Weismann (Eds.), *Kultur – Propaganda – Öffentlichkeit* [Cultural affairs – propaganda – publicity] (pp. 135–169). Berlin: Metropol.

Goldstein, E. B. (2001). Pictorial perception and art. In E. B. Goldstein (Ed.), *Blackwell handbook of perception* (pp. 344–378). Malden, Mass.: Blackwell.

Hahn, H. H., & Hahn, E. (2002). Nationale Stereotypen. Plädoyer für eine historische Stereotypenforschung [National stereotypes. promoting historical studies on stereotypes]. In H. H. Hahn (Ed.), *Stereotyp, Identität und Geschichte. Die Funktion von Stereotypen in gesellschaftlichen Diskursen* [Stereotype, identity, and history. The functions of stereotypes in social discourses] (pp. 17–56). Frankfurt am Main: Peter Lang.

Hall, S. (1999). Encoding, Decoding. In S. During (Ed.), *The cultural studies reader* (2nd ed., pp. 507–517). London and New York: Routledge.

Hinton, P. R. (2000). *Stereotypes, cognition, and culture*. Philadelphia: Psychology Press.

Höhler, G. (2011, June 21). *Stolz und Vorurteil [Pride and prejudice]*. Retrieved from www.tagesspiegel.de/politik/deutsche-und-griechen-stolz-und-vorurteil/4310140.html

Huntington, S. (1993). The clash of civilizations? *Foreign Affairs, 72*(3), 22–49. Retrieved from http://www.foreignaffairs.com/articles/48950/samuel-p-huntington/the-clash-of-civilizations

Ichijo, A., & Uzelac, G. (2005). Introduction. In A. Ichijo & G. Uzelac (Eds.), *When is the nation?* (pp. 1–6). London and New York: Routledge.

Jeřábek, M. (2011). *Deutschland und die Osterweiterung der Europäischen Union* [Germany and the European Union enlargement to the east]. Wiesbaden: VS.

Keller, R. (2007). *Diskursforschung. Eine Einführung für SozialwissenschaftlerInnen* [Discourse studies. An introduction for social scientists] (3rd. ed.). Wiesbaden: VS Verlag.

Kindervater, A. (2007). *Stereotype versus Vorurteile: Welche Rolle spielt der Autoritarismus? Ein empirischer Beitrag zur Begriffsbestimmung* [Stereotypes versus prejudices: What role does authoritarianism play?]. Frankfurt am Main: Peter Lang.

Krah, H. (2011). Semantik und Semantisierung [Semantics and semantization]. In H. Krah & M. Titzmann (Eds.), *Medien und Kommunikation. Eine interdisziplinäre Einführung* [Media and communication. An interdisciplinary introduction] (pp. 31–52). Passau: Stutz.

Küpper, B., & Zick, A. (2005). Status, Dominanz und legitimierende Mythen. Eine kritische Bestandsaufnahme der Theorie der Sozialen Dominanz [Status, dominance, and legitimising myths: A critical review of social dominance theory]. *In Zeitschrift für Politische Psychologie, 13,* 31–51.

Marotzki, W., & Stoetzer, K. (2006). Die Geschichte hinter den Bildern. Annäherungen an eine Methode und Methodologie der Bildinterpretation in biographie- und bildungstheoretischer Absicht [The story behind the Images. An approach to the method and methodology of image interpretation based on biographical and educational concepts]. In W. Marotzki & H. Niesyto (Eds.), *Bildinterpretation und Bildverstehen. Methodische Ansätze aus sozialwissenschaftlicher, kunst- und medienpädagogischer Perspektive* [Image interpretation and image comprehension. Methodological approaches from the perspective of social science, art and media pedagogy] (pp. 15–44). Wiesbaden: VS Verlag.

Mathieu, M. (1978). *Akropolis adieu* [Acropolis adieu]. Retrieved from https://www.youtube.com/watch?v=qDc4udA_Y4g

Meid, C. (2012). *Griechenland-Imaginationen*. [Images of Greece]. Berlin: de Gruyter.

Mouskouri, N. (1961). Weiße Rosen aus Athen [White rose of Athens]. Retrieved from https://www.youtube.com/watch?v=b0_gDCbCRM8&index=1&list=RDb0_gDCbCRM8

Panagiotarea, E. (2013). *Greece in the Euro: Economic delinquency or system failure?* Colchester: ECPR.

Panofsky, E. (1932). Zum Problem der Beschreibung und Inhaltsdeutung von Werken der bildenden Kunst [On the problem of describing and interpreting works of fine art]. *Logos. Zeitschrift für systematische Philosophie, 21*(2), 103–119. Retrieved from http://opac.mpisoc.mpg.de/Record/ 1812956487

Panofsky, E. (1978). *Sinn und Deutung in der Bildenden Kunst* [Sense and meaning in the fine arts]. Köln: DuMont.

Papadimitriou, E. (1995). *Deutsche Urlauber in Griechenland.* [German tourists in Greece]. Göttingen: Cuvillier.

Petersen, T., & Schwender, C. (Eds.). (2009). *Visuelle Stereotype* [Visual stereotypes]. Köln: Herbert von Halem Verlag.

Quinn, K. A., Macrae, C. N., & Bodenhausen, G. V. (2010). Stereotyping and impression formation: How categorical thinking shapes person perception. In M. A. Hogg & J. Cooper (Eds.), *The SAGE handbook of social psychology,* (2nd ed., pp. 68–92). Los Angeles: Sage.

Rondholz, E. (2012). Anmerkungen zum Griechenland-Bild in Deutschland [Comments on the image of Greece in Germany]. *Zeitschrift für Außen- und Sicherheitspolitik, 35–37,* 49–54. Retrieved from http://www.bpb.de/apuz/142839/griechenland-bild-in-deutschland?p=all

Schneider, D. J. (2004). *The psychology of stereotyping.* New York: Guilford Press.

Schrag, W. (2007). *Medienlandschaft Deutschland* [Media landscape Germany]. Konstanz: UVK Verlagsgesellschaft.

Schweinitz, J. (2006). *Film und Stereotyp. Eine Herausforderung für das Kino und die Filmtheorie. Zur Geschichte eines Mediendiskurses* [Film and stereotype. a challenge for cinema and film theory]. Berlin: Akademie-Verlag.

Sidanius, J., & Pratto, F. (1999). *Social dominance: An intergroup theory of social hierarchy and oppression.* New York: Cambridge University Press.

Smith, A. D. (1991). *National identity.* London: Penguin.

Smith, E. R., & Queller, S. (2001). Mental representations. In A. Tesser & N. Schwarz (Eds.), *Blackwell handbook of social psychology: Intra individual processes* (pp. 111–132). Oxford: Blackwell.

Stanzel, F. K. (1998). *Europäer. Ein imagologischer Essay* [Europeans. an imagological essay]. Heidelberg: Winter.

Tajfel, H., & Turner, J. C. (1986). The social identity theory of intergroup behaviour. In S. Worchel & W. G. Austin (Eds.), *Psychology of intergroup relations* (pp. 7–24). Chicago: Nelson-Hall.

Thanopulos, G. I. (1987). *Das deutsche Neugriechenland-Bild 1918–1944.* [The German image of new Greece 1918–1944]. München: Hieronymus.

Todorova, M. (1997). *Imaging the Balkans.* New York and Oxford: Oxford University Press.

Turner, J. C. & Reynolds, K. J. (2012). Self-categorization theory. In P. M. V. Lange, A. W. Kruglanski & E. T. Higgings (Eds.), *Handbook of theories of social psychology,* (pp. 399–417). London: Sage.

Urquhart, D. (2008). *Im wilden Balkan. Vom Berg Olymp bis zur albanischen Adriaküste* [In the wild balkans. from mount olympus to the albanian adriatic coast, original written around 1830]. Wiesbaden: Edition Erdmann.

Voss, M. (2006). *Symbolische Formen. Grundlagen und Elemente einer Soziologie der Katastrophe* [Symbolic forms. foundations and elements of a sociology of a catastrophe]. Bielefeld: Transcript.

Warnke, M. (2005). *Bildwirklichkeiten* [Image realities]. Göttingen: Wallstein.

Wippermann, W. (1981). *Der deutsche Drang nach Osten. Ideologie und Wirklichkeit eines politischen Schlagwortes* [The German drive to the east. ideology and reality of a political catchphrase]. Darmstadt: Wissenschaftliche Buchgesellschaft.

Zerbst, M., & Waldmann, W. (2006). *Du Mont's Handbuch Zeichen und Symbole. Herkunft, Bedeutung, Verwendung* [Du mont's handbook on signs and symbols. origin, meaning, and application]. Köln: DuMont.

7 Imag(in)ing the eurocrisis

A comparative analysis of political cartoons

Matti Van Hecke

ABSTRACT

Political cartoons enable the public to understand and interpret otherwise very complex problems. However, while all cartoons agree that the European Union has been suffering from a major crisis, agreement on what kind of crisis is far less uniform. By executing a comparative analysis of 400 political cartoons across 12 countries, this paper examines how cartoons frame the eurocrisis and argues that its definition, causal interpretation and moral evaluation, is constructed along national or cultural lines. In northern Europe, the eurocrisis is primarily associated with a crisis of responsibility. In southern Europe, a crisis of solidarity is the dominant frame.

Introduction

The eurocrisis led to a remarkable peak in the volume of political cartoons covering European affairs. While the gradual increase in domestic media attention for European Union (EU) events has been observed for some time now (Sifft, Brüggemann, Königslöw, Peters, & Wimmel, 2007), these events never seemed able to capture the imagination of political cartoonists. Due to the eurocrisis, media forms that previously disregarded 'Brussels' as a place far away with little relevance to the day-to-day lives of their audience, found their way to the EU level. As such, it has inspired artists across Europe providing a unique supply of political cartoons. However, while all these cartoons seem to agree that the EU is suffering from a major crisis, agreement on what kind of crisis is far less evident. This paper offers an exploratory and descriptive account of how political cartoons frame the eurocrisis and how their (dis)agreement on the frame is structured across Europe.

When stripped from meaningful interpretation and moral evaluation, the so-called eurocrisis can best be understood as the result of a monetary union that was not backed by a common fiscal policy. During this crisis, the EU members, who had entered into monetary union, attempted to prevent the risk of national debt defaults by several member countries that would destabilize the whole currency zone. In response, EU-level negotiations among national executives resulted into common policies for financial bailouts for indebted countries in return for the implementation of stringent national austerity policies. These negotiations have been dominated by Germany and France, who have called the shots and acted through the ECB with support from the IMF (Statham & Trenz, 2012).

These new monetary policies, however, have clear redistributive consequences and have – to a varying extent – a potentially damaging political, social and economic impact on the EU population. As a result, the pooling of EU sovereignty can no longer be publicly justified as a 'positive sum game' with the promise of benefits for all. Instead, the eurocrisis has an extraordinary high potential for generating a deep and ongoing politicization within and across national domestic politics across the region (Majone, 2011). This creates political opportunities for a framing competition within Europe contesting what the essence of the crisis is, to whom causalities and responsibilities should be attributed and which countries and/or social constituencies are the 'winners' and 'losers' of European integration.

This paper argues that political cartoons, as part of a mediated filtering system, have the potential to frame the eurocrisis by 'selecting some aspects of a perceived reality and make them more salient, in such a way as to promote a particular problem definition, causal interpretation, moral evaluation, and/or treatment recommendation' (Entman, 1993, p. 52). This way, cartoons can help to render infinite amounts of detail into straightforward interpretative packages that capture the essence of an otherwise very complex issue or event. In doing so, they explain events in ways that have first and foremost to do with the attribution of blame and responsibility (Greenberg, 2002). As the guest editors touched upon in their introduction, it is precisely when conflicts become a 'blame game' that identity politics, – for example, 'sovereign national people versus EU monetary technocrats' or 'Germans versus Greeks' – enters the stage, reinforcing cultural and national stereotypes. Research on how political cartoons frame the eurocrisis is therefore relevant, since it might reflect how national publics across Europe have come to interpret the nature of the crisis.

This paper asks two research questions. Firstly, what frames do political cartoons use to give meaning to the eurocrisis? The aim here is to present a descriptive overview of how political cartoons channel the discursive possibilities for making sense of the eurocrisis and to empirically show the controversy among cartoons that the eurocrisis brings about. Secondly, how is the frequency of certain frames distributed across Europe? One can expect that some frames will be more prominent within some national contexts than in others as a result of diverging audience expectations. Therefore, the aim is to explore whether we can observe variation in the use of frames across EU nations.

To answer these research questions, I first build a theoretical framework where I conceptualize communication about the eurocrisis as a framing contest and political cartoons as a tool for framing the eurocrisis. Following, I execute a framing analysis of 400 political cartoons created by 18 unique artists originating from 12 European countries. Next, the four frames that were most often used by political cartoons, that is, the eurocrisis as 'crisis of solidarity', 'crisis of responsibility', 'crisis of democracy' and 'crisis of governance', are discussed in detail. Finally, by controlling for the national background of the cartoonist, I discern a pattern concerning the relative frequency of these frames. While in northern and western Europe 'crisis of responsibility' is the dominant frame, the 'solidarity' frame prevails in southern Europe. In old and large member states such as Germany, France and the UK, cartoons dominantly frame the eurocrisis as a 'crisis of democracy'. These results are further discussed in the conclusion.

Crises as a framing contests

The eurocrisis is structural and deep and has a direct impact on the daily lives of thousands of citizens. However, issues and events often become the foci of collective concern or anxiety, not by the objective severity of the issue or event in question, but by how people subjectively encounter them. As starting point for the theoretical framework, I draw on social constructionist theories arguing that crises can be usefully understood as socially constructed problems (Berger & Luckmann, 1966; Fairhurst & Grant, 2010). As a result, the potential impact of crises is not necessarily determined by the events on the ground, but by their public perception and interpretation. Accordingly, this paper defines a crisis as 'an event or development that is widely perceived by members of relevant communities to constitute an urgent threat to some core community values and structures' (Boin, 't Hart, & McConnell, 2009, pp. 83–84).

Notwithstanding that, it is essential to note that no set of events or developments is likely to be perceived uniformly by the members of a political community. In any polity, major disturbances tend to give rise to different interpretations concerning the nature and severity of a crisis, its causes, the responsibility of its occurrence or escalation and implications for the future. Perceptions of crises are likely to vary within and across communities, reflecting the different biases of stakeholders as a result of different values, positions and interests. These interpretations and perceptions do not only differ, but are potentially conflicting at the same time (Boin et al., 2009).

Accordingly, this paper argues that the eurocrisis can be usefully understood in terms of a 'framing contest' between frames and counter-frames to interpret the crisis, its causes, and the responsibilities and lessons involved (see also Candel, Breeman, Stiller, & Termeer, 2014). Frames, here, thus refer to relatively distinct and coherent sets of meaning attributed to the eurocrisis (Dewulf et al., 2009). Proponents of these conflicting frames, manoeuvre, debate and negotiate in order to ensure that their frame prevails (Stone, 2001). A frame prevails when it becomes accepted by public opinion as the dominant narrative, and enjoys majority support in relevant political arenas 'processing' the crisis.

News media plays a crucial role in the framing contest that ensues in the wake of a crisis (Entman, 1993). It can be seen as an arena within which institutions, groups and individuals struggle over the definition and construction of social reality (Hilgartner & Bosk, 1988). When considered as a claims-making arena where the cultural meanings of circumstances and events are constructed, news media provides a rich source of data for examining how everyday issues or events come to be defined as 'social problems' and offers clues as how meaning will be negotiated and understood by the public. However, while scholars from differing theoretical and methodological perspectives suggest that media content plays a particularly important role in constructing, shaping and reinforcing perceptions of news events, the concept of 'framing' lacks a common shared theoretical model (Iorgoveanu & Corbu, 2012).

From a constructionist perspective, scholars have defined media frames a central organizing idea or story line that 'organizes everyday reality' (Tuchman, 1980) by providing 'meaning to an unfolding strip of events' (Gamson & Modigliani, 1987, p. 143) and 'promoting particular definitions and interpretations of political issues' (Shah, Watts, Domke, & Fan, 2002). According to Gitlin (2003, p. 7), media frames are 'persistent patterns of cognition, interpretation, and presentation, of selection, emphasis and exclusion, by which symbol-handlers routinely organize discourse, whether verbal or visual'. Entman (1993, p. 53) even extends their remit in suggesting that frames serve to explain causal factors of events and provide moral evaluations or recommendations. Summing up, the frame suggests what the core meaning of the controversy is about, the essence of the issue – or in this case – the essence of the crisis.

Cartoons as a tool for framing

When media frames are conceptualized as above, one can subsequently argue that political cartoons constitute an important medium for framing social crises (Abraham, 2009). Cartoons are part of a mediated filtering system that helps the construction and framing of social reality. They reinforce and reproduce the commentary of opinion columnists, editorial writers and other claim-makers or opinion formulators featured more prominently in media discourse: they draw upon topics that have already been established in the mainstream media as being worthy of public attention. Cartoons intend to transform otherwise complex events and situations into quick and easily readable depictions that facilitate the comprehension of social issues and events (Abraham, 2009, p. 119). Due to their spatial limitation, they need to condense complex social issues into a single, visual frame that captures the essence of an issue at a single glance (Streicher, 1967, p. 434). Because of this, cartoons are easier to understand and more accessible for lower social and intellectual classes when compared to more traditional media.

Moreover, political cartoons are opinion messages, not factual reports. They are considered social and political commentary providing a safe avenue for expressing opinions (Conners, 1995). While news reporters, emphasizing professional goals of value neutrality and objectivity, strive to create reports, the content of which are 'deliberately void of meaningful interpretation of events' (Streicher, 1967, p. 439), cartoonists are free to choose sides. Cartoons, therefore, reveal themselves as more explicitly political and constructed, rather than as attempts at objective renditions of social events (Abraham, 2009, p. 120). Some argue that because of their visual, satirical and humorous nature, cartoons might be even more provocative or controversial than other forms of opinion discourse since they are considered to be held less accountable to their 'artistic expression': cartoons may convey meanings that 'might meet with greater audience resistance if they were conveyed through words' (Abraham & Appiah, 2006, p. 190). Others have emphasized that the satirical, humorous and moralistic nature of cartoons often makes them mean and cynical, and because of that, they are more likely to insult certain social, religious, political or ethnic groups that are the object of ridicule (Kuipers, 2011). The Danish cartoon crisis in 2004, and more recently, the attack on the offices of the French satirical weekly newspaper *Charlie Hebdo* provide proof for their claims. Anyway, even if they speak of the world in hyper-figurative terms, political cartoons enable the public to actively classify, organize and interpret what they see and experience in meaningful ways.

Finally, this theoretical framework elaborates on why one would expect variation in the frequency of frames promoted by political cartoons. One view in the literature suggests that political entrepreneurs are to a varying degree effective in 'selling' their frame to the media (Boin et al., 2009, p. 96). Here, the media constitutes a prime arena in which crisis actors need to convince news-makers to pay attention to their particular crisis frame, and, if possible support it. The rivalling – and more convincing – view suggests that the media pursues their own agenda in crisis reporting, and that the crisis communication performance by any of the actors matters less than the degree to which the colour of the frame they put forward fits with the pre-existing biases of the main media outlets (Streitmatter, 2011). This approach implies that cartoonists and editors are embedded in a certain social environment and will therefore select those frames that resonate best with the dominant values and interests of their perceived audience (Clausen, 2004, p. 28).

An understanding of expectations is thus crucial in understanding the variation in use of media frames. Media casts far-away events in frameworks that render these events comprehensible, appealing and relevant to domestic audiences, by constructing the meanings of these events in ways that are compatible with the culture and the dominant ideologies of the societies they serve: 'although the media are required to reflect all sides of a story, retaining values and beliefs of the target audience is not only expected, it is also indispensable' (Fahmy, 2005, p. 120; see also Clausen, 2004). Political cartoonists as well are considered to 'construct their account of news against a backdrop of assumptions about the social world, that they expect to share with an implied readership community' (Greenberg, 2002, p. 195). Therefore, this paper expects that cartoonists shape the form and content of their accounts with a particular understanding about who their readers are and what they will find interesting, informative and humorous.

Data and methodology

To identify the different frames political cartoons use to give meaning to the eurocrisis, I applied a frame analysis consisting of several steps. In a first step, I collected political cartoons that treated the eurocrisis as their central theme. Nowadays, print media routinely purchase political cartoons they wish to publish from syndicated artists, rather than hire their own editorial cartoonists. The motivation behind the shift from full-time artists to syndicated artists can be attributed to money (syndicated cartoons can cost as little as a few dollars), as well as to editors' and owners' fear of retribution from irritated readers, and political pressure to remain 'politically balanced' (Lacity & Rudramuniyaiah, 2009, p. 202). Whereas magazines and newspapers are facing severe challenges in the digital age, cartoons manage to stay popular and relevant. The internet has provided substantial and highly accessible online platforms to professional and amateur cartoonists (Bal, 2011, p. 135). Accordingly, a search for political cartoons was carried out on Daryl Cagle's syndicated website, politicalcartoons.com, the largest searchable online database of political cartoons.[1]

In the online archive, I looked for cartoons that appear when using the search term 'euro', and were published online in the period between 1 January 2010 and 30 June 2012. These dates can arguably be considered the starting and ending point of the eurocrisis, or at least of its most acute phase. Near the end of the year 2009, Greece's prime minister announced that the government had been tampering with the country's financial statistics, initiating intense speculation on the financial market. Most of this financial speculation came to an end when the ECB announced at the end of June 2012 that it would act as a de facto lender of last resort. The search yielded a total of 1000 results. This initial sample of 1000 cartoons was filtered based on several criteria. Firstly, as I wish to analyse the extent of the variation of frames within Europe, only cartoons that were created by European artists were selected. Secondly, in the case that the original sample included both a coloured version of the cartoons as well as a black-and-white version, the latter was deleted from the dataset. Thirdly, cartoons that – although they were summoned by the use of the search term 'euro' – had nothing to do with the euro-crisis, were deleted from the dataset as well. For example, this included cartoons that covered the European Football Championship, 'Euro 2012'. These criteria resulted in a sample of 400 political cartoons by European artists, all covering the eurocrisis between 1 January 2010 and 30 June 2012.

These 400 political cartoons were created by 18 unique artists originating from 12 different European countries (see Table 1). These countries include the Netherlands, Austria, Sweden, Bulgaria, France, Switzerland, Slovakia, the UK, Romania, Greece, Spain and Germany. Of the group of unique artists, 16 had ten or more cartoons in the sample. The largest share of cartoons in the sample are the work of Arend Van Dam with 14.2% of all cartoons. In terms of countries, Dutch cartoons were most present, repre-senting 32.8% of all cartoons (Table 2).

Next, a coding scheme was developed to reveal the frames hidden within these car-toons. The methodological concept of a frame originates from communication and media studies (Gorp, 2005; Semetko & Valkenburg, 2000), and can be described as a 'cluster of logical organized devices that function as an identity kit for a frame' (Van Gorp, 2007, p. 64). As such, I understand a frame as a certain pattern in a cartoon that is composed of several elements. Rather than directly encoding the entire frame, I follow Van Gorp's suggestion of splitting it up into its separate 'frame elements' or 'reasoning devices': 'explicit and implicit statements that deal with justifications, causes, and conse-quences in a temporal order' (2007, p. 64). When these elements group together

Table 1. Frequencies by cartoonist.

Artist	#Cartoons	% Total dataset
Arend Van Dam	57	14.2
Petar Pismestrovic	46	11.5
Christo Komarnitski	33	8.3
Frederick Deligne	33	8.3
Tom Janssens	33	8.3
Olle Johansson	26	6.5
Joep Bertrams	23	5.8
Patrick Chappatte	22	5.5
Martin Sutovec	20	5.0
Pavel Constantin	19	4.8
Hajo De Reijger	18	4.5
Michael Kountouris	17	4.3
Iain Green	14	3.5
Kap	11	2.8
Riber Hansson	11	2.8
Rainer Hachfeld	10	2.5
Brian Adcock	6	1.5
Jozef Danglar Gertil	1	0.3
Total	400	100

Table 2. Frequencies by country.

Country	#Cartoons	% Total dataset
The Netherlands	131	32.8
Austria	46	11.5
Sweden	37	9.3
Bulgaria	33	8.3
France	33	8.3
Switzerland	22	5.5
Slovakia	21	5.3
UK	20	5.0
Romania	19	4.8
Greece	17	4.3
Spain	11	2.8
Germany	10	2.5
Total	400	100

systematically in a comprehensible way, they form a pattern that can be identified across several cartoons in the sample. These patterns I call frames.

For this method, a frame concept that provides a clear operational definition of frame elements is needed. Following the definition of Entman (1993, p. 53), a frame consists of a problem definition, causal interpretation, moral evaluation and/or a treatment recommendation. The satirical nature of political cartoons has the effect that they are more inclined to humorously offer social criticism concerning particular social problems, rather than suggesting concrete solutions to solve them. Therefore, I do not include 'treatment recommendation' into the coding scheme. For the purposes of this particular research, I define the remaining frame elements as in Table 3. This operationalization runs parallel with the claim that political cartoons reduce the complexity of a problem or event to a binary struggle that has foremost to do with the allocation and attribution of responsibility to the parties involved (Greenberg, 2002).

I understand these elements as variables that can have several categories. In a first round, these variables were coded. Subsequently, the codes were compared with each other and were made uniform. Eventually these different codes were systematically grouped together in a logical way, thereby forming a pattern that could be identified across the cartoons in the sample. For example, when the problem of the eurocrisis was defined as, 'lack of efficient measures', 'lack of unity', 'lack of leadership' or 'corruption', these codes were put together since they all point to the same meta-narrative: the eurocrisis is a crisis of governance. These patterns led to causal frames, which were put into separate frame matrixes (see Table 4). These matrixes formed the basis for the description of the various frames in the results section.

Results

In this section, I describe the various frames that political cartoons use to give meaning to the eurocrisis. The analysis described above yields 10 different frames in which the essence

Table 3. Frame elements.

Frame elements	Description
Problem definition	What is the problem of the eurocrisis?
Causal interpretation	Who is deemed responsible for the eurocrisis? To whom is blame attributed?
Moral evaluation	Who is portrayed as the victim of the eurocrisis? Who is the loser of monetary integration?

Table 4. Schematic overview of frames.

	Problem definition (what is the problem?)	Causal interpretation (who is to blame?)	Moral evaluation (who is the victim?)
Crisis of solidarity	• Lack of solidarity • Insistence on austerity • Economic suffering of peripheral countries • Stringent bailout conditions	• European Union • European institutions • IMF • The euro • Governments of lender countries (Germany, northern Europe)	• Peripheral countries • PIIGS (Portugal, Italy, Ireland, Greece, Spain) • Governments of debtor countries
Crisis of responsibility	• Lack of fiscal responsibility • Financial transfers • Moral hazard • Costs of bailouts • Waste of money	• Peripheral countries • PIIGS (Portugal, Italy, Ireland, Greece, Spain) • Governments of debtor countries	• European Union • European taxpayer • Germany • Governments of lender countries (Germany, northern Europe)
Crisis of democracy	• Unequal power relations • Neo-imperialism • Domination by large countries • Impact on domestic politics	• Governments of large countries (France, Germany) • European institutions (EC, ECB) • IMF • Financial markets	• National democracy • National sovereign people • National political leaders (Papandreou, Berlusconi) • National voters
Crisis of governance	• Lack of effective crisis countermeasures • Lack of efficient crisis countermeasures • Corruption • Lack of leadership • Lack of unity	• European institutions (Van Rompuy, Barroso) • Heads of government • Corrupt political leaders and officials	• European Union • European citizens • Euro

of the eurocrisis is captured differently, each involving distinct culprits and victims. I will only focus on four frames that were identified most often.[2] These frames portray the eurocrisis as a crisis of solidarity, a crisis of responsibility, a crisis of democracy and a crisis of governance, and account for a total of 70% of all cases.

Crisis of solidarity

The first frame revolves around a storyline that considers the eurocrisis first and foremost as a crisis of solidarity. A first important implication of this frame is that the peripheral Eurozone countries did not cause the eurocrisis. What is more, it suggests that it is not Greece that is responsible for the eurocrisis, but it is the euro that is responsible for the Greek crisis. Hence, this interpretation of the eurocrisis portrays Greece and other countries in financial difficulties as the main victims of the eurocrisis instead of the ones who should be blamed for it (see Figure 1).

This frame builds on the notion that the eurocrisis is first and foremost the result of structural defects in the architecture of the European Monetary Union. As the causal story goes, the global financial and economic crisis of 2008 suddenly brought an end to the cheap loans that flooded the peripheral economies since the introduction of the common currency. As a result, strong economic growth came to a halt and several

Figure 1. EU rescuing Greece.

governments were forced to rescue their banks with public money. These two developments had disastrous consequences for the national budgets of the member states. However, since these countries were part of a currency union, they did not possess the necessary policy instruments to solve the crisis. Since monetary policy was now the sole competence of the European Central Bank (ECB), a devaluation of the currency to make their export competitive again was no longer an option. As the financial markets became aware of this, they lost confidence in these countries and were no longer willing to buy sovereign bonds.

A second implication of the solidarity frame is that responsibility for the crisis is attributed to actors and objects that symbolize the EU and the national governments of some member states. This claim relates to the architectural flaw that failed to foresee a rescue mechanism in case a crisis were to occur. When, after months of discussion, a European emergency fund was finally set up, its bailout loans were linked to very strict conditions. Greece, Portugal and Ireland were commissioned to carry out stringent cuts what led to a wave of social protest. Moreover, the austerity programmes pushed the peripheral economies even deeper into recession. However, the EU and in particular the creditor countries were not prepared to grant the loans without these conditions. This frame considers that it is this lack of solidarity that is at the heart of the eurocrisis (Figures 2 and 3).

Figure 2. EU saves Greece.

Figure 3. Deeper.

Crisis of responsibility

For the responsibility frame, it is essential that politically or socially defined communities, that is, nations, should be responsible for their own revenues and expenses. Since proponents of the frame suggest that bailout loans are being financed by north-European tax payers, it is argued that the EU is suffering from a crisis of responsibility leading to moral hazard. This frame attributes the responsibility for the eurocrisis to 'lazy southern Europeans' who uphold their living standards with money earned on the back of 'hard-working northern Europeans'. This frame considers the debtor nations as the culprit and the creditor nations as the victim and political cartoons employing this frame depict them as such.

The causal story goes that peripheral economies – by means of cheap loans made possible by the euro – lived beyond their means for many years. The upgrading of wages and social protection that followed was not based on a true perception of the capabilities of their economy. To rectify this, they must now undergo painful cuts and reforms. This frame suggests that it is not up to the rest of Europe to now pay for the living standard that the south of Europe got accustomed to. This is especially the case for Greece that has been accused of tampering its budget figures. It is therefore considered only natural that certain conditions need to be set in order to ensure that one day these loans will be paid back (Figures 4 and 5).

Crisis of democracy

The third frame considers the eurocrisis primarily as a crisis of national democracy and sovereignty. One of the main problems this frame identifies are the unequal power relations that have arisen within the EU as a result of the crisis. In a first instance, proponents of the frame argue that this is caused by large and solvent member states who cling to decision-making powers. This is supposed to lead to a 'creditocracy': governance by those who pretend to be on the giving side of Europe. Especially, the dominant role of Angela Merkel is criticized frequently within this frame, claiming that she wants to create a 'German Europe' with German cultural and economic standards. Expressed

Figure 4. Bankrupt threat.

most radically, this frame fears that Germany tries to achieve by economic means, what it has failed to achieve by military means during the Second World War: the expansion of a 'Fourth Reich'. The frame points to the irony that the common currency was historically launched as a project to make a newly unified Germany more European, while today it seems that Germany is making Europe more German (Figure 6).

The democracy frame focuses next to Germany also on European institutions as a threat to national democracy and sovereignty. The frame argues that armed with new policy measures such as the 'Sixpack' and the 'Fiscal Compact', the European Commission is acquiring more and more powers to impose its will on member states. Moreover, the frame points out and criticizes the influence and control that foreign European governments, non-directly elected institutions (EC, ECB and IMF) and financial markets have over the fate of domestic politics. Illustrative here are the various governments that fell

North-West Europe...

...and Southern Europe

Figure 5. Europe North-West and South.

Figure 6. A European Shotgun wedding.

over the crisis, such as in Ireland, Portugal, Spain, Greece and the Netherlands. The former Italian prime minister Silvio Berlusconi, who was forced to resign a couple of days after he had made some unfortunate statements at the G20 and European summit and was promptly replaced by an ex EU-official, is a popular example here. Especially, since the Italian justice system and opposition unsuccessfully tried to get rid of him for several years. A very similar story can be applied to the Greek prime minister, Giorgos Papandreou (Figures 7 and 8).

Crisis of governance

The final frame identifies the essence of the eurocrisis as a crisis of governance. It argues that the primary problem is the way in which European decision-makers have tried to handle the crisis so far. Firstly, the proponents of this frame argue that the EU decision-making in the EU is far from being efficient. On the contrary, they portray it as being slow and lagging behind the events on the ground. This runs in stark contrast to the

Figure 7. Berlusconi resigns.

Figure 8. Greek taxpayer.

financial markets who swiftly react to international events. The frame is highly critical of EU decision-making that – with all its checks and balances – is not suitable to rapidly implement big changes, while at the same time the crisis demands a quick response (Figures 9).

Secondly, the frame labels EU decision-making as ineffective. It argues that promulgated anti-crisis measures soon proved to be obsolete and therefore insufficient to combat the crisis. The frame identifies the lack of leadership as the main cause for the inefficient and ineffective approach to the crisis. In some instances, the frame even invokes doubts concerning corruption within the EU institutions. According to this frame, the euro-crisis is a crisis of governance and blame is assigned to EU decision-makers and policy-makers, including heads of government and EU-officials. Here, the rest of the EU is the main victim of their poor crisis management (Figures 10).

Figure 9. Europe indecisive.

Figure 10. 130000000000.

Distribution of frames

This section describes the variation in the use of the four main frames as identified above. Out of the 400 political cartoons that made up the dataset, there were 52 cartoons that did not promote a particular frame. These were very simple images where no blame was attributed or victims were identified. Examples include cartoons that draw an image of the EU as a 'sinking ship' or Greece as an ancient broken piggybank. The 348 other cartoons promoted one or more frames. To 91 cartoons 2 frame codes were applied and to 9 cartoons 3 frame codes were applied. In case a cartoon promoted more than one frame, all frames codes were given equal weight of one. This amounts to a total of 448 frame codes that have been attributed to political cartoons. Figure 11 offers an overview of the frequency of these frame codes.

Figure 11 shows that the four frames described above – crisis of solidarity, crisis of responsibility, crisis of democracy and crisis of governance – cover an overwhelming majority (70%) of the frame codes. Furthermore, the plurality of political cartoons included in the dataset frame the eurocrisis as a 'crisis of democracy' (23.7%). 'Crisis of responsibility' is a very close second with 23.2%. The third and fourth places are, respectively, occupied by 'crisis of governance' (12.7%) and 'crisis of solidarity' (11.2%) (Figure 11).

However, this ranking in the use of frames among cartoons is not very representative for the 'European' cartoonist. The composition of the dataset gives a distorted picture. As shown in Table 2, there is a strong bias in the national background of cartoonists in favour of northern Europe. Artists originating from three north-European countries – the Netherlands, Sweden and Austria – provide more than half (53.6%) of all the cartoons. Therefore, a look at the distribution of the frames is needed, taking account of inter-country differences.

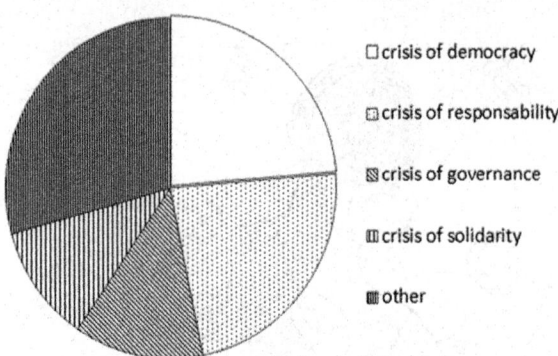

crisis of democracy

crisis of responsability

crisis of governance

crisis of solidarity

other

Figure 11. Distribution of frames on aggregate.

Table 5. Distribution of frames per country.

	Crisis of			
	solidarity (%)	Responsibility (%)	Democracy (%)	Governance (%)
Greece	**37.5**	12.5	25	25
Spain	**37.5**	12.5	37.5	12.5
Sweden	4.3	**65.2**	17.4	13
Bulgaria	9.7	**45.2**	41.9	3.2
Switzerland	18.8	**37.5**	31.3	12.5
The Netherlands	15.5	**37.1**	21.6	25.8
Slovakia	22.7	**31.8**	27.3	18.2
Austria	5.7	20	**60**	14.3
Germany	0	22.2	**55.5**	22.2
France	22.6	16.1	**48.4**	12.9
The UK	15.8	31.6	**42.1**	10.5
Romania	20	30	10	**40**

Table 5 shows the distribution of frames per country. I consider the frame that is relatively used most often by cartoonists of the same country as the dominant frame of that country. These have been highlighted in bold. This way, big differences concerning the dominant frame of countries emerge. Political cartoonists originating from southern-European countries such as Greece and Spain frame the eurocrisis most often as a crisis of solidarity. In northern and eastern Europe, including Sweden, the Netherlands, Bulgaria and Slovakia, the eurocrisis is most often framed in terms of a crisis of responsibility. The 'crisis of democracy' frame is most popular in member states that are part of the geographical core of Europe, including Austria, Germany and France. Finally, cartoons originating from Romania frame the eurocrisis predominantly as a crisis of governance. These results will be further discussed and interpreted in the following section.

Discussion and conclusion

This paper demonstrates that cartoons actively frame the eurocrisis by promoting a problem definition and identifying the 'winners' and 'losers' of the crisis. By using symbols and metaphors, they make claims about who should be blamed for causing the crisis and who should be considered as the victim. They do so in a way that is more provocative than we can expect from traditional media. For example, one cartoon not showed in the analysis above depicts the Greek taxpayer as a prisoner in an Auschwitz-like setting whereby the Star of David is replaced by a Euro sign and the watchtower reads to word 'Troika'. To fully understand how the framing by political cartoons relates to other types of media discourse, a more elaborate comparative research design is required. Yet, by oversimplifying a very complex issue, cartoons offer black-and-white accounts of the eurocrisis that resonate well within certain national contexts.

Despite the observation that all cartoons seem to agree that the EU is suffering from some kind of crisis, this paper's findings indicate that the meanings these cartoonists attach to the crisis show great variation. On the basis of a framing analysis, I identified a total of 10 frames and focused on the 4 most relevant ones for interpreting the eurocrisis. These claim that the eurocrisis should be understood first and foremost as a crisis of solidarity, a crisis of responsibility, a crisis of democracy or a crisis of governance. Each frame has its own definition, causal analysis and moral evaluation of the eurocrisis which are not necessarily mutually exclusive. It is possible, for example, to consider the eurocrisis as a crisis of democracy, as well as a crisis of governance. Both frames just emphasize different but potentially complementary aspects of a perceived reality. In some cases, however, these causal elements are rivalling and in conflict with one another. Conflict particularly arises when the victims of the crisis suggested in one frame are identified as the main perpetrators of the crisis in another frame. For example, political cartoons employing the solidarity frame claim that the EU and especially the governments of the lender countries are responsible for the economic crisis which has devastating consequences for the peripheral countries, that is, the victim. The responsibility frame, on the other hand, reverses this order of causality by blaming the peripheral countries for causing the crisis and portraying the lender countries as the losers of a redistributive conflict. While according to the solidarity frame a lack of solidarity is the main issue, the responsibility frame argues that the main issue consists precisely in these utterances of solidarity: financial bailouts leading to moral hazard. These diverging interpretations of the eurocrisis are impossible to reconcile.

The extent to which these frames are employed by cartoons varies strongly across countries, suggesting that the interpretation of the eurocrisis by political cartoons is somehow determined by its national background. Cartoonists from south-European countries, such as Greece and Spain countries, frame the eurocrisis first and foremost as a crisis of solidarity, while in the north of Europe, the 'responsibility' frame is most prominent. By and large, the literature suggests that visual media, including political cartoons, from different cultural and political perspectives create different images of a conflict that align with the dominant perceptions of their implied readership (Diamond, 2002; Greenberg, 2002). Accordingly, it is not all that surprising that south-European cartoonists are less likely to blame their own political and cultural community for the eurocrisis, for example, the 'crisis of responsibility' frame. The same goes for north-European cartoonists. In contrast, it is somewhat counter-intuitive that the 'crisis of democracy' frame is most prominent among cartoonists from large powerful countries such as France, Germany and the UK to whom responsibility for the crisis is attributed. One explanation could be that in large and powerful countries, cartoonists are more critical towards their own government, or are more sensitive to loss of sovereignty.

To explain why cartoonists chose certain frames and what role nationality plays in this process, however, explanatory research involving hypothesis-testing must be conducted.

In this case, it would additionally be interesting to test for the effect of intended audiences. Since the cartoons in the sample were drawn from an online database, I only have information available for the nationality of the cartoonist. In the event that the nationality of the cartoonist and the nationality of the intended audience differs, it would be interesting to see which would be a better predictor of the frame of a cartoon. In other words, what drives a cartoonist when constructing social reality, his own set of values, beliefs and possibly stakes or those of his readership? To fully understand the effect of 'nationality', as well as other possible predictors such as 'left/right ideology', we need data on cartoonists as well as the media outlets and their implied readership in which the cartoon was published across Europe.

In sum, these conclusions support the theoretical proposition of this paper that crises generate framing contests that reflect the different positions of stakeholders. Political cartoons contribute to this through the act of framing. Since little of the work examining framing of news events has focused on visual images (Fahmy, 2010, p. 697), this study contributes to the literature that conceptualizes political cartoons as a tool for framing social meaning (Abraham, 2009). Moreover, the research offers new insights by exploring differences and similarities of visual framing in a cross-cultural and trans-national context.

From a societal point of view, it is not problematic that there are several ways in which political cartoons frame social problems. It can even be argued that the exposure to different frames is healthy for the formation of public opinion in a democratic polity. However, I found that for one, some of these frames are mutually exclusive and secondly, the frequency by which these frames occur are delineated by national or cultural borders. When different conflicting frames prevail in different parts of Europe, it puts severe limitations on the legitimacy of the EU. As such, the lack of a European public sphere brings to bear the true nature of the crisis: how can EU policy-makers formulate an efficient, effective and legitimate solution to a problem that is perceived and interpreted differently across national and cultural contexts?

Notes

1. For other articles using Daryl Cagle's online database, see Wiid, Leyland, and Engstrom (2011) and Lacity and Rudramuniyaiah (2009).
2. The six other identified frames include 'crisis of the financial system', 'crisis of the EU's position in the world', 'crisis of the monetary system', 'crisis of morality', 'crisis of interconnectedness'. and 'crisis of unity' (For a complete overview and discussion of all identified frames, see Van Hecke, 2012.)

Disclosure statement

No potential conflict of interest was reported by the author.

References

Abraham, L. (2009). Effectiveness of cartoons as a uniquely visual medium for orienting social issues. *Journalism & Communication Monographs, 11*(2), 117–165. doi:10.1177/152263790901100202

Abraham, L., & Appiah, O. (2006). Framing news stories: The role of visual imagery in priming racial stereotypes. *Howard Journal of Communications, 17*(3), 183–203. doi:10.1080/10646170600829584

Bal, A. S. (2011). Cartoons: When politics are too serious to be left to politicians. Introduction to the special issue, cartoons and political marketing: Challenges in an age of new media. *Journal of Public Affairs, 11*(3), 135–136. doi:10.1002/pa.405

Berger, P. L., & Luckmann, T. (1966). *The construction of social reality: A treatise in the sociology of knowledge.* New York: Anchor.

Boin, A., 't Hart, P., & McConnell, A. (2009). Crisis exploitation: Political and policy impacts of framing contests. *Journal of European Public Policy, 16*(1), 81–106. doi:10.1080/13501760802453221

Candel, J., Breeman, G., Stiller, S. J., & Termeer, C. (2014). Disentangling the consensus frame of food security: The case of the EU common agricultural policy reform debate. *Food Policy, 44*(1), 47–58.

Clausen, L. (2004). Localizing the global: 'Domestication' processes in international news production. *Media, Culture & Society, 26*(1), 25–44. doi:10.1177/0163443704038203

Conners, J. (1995, August). *Representations of Saddam Hussein as the enemy: Political cartoons during the Persian Gulf crisis.* Paper presented to the Mass Communication and Society Division, Association for Education in Journalism and Mass Communication, Washington, DC.

Dewulf, A., Gray, B., Putnam, L., Lewicki, R., Aarts, N., Bouwen, R., & Woerkum, C. van. (2009). Disentangling approaches to framing in conflict and negotiation research: A meta-paradigmatic perspective. *Human Relations, 62*(2), 155–193. doi:10.1177/0018726708100356

Diamond, M. (2002). No laughing matter: Post-September 11 political cartoons in Arab/Muslim newspapers. *Political Communication, 19*(2), 251–272. doi:10.1080/10584600252907470

Entman, R. M. (1993). Framing: Toward clarification of a fractured paradigm. *Journal of Communication, 43*(4), 51–58. doi:10.1111/j.1460-2466.1993.tb01304.x

Fahmy, S. (2005). Photojournalists' and photo editors' attitudes and perceptions: The visual coverage of 9/11 and the Afghan war. *Visual Communication Quarterly, 12*(3–4), 146–163. doi:10.1080/15551393.2005.9687454

Fahmy, S. (2010). Contrasting visual frames of our times: A framing analysis of English- and Arabic-language press coverage of war and terrorism. *International Communication Gazette, 72*(8), 695–717. doi:10.1177/1748048510380801

Fairhurst, G. T. & Grant, D. (2010). The social construction of leadership: A sailing guide. *Management Communication Quarterly, 24*(2), 171–210.

Gamson, W. A., & Modigliani, A. (1987). The changing culture of affirmative action. In R. G. Braungart & M. M. Braungart (Eds.), *Research in political sociology* (pp. 137–177). Greenwich, CT: JAI Press.

Gitlin, T. (2003). *The whole world is watching: Mass media in the making and unmaking of the new left, with a new preface* (First Edition, with a new preface edition). Berkeley: University of California Press.

Gorp, B. V. (2005). Where is the frame? Victims and intruders in the Belgian press coverage of the asylum issue. *European Journal of Communication, 20*(4), 484–507. doi:10.1177/0267323105058253

Greenberg, J. (2002). Framing and temporality in political cartoons: A critical analysis of visual news discourse. *Canadian Review of Sociology/Revue Canadienne de Sociologie, 39*(2), 181–198. doi:10.1111/j.1755-618X.2002.tb00616.x

Hilgartner, S. & Bosk, C. L. (1988). The rise and fall of social problems: A public arenas model. *American Journal of Sociology, 94*(1), 53–78.

Iorgoveanu, A., & Corbu, N. (2012). No consensus on framing? Towards an integrative approach to define frames both as text and visuals. *Romanian Journal of Communication and Public Relations, 14*(3), 91–102.

Kuipers, G. (2011). The politics of humour in the public sphere: Cartoons, power and modernity in the first transnational humour scandal. *European Journal of Cultural Studies, 14*(1), 63–80.

Lacity, M., & Rudramuniyaiah, P. (2009). Funny business: Public opinion of outsourcing and offshoring as reflected in U.S. and Indian political cartoons. *Communications of the Association for Information Systems, 24*(1), 199–224.

Majone, G. (2011). *Monetary union and the politicization of Europe*. Euroacademia International Conference. Vienna.

Semetko, H., & Valkenburg, P. (2000). Framing European politics: A content analysis of press and television news. *Journal of Communication, 50*(2), 93–109. doi:10.1111/j.1460-2466.2000.tb02843.x

Shah, D. V., Watts, M. D., Domke, D., & Fan, D. P. (2002). News framing and cueing of issue regimes: Explaining Clinton's public approval in spite of scandal. *The Public Opinion Quarterly, 66*(3), 339–370.

Sifft, S., Brüggemann, M., Königslöw, K. K.-V., Peters, B., & Wimmel, A. (2007). Segmented Europeanization: Exploring the legitimacy of the European Union from a public discourse perspective. *JCMS: Journal of Common Market Studies, 45*(1), 127–155. doi:10.1111/j.1468-5965.2007.00706.x

Statham, P., & Trenz, H.-J. (2012, January). *The politicization of the European Union: From constitutional dreams to Euro-Zone crisis nightmares*. Paper presented at the 3rd International Conference on Democracy as Idea and Practice, Oslo. Retrieved from http://www.uio.no/english/research/interfaculty-research-areas/democracy/news-and-events/events/conferences/2012/papers-2012/Statham-Trenz-wshop3.pdf.

Stone, D. (2001). *Policy paradox: The art of political decision making* (3rd ed.). NY: W. W. Norton.

Streicher, L. H. (1967). On a theory of political caricature. *Comparative Studies in Society and History, 9* (4), 427–445. doi:10.1017/S001041750000462X

Streitmatter, R. (2011). *Mightier than the sword: How the news media have shaped American history* (3rd ed., Third Edition edition). Boulder, CO: Westview Press.

Tuchman, G. (1980). *Making news* (Later Printing edition). New York, NY: Free Press.

Van Gorp, B. (2007). The constructionist approach to framing: Bringing culture back in. *Journal of Communication, 57*(1), 60–78. doi:10.1111/j.0021-9916.2007.00329.x

Van Hecke, M. (2012). *Beeldvorming van de Eurocrisis in Comparatief Perspectief: een analyse van Politieke Cartoons* (Unpublished master's thesis). University of Antwerp, Belgium.

Wiid, R., Leyland, F. P., & Engstrom, A. (2011). Not so sexy: Public opinion of political sex scandals as reflected in political cartoons. *Journal of Public Affairs, 11*(03), 137–147. doi:10.1002/pa.401

Epilogue

Insisting on complexity

Christian Karner and Aline Sierp

Since the papers compiled here were first published, the European Union has rushed from one crisis to another. News headlines proclaiming the EU's likely, or at least possible, disintegration have been reaching us with increased frequency over recent years. While dispassionate observers may conclude, in intertextual allusion to Mark Twain, that such predictions of an actually very resilient EU's imminent death have thus far been exaggerations, those of us more invested in the European project can certainly be forgiven for feeling more concerned. After all, since the height of 'Euro-crisis', which constitutes the focal point and backdrop to the papers assembled here, the political geometry both within and beyond the European Union has shifted profoundly and in directions that make further European integration, at least, less likely. With Brexit now an uncomfortably and unpredictably unfolding reality, and with EU-skeptical-, in some cases positively EU-phobic, parties now either in coalition governments or putting them under serious pressure across much of the EU, our institutional future seems less certain than it has for many years. Centrifugal forces, it appears, are now acting on the European Union from outside and from within. Arguably, a process of 'renationalization' (e.g. Hartleb 2012) is afoot, with those just-mentioned forces of EU-skepticism and EU-phobia, firmly opposed as they are to any (further) European integration, eagerly waiting to re-entrench and re-celebrate national boundaries that until not very long ago were widely seen as mere relics of the continent's recent and darkest historical chapter.

Yet, and as argued elsewhere (Karner and Kopytowska 2017), at present several outcomes are equally imaginable as the possible future endpoint to a period of protracted, multiple crises – from a still unresolved debt- and austerity crisis, via the much-discussed 'refugee crisis', to profound environmental and demographic challenges – affecting localities, nation-states as well as the supranational institutions of the European Union. Such possible outcomes undoubtedly include a possible unravelling of the European project, in which case what started as a British exit driven, in no small part, by a 'post-imperial melancholia' (Gilroy 2004) and a lack of collective engagement with European- rather than national memories of the recent past, will have spread much further and done much greater damage. This having been said, such possible disintegration, if it was to occur, would also have other reasons, including the national egoisms that have thus far featured prominently in the lack of a common, European response to the migration flows from the Middle East, Asia and Africa witnessed since 2015. Alternatively, however, closer European integration amongst the remaining 27, albeit an integration that would perhaps be largely an instrumental response to global geopolitics, is similarly thinkable. Finally, and with the worst of the economic downturn that has plagued Europe since 2008 now seemingly behind us, this scenario is not a priori less plausible than the others, it is also conceivable that we will continue to see more of the same: i.e. a European Union largely (albeit only loosely) held together by economic rationality and able to generate shared strategies only when faced with the next in a series of acute crises. In any case, the question as to 'which Europe' we want to live in looks set to preoccupy politicians, journalists, academics, cultural creators and many 'ordinary citizens' for a long time yet.

Social scientists' and historians' record in predicting the near future is at most mixed. As such, we offer these reflections not as competing prognoses or hypotheses for what might happen next, but as a way of contextualizing the preceding papers in relation to important events and shifts that have occurred since their first publication. Put differently, though still recent, the research contained in this book's constitutive chapters is further enriched, we believe, by being related to yet more recent and current affairs. Our primary objective in this epilogue, however, is to return to the conceptual level, with which we started our introduction. Instead of reiterating points already made there, we would like to add to them, in light of the insights our contributing authors offer and the wider reflections they encourage. Simply put, by way of some concluding thoughts it is worth asking again what recent and current European crisis-responses suggest about the political uses and dangers of stereotypes. The preceding pages have offered ample evidence of unjust distortions, pejorative depictions of various 'others', of formulae that demonize 'them', defined nationally, while presenting national in-groups positively, as purported heroes, victims or martyr-like collectives allegedly being taken advantage of by others. The critical, analytical insight that such problematic portrayals are as decontextualized and selective as they are self-interested is as important as it is obvious; so obvious, in fact, that this critical conclusion barely needs repetition yet so important as to demand reiteration. The real questions, then, must probe *why* national/ ethnic stereotypes have (re)acquired, in the context of recent and ongoing crises, the political and discursive prominence, to which our chapters testify.

In order to sketch the beginnings of one plausible answer to this important question, we may (re)turn to an argument first proposed by Rogers Brubaker, Mara Loveman and Peter Stamatov (2004) in the study of ethnicity and, by extension, nationalism. These inter-disciplinary fields, Brubaker et al. argued, had begun to take a 'cognitive turn'. By this they meant that two sets of psychological insights into human cognition had rightly begun to enrich the social scientific study of ethnicity. The first of these insights pertains to the cognitive importance of classification, for categories 'make the natural and social worlds intelligible, interpretable, communicable … Without [them] … experience and action as we know them would be impossible' (Brubaker et al. 2004: 32). Three important caveats are needed here. First, it is but a small step from observing the cognitive importance of cat-egorization to postulating that the need for *perceived* order – or, in these authors' termin-ology, for intelligibility, interpretability and communicability – is likely to be heightened in moments or periods of crises (see also Bourdieu 1977; Karner 2007). Put differently, crises often add to the psychological and social utility of categories. Second, although stereo-types are an obvious example of people thinking in larger categories, the latter need not necessarily be defined stereotypically. Put differently, a category *becomes* stereotypical when it is ascribed essentializing content, when it reifies, naturalizes and precludes or overlooks individual variations and diversities within the categories being used (see our introduction). Such ascriptions, in other words, involve very particular social processes that are not inevitable and that are profoundly political. And it is around this insight that the cru-cial question as to when exactly an arguably necessary cognitive practice (i.e. classification per se) becomes unjust, totalizing and dangerous (i.e. classification of a particular kind) by necessity revolves. Third, categories may indeed be necessary cognitive devices, through which individuals make sense of the world surrounding them. However, a cognitive device should not be mistaken for an epistemologically unproblematic mirror of reality. In other words, a particular category may indeed be psychologically helpful and yet a complete distortion of what or whom it groups. Those of us who teach issues of identity politics will recognize this as a pedagogical moment that can be profoundly challenging and productive in equal measure: i.e. when students begin to interrogate the slippery slope that leads arguably socially or psychologically helpful classifications to develop pejorative and exclusivist political momentum. Put more simply: the question as to when a category becomes xenophobic, racist or otherwise 'unsavoury' (Fraser 2012) is crucial here.

Importantly, the 'cognitive turn' detected by Brubaker et al. includes more than a recognition of the psychological and social prominence of categories. Ethnicity, they argue, also entails broader 'ways of seeing' – and hence interpreting – the world. Drawing on the psychological concept of *schemas* – or 'complex knowledge structures' that 'guide perception and recall, interpret experience, generate inferences and expectations, and organize action' (Brubaker et al. 2004: 43; 41) – Brubaker and his co-authors argue that ethnic membership provides access to culturally shared, largely taken-for-granted and often unreflexively applied theories of the world. Although often applied 'automatically', such schematic models for interpreting reality are 'not forever barred from awareness … it is entirely possible to foreground and describe [them]' (Strauss and Quinn 1997: 46). Here one further caveat and a, to our mind, crucial question need to be inserted. Similar to our earlier point, for a schema to economically order and interpret perceptual input is one thing; for it to accurately represent that which is being interpreted is quite another. Or in other words: cognitive utility does not automatically translate into epistemological/ ontological 'truth'. In fact, it is arguably very much a core part of our responsibility as social scientists and historians to tell the difference between them. Stereotypes of the kind reported and analyzed in this book work with categories but they also formulate larger theories of the world. In other words, and in keeping with Brubaker et al., national stereotypes are also schematic 'ways of seeing'. As re-emphasized earlier and throughout this book, they can be politically highly dangerous schemata, which select, decontextualize, simplify and universalize. They are, sociologically speaking, schemata that commit acts of symbolic violence on those being classified and ascribed particular meanings.

The important issue this raises for us is what, as social scientists, we may add to this. In particular, the question arises as to how – across various domains – so-called 'ordinary social actors' formulate broader theories of the world, some of which may manifest as (national) stereotypes. Either anecdotally, or through sustained empirical research, we all know that the people we listen to, whose accounts we record, and whose perspectives on the world we analyze, formulate their theories of the world in terms that are usually anything but abstract. Social actors are skilled at citing what appears to them as corroborating 'evidence', or everyday verification, of their stereotypical postulates. It is indeed rare to encounter articulations of xenophobic or otherwise exclusionary rhetoric that do not offer particular, *purported illustrations* of what it is being claimed about someone else to an intended audience. In the empirical settings examined by our contributors, this manifests in people claiming to have specific instances to hand: i.e. be they instances of a 'cold' or 'dehumanizing' Protestant or 'Germanic-Northern' work ethic in operation; or instances allegedly testifying to 'social problems' local actors perceive as being 'caused' not just by migration but by a particular migrant they remember; or instances cited as 'evidence' of structural inadequacies that allegedly define southern European political structures or – note the stereotyping category at work – 'mentalities' in particular.

When thus confronted by social actors 'armed' with examples that are taken, so they claim, from a lifeworld only insiders will ever understand, how are we – as social researchers and analysts – to respond, particularly in contexts where there is evidently much at stake, socially, politically and ethically? The particular illustrations we are offered can be hard to dismiss out of hand. More than that, they need to be taken seriously, this is a core part of our scientific craft and of our obligation to fellow human beings. After all, we here also come face to face with people demonstrating, in Charles Lemert's terminology (2005), that they themselves are 'sociologically competent'; that they reflexively engage with the world around them, attempting to detect patterns, communicating meanings, and struggling to get by in contexts of scarcity and, seemingly, multiplying crises.

Our suggested answer to this recurring social scientific conundrum consists of two parts. First, we would like to suggest another return to a very particular contribution to the literature. Les Back, in his masterly *The Art of Listening*, poses arguably the most important epistemological question underpinning social scientific research; and yet it is a question that seems all too often to be left unexamined or even unarticulated. Is anyone, Back (2007: 12ff.) encourages us to ask, 'expert in their own lives'? Or, conversely, is social understanding always partial and 'incomplete'? Our chosen answer to these questions inevitably shapes our approach to scholarship and our understanding of the relationship between academic knowledge claims and everyday knowledge claims. And we would like to continue with Back for one further argumentative step: the former (i.e. academic knowledge claims) cannot be automatically assumed to be superior to the latter (i.e. everyday claims to knowledge). All knowledge claims, those made by the people we study as well as those arrived at through carefully designed and rigorously conducted empirical research, are partial and 'incomplete'. However, and with this we move to the second part of our suggested answer, academic knowledge claims carry a stronger, professionally enforced, two-fold obligation: i.e. the obligation to reflect on one's own and other people's premises and ways of arriving at 'knowledge'; and the obligation to thoroughly contextualize our and others' portrayals of reality. Jointly, these obligations issue powerful warnings against what may be termed an *inductive trap*: the tendency to formulate generalizing, highly oversimplified theories of the world on the basis of singular or very few, isolated and utterly decontextualized 'examples'; to see causation where there is none; to detect patterns that are in the 'eye of the beholder' only. Reflexivity and contextualization of any claim can and need to be used to challenge generalizations, however appealing or cognitively 'useful' they may be to those articulating them, especially in crisis scenarios. Stereotypical schemata and the 'theories of the world' they contain can thus be shown to be underpinned, at most, by a deeply flawed logic that judges from one to many, whilst constructing a category that may be entirely out of step with the lived experiences of those it classifies. And at worst, stereotypical schemata will be shown to not even be trapped in such a false (since highly selective) inductive 'logic': namely when the classifications and interpretations proposed are mere expressions of self-interest, of pre-judgment, or of fear of the unfamiliar. In all such cases, and to state the obvious, we must be alert to the traps of induction as well as to other claims that do not even wrongly generalize, but merely assert, wherever they occur – in everyday claims to 'knowledge' as much as in academic accounts.

Social scientific engagement with stereotypes and prejudice of the types examined in this book is inevitably political; it brings us face to face with meaning-making that at the same time fosters and perpetuates divisions or exclusions. It demands more than a recording and detached analysis of the accounts we encounter. It requires us to ask why human beings formulate their particular theories of the world, in their lifeworlds and at particular historical junctures. As such, and as we have seen, this is an intrinsically inter-disciplinary undertaking. Further, it requires a delicate balancing act between contextual-izing, Weberian *Verstehen* and critical engagement with false or at least hugely problematic and distorting claims. Such a balancing act, in turn, can have different outcomes and trajec-tories, as is demonstrated by the contributions assembled here.

References

Back, L. (2007) *The Art of Listening*, Oxford: Berg.

Bourdieu, P. (1977) *Outline of a Theory of Practice*, Cambridge: Cambridge University Press.

Brubaker, R., Loveman, M. and Stamatov, P. (2004) 'Ethnicity as cognition', *Theory and Society* 33 (1), 31–64.

Fraser, N. (2012) 'Marketization, social protection, emancipation: toward a neo-Polanyian conception of capitalist crisis', http://sophiapol.hypotheses.org/files/2012/02/Texte-Nancy-Fraser-anglais.doc, last accessed 22 July 2013.

Gilroy, P. (2004) *After Empire*, Abingdon: Routledge.

Hartleb, Florian (2012) 'European project in danger?' *Review of European Studies* 4 (5), 45–53.

Karner, C. (2007) *Ethnicity and Everyday Life*, London/ New York: Routledge.

Karner, C. and Kopytowska, M. (eds.) (2017) *National Identity and Europe in Times of Crisis*, Bingley: Emerald.

Lemert, C. (2005) *Social Things*, New York: Rowman & Littlefield.

Strauss, C. and Quinn, N. (1997) *A Cognitive Theory of Cultural Meaning*, Cambridge: Cambridge University Press.

Index

Note: Page numbers in *italic* refer to figures; page numbers in **bold** refer to tables.